WORLD WAR II AND THE AMERICAN DREAM

WORLD WAR II AND THE AMERICAN DREAM

How Wartime Building Changed a Nation

Exhibition Organized and
Catalog Edited by **Donald Albrecht**

Essays by
Margaret Crawford, Joel Davidson,
Robert Friedel, Greg Hise,
Peter S. Reed, and Michael Sorkin

National Building Museum, Washington, D.C. • **The MIT Press,** Cambridge, Massachusetts, and London, England

This book is published in conjunction with the exhibition *World War II and the American Dream: How Wartime Building Changed a Nation,* presented at the National Building Museum, Washington, D.C., November 11, 1994–December 31, 1995.

Curator and Supervising Editor: Donald Albrecht
Editors: Georgette Hasiotis/Jane Fluegel

The exhibition and this publication are made possible by the Legacy Resource Management Program of the Department of Defense. Additional funding has been provided by the Martin Marietta Corporation, the College of Fellows of the American Institute of Architects, and the United States Gypsum Company. The Museum also wishes to acknowledge the assistance of the National Park Service.

This book was set in New Century Schoolbook by Graphic Composition, Inc., and was printed and bound in the United States of America.

Library of Congress Cataloging-in-Publication Data

World War II and the American dream : how wartime building changed a
    nation / exhibition organized and catalog edited by Donald Albrecht ;
    essays by Margaret Crawford . . . [et al.].
        p.   cm.
    Catalog of an exhibition held at the National Building Museum, Nov.
11, 1994–Dec. 31, 1995.
    Includes bibliographical references and index.
    ISBN 0-262-01145-X (alk. paper).—ISBN 0-262-51083-9 (pbk. : alk.
paper).
    1. Housing—Social aspects—United States—History—20th century.
2. Building—Social aspects—United States—History—20th century.
3. World War, 1939–1945—Economic aspects—United States. 4. United
States—Social life and customs—1918–1945.   I. Albrecht, Donald.   II.
Crawford, Margaret.   III. National Building Museum (U.S.)
HD7293.W67   1995
363.5'0973—dc20   94-38871
                                                                                    CIP

Contents

Awards ceremony, Fort Leonard Wood, Missouri, 1942. Courtesy Office of History/Army Corps of Engineers.

Foreword

Dear Friends,

It is a pleasure to be able to join with the National Building Museum, the National Park Service, and the Legacy Resource Management Program of the Department of Defense in opening the exhibition *World War II and the American Dream: How Wartime Building Changed a Nation*. This exhibition and its accompanying catalog commemorate the architectural and design achievements of the American building industry, as well as the spirit of sacrifice and public-private cooperation that helped make victory possible nearly half a century ago.

I believe that the character of a people is strongly expressed in its architecture. In all of its myriad forms, architecture represents humanity's striving for permanence—an effort to find the optimum balance between function and artistic expression. This, at least, is the condition that prevails in times of peace. War, however, imposes entirely new and unique demands on the builder, demands that reflect the unsettling conditions of austerity, uncertainty, and expediency that mark a nation in arms. Faced with the practical concerns of survival, wartime building takes on special characteristics. Factories are optimized for rapid erection and mass production, defense installations are strengthened, and housing is simplified and standardized for quick large-scale assembly.

Fifty years ago, this wartime transformation had a profound impact on our national life. In the span of a single decade, we moved from being a nation of predominantly rural and insular outlook to one with a decidedly urban, industrial, and utilitarian focus. Following the war, pent-up consumer demand led to a burst of economic activity, while desire for a stable home life led millions of veterans and their families to settle in newly created suburban communities. *World War II and the American Dream* chronicles the nation's extraordinary journey through this decisive decade of change. As seen through the prism of engineering, architecture, and community planning, the exhibition examines the influence of war and peace on the signature artifacts of our civilization—America's buildings.

This exhibition is made possible in large part by a grant from the Department of Defense's Legacy Resource Management Program. Established by an Act of Congress in 1991, the Legacy Program is one of our nation's premier conservation initiatives. It is devoted to the protection and enlightened management of all significant biological, historical, cultural, and geophysical resources on twenty-five million acres of Department of Defense land in every state, the District of Columbia, and United States territory.

Through a special program devoted to the preservation of historically significant objects and documentary records, Legacy strives to ensure that the images and artifacts of this influential period remain part a of our national consciousness. *World War II and the American Dream* is intended to provide insight into an important part of our nation's past, and to celebrate the creative accomplishments of the American people under the most trying of circumstances.

As Chairman of the Senate Defense Appropriations Subcommittee, the author of the Legacy Program, and a veteran of World War II, it gives me great honor to contribute to this exhibition on the fiftieth anniversary of the end of this century's most devastating conflict. It is my sincere hope that all who visit this exhibition or read this catalog will gain a fuller appreciation of the inventiveness and perseverance of all those men and women, civilian and military, whose ingenuity and hard work both sustained and transformed our great nation.

Daniel K. Inouye
U.S. Senator

Preface

World War II shaped the expectations and values of an entire generation of Americans. For the past five decades, the nation has drawn its leadership, inspiration, and world view from among the ranks of those who considered this struggle to be the epochal event of their lives. Now, a half-century later, with the wartime generation passing from our national scene, the postwar generation is succeeding to political and cultural leadership. To most Americans under fifty, the experience of living through a war for national survival is entirely foreign; war is something that goes on somewhere else, brought home chiefly through the mass media. Our nation has not fought anything approaching a total war during the last fifty years, and, with the proliferation of ever-deadlier technologies and the rise of a new world order, all-out national mobilization may be as obsolete an idea as the citizen militia our founders envisioned.

Yet World War II left another, more permanent legacy—a massive building program that created thousands of factories, homes, even entire cities throughout the country. Many of these structures still stand, the physical manifestation of an unprecedented effort to harness the power and resources of a people to defend their very existence. *World War II and the American Dream: How Wartime Building Changed a Nation* explores this long-ignored topic, one that is vital to an understanding of modern American life. Both exhibition and catalog acknowledge the inventiveness and sacrifices of the American people, while examining how total war transformed not only ideology and habits but also the physical structures of our communities, workplaces, and landscapes. By documenting the material changes that took place on the American home front during that decisive half-decade, *World War II and the American Dream* is intended to give visitors and readers a greater appreciation for the lasting impact of the war, and a clearer understanding of the scale and breadth of the effort undertaken in defense of our freedom some fifty years ago.

World War II and the American Dream grew out of an interest by the Department of Defense in studying and documenting the historical significance of troop barracks and other structures located on military reservations throughout the country. During discussions between David Chase, former Curator of

Exhibitions at the National Building Museum, and Constance Werner Ramirez, then Historic Preservation Officer for the Department of the Army, the idea for an exhibition encompassing the entire wartime building program was born.

This exhibition and catalog are the creation of a dedicated team at the National Building Museum who have worked over the last two-and-a-half years to bring the project to fruition. The exhibition team was led by Guest Curator and Consultant Donald Albrecht, and included Guest Historian Joel Davidson, Curatorial Assistant Heather Burnham, and Curatorial Assistant Mark Strassman. Their efforts were supplemented by the work of volunteers Wilbur Leventer, Delbert Lewis, and Susan Reed, who gave generously of their time and talents, while student interns Jean Beinart, Laura Delmonico, Karen Lewinnek, and Robin Tannenbaum contributed much enthusiasm and energy.

Funding for this project is provided through a generous grant from the Legacy Resource Management Program of the Department of Defense. The project team received helpful guidance from Constance Werner Ramirez of the Department of Defense, H. Ward Jandl and Thomas Jester of the Preservation Assistance Division of the National Park Service, General Claude Kicklighter of the Department of Defense 50th Anniversary of World War II Commemoration Committee, and Dr. J. Bernard Murphy, Federal Preservation Officer of the Department of the Navy.

As the people of this country prepare to confront the challenges of a new millenium, the experience of World War II should help to remind us of what we can accomplish as a unified society of dedicated individuals. The buildings erected for the war are indicative of both the achievements and the cost of this mammoth effort; in producing this exhibition and catalog the National Building Museum fosters awareness of our rich building heritage. By reflecting on how the imperatives of war were expressed in physical structures, we can better understand the subtle and often unseen ways that our past influences our present lives.

Susan Henshaw Jones
President and Director, National Building Museum

Acknowledgments

World War II and the American Dream drew on numerous sources to document the rich legacy of wartime construction and its postwar repercussions. The National Building Museum is indebted to the many organizations, both public and private, that helped the exhibition team locate and obtain vital artifacts. The Museum is especially grateful for the help given by the staffs of the following official record repositories: David Taylor Model Basin; National Archives Cartographic Branch; National Archives Modern Military Branch; National Archives Motion Picture, Sound, and Video Branch; National Archives Still Pictures Branch; Office of History/Army Corps of Engineers; Pentagon Office of History; Prints and Photographs Division of the Library of Congress; U.S. Army Center for Military History; U.S. Army Military History Institute; U.S. Department of Housing and Urban Development; U.S. Forest Products Laboratory; U.S. Navy NAVFAC Historical Program at Port Hueneme, California; and Vancouver Housing Authority.

The following museums and historical groups also generously provided access to their collections: Baltimore Museum of Industry; Bancroft Library/University of California at Berkeley; Buckminster Fuller Institute; Casemate Museum; Chicago Historical Society; Cobb Landmarks and Historical Society; Cooper-Hewitt/National Museum of Design/Smithsonian Institution; Egmont Arens Collection, Russel Wright Collection, and William Lescaze Collection/Department of Special Collections/George Arents Research Library/Syracuse University; Frank Lloyd Wright Foundation; Graduate Aeronautical Laboratories/California Institute of Technology; Harbor Defense Museum; Henry Ford Museum and Greenfield Village; Huntington Library; Institute Archives and Special Collections/MIT Libraries; Japanese American National Museum; Levittown Public Library; Los Alamos Historical Museum; Marinship Museum; MIT Museum; Museum of Modern Art, New York; National Air and Space Museum/Smithsonian Institution; National Museum of American History/Smithsonian

Institution; New England Air Museum; Oakland Museum; Oklahoma Historical Society; Oregon Historical Society; P.T. Boats, Incorporated; Post Street Archives; Richard J. Neutra Archive/Special Collections/University Research Library/University of California at Los Angeles; Richmond Museum of History; RV and Manufactured Home Heritage Foundation; San Diego Historical Society; University of California at Los Angeles Department of Geography; U.S. Air Force Museum, Dayton, Ohio; U.S. Army Ordnance Museum; U.S. Army Quartermaster Museum; Vallejo Naval and Historical Museum; Watervliet Arsenal Photograph Collection; Whittington Collection/Department of Special Collections/University of Southern California; and Yankee Air Museum.

Corporations and private individuals contributed generously of their time in providing the Museum with otherwise unobtainable artifacts and information. The project was immensely enhanced by the help provided by the staffs of Albert Kahn Associates, Baltimore Gas and Electric Company, Black and Decker Corporation, Boeing Company, Butler Manufacturing Company, Dow Chemical Company, Hughes Aircraft Company, J. A. Jones Construction Company, Lockheed Corporation, Martin Marietta Corporation, McDonnell-Douglas Corporation, Rohm and Haas, and Summa Corporation.

The Museum also acknowledges the help of the following individuals: Tom Alison, Carole J. Ancelin, W. P. Atkinson, William F. Atwater, Alfred Bachmeier, Rex Ball, Mary Bandziukas, Edward Larrabee Barnes, Judson E. Bennett, Jr., Leo Bobo, David Brinkley, Shirley Camarata, Cristina Carbone, Vernon DeMars, Lucia Eames Demetrios, Eugenie Devine, Tom Dietz, Debra J. S. Dietzman, Katherine Dirks, George Dudley, Diane Dunnigan, Keller Easterling, Lucinda Eddy, J. B. Eklund, James H. Epperson, Cynthia Field, Rand Fishbein, Jon P. Flaesch, Russell Flinchum, Alfred Goldberg, Bertrand Goldberg, Bonnie Goldstein, Martin Gordon, Gerri Gray, Roy Eugene Graham,

J. Phil Huber, Senator Daniel K. Inouye, H. Ward Jandl, Thomas Jester, Mary Ellen Jones, Terrance Keenan, Barbara Kelly, James Kern, General Claude Kicklighter, James Lakey, Catherine Lavoie, Michael Lawrence, Doris Leggat, E. R. Lewis, Richard Longstreth, Dorothy Madsen, Edward Marshall, Richard McCleary, Joseph Meagher, Shelley Mills, Senator Daniel Patrick Moynihan, J. Bernard Murphy, Georgette Myers, C. Ford Peatross, Richard Prelinger, Arthur Pulos, Ralph Rapson, Marguerite C. Rodney, Alex Roland, Rodris Roth, Kathleen Rupley, Joel Sabadasz, Kelly A. Saunders, Natalie Shivers, Jeffrey P. Shrimpton, Julius Shulman, Richard Slavin, Commander Luanne Smith, Suzanne Smith, Ken Smith-Christmas, Kevin Starr, William H. Straus, Brenda Tenberg, Lloyd Thoburn, Heidi Umbhau, Jacob van der Meulen, Colonel E. J. Vincent, Robert H. Waldo, Lewis D. Walker, Louis S. Wall, Paul Williams, Geraldine Yarnell, and James Zehnder.

The exhibition and catalog have benefited from the talents of many: the staff of the National Building Museum; the Michael Sorkin Studio and Design Writing Research, the exhibition's designers; George Sexton Associates, its lighting designer; R. H. Guest, Inc., its fabricator; Merrick Communications, audiovisual producer; Sharon Blume and Sharon Wyse, interpretive exhibition text writers; and Georgette Hasiotis and Jane Fluegel, catalog editors. Exhibition models were made by Alastair Reilly; Daniel Wood, Richard Sturgeon, and Carol Patterson of Mesa Modelmakers; and Gregory K. Hunt's students at the Washington-Alexandria Center/College of Architecture and Urban Studies/Virginia Polytechnic Institute and State University. Talbot McLanahan and Michael Cook provided renderings, and the members of Local 37 of the International Association of Bridge, Structural, and Ornamental Iron Workers volunteered their time and services to prepare the Quonset hut for the exhibition.

Most of all, I am deeply indebted to Constance Werner Ramirez, who initiated the project and remained a guiding force throughout; Robert Duemling, former director of the Museum, who first supported the idea; and Susan Henshaw Jones, current director, who saw the project through to completion. Roger Conover of the MIT Press deserves thanks for his enthusiastic commitment to the catalog, as do editor Jenya Weinreb, designer Jean Wilcox, and all the catalog contributors. David Chase is to be thanked for originating the exhibition, as is his assistant, Mark Strassman. We were fortunate to have the help of volunteers Wilbur Leventer, Delbert Lewis, and Susan Reed, and interns Jean Beinart, Laura Delmonico, Karen Lewinnek, and Robin Tannenbaum. And finally I am especially grateful to Joel Davidson, Heather Burnham, and Melissa McLoud of the Museum, all of whom provided constant support, patience, and expertise beyond the call of duty, both military and civilian.

Donald Albrecht
Guest Curator

Introduction

Donald Albrecht

From the fall of France in the summer of 1940 to V-J Day in August of 1945, more than seventeen million Americans, or fourteen percent of the population, served in the armed forces of World War II. More than four hundred thousand lost their lives; almost seven hundred thousand were wounded. Yet for millions of Americans at home, a booming wartime economy produced a remarkable prosperity that ended the Great Depression, sparked a postwar economic miracle, and made the American dream of suburban homes, shopping centers, and modern kitchens a reality.

"War," wrote cultural historian Lewis Mumford in 1934, "is the health of the machine." Mumford's assertion was borne out by World War II, the first truly mechanized war in history. After instituting the first peacetime draft in 1940, the government funded a massive building program that facilitated the nation's largest military mobilization. In less than a year, Army camp capacity quadrupled through the rapid construction of standardized barracks, mess halls, and other structures. These simple buildings, marching like soldiers toward the horizon, captured a wartime ethos of conformity and consensus that later proved valuable to many who traded their Army fatigues for gray flannel suits. The same spirit of functional consequence gripped every facet of wartime construction, from the steady stream of more than one hundred seventy thousand Quonset huts made and shipped overseas to the network of coastal defenses that guarded our shores against the possibility of enemy attack. At the same time, the nation's industrialists, driven by patriotism and profit, entered into lucrative partnerships with the Federal government. Titans like Henry Ford and Henry J. Kaiser revved up America's prewar consumer economy into a hyperactive wartime engine. They converted, expanded, and built thousands of new factories, and produced unheard-of numbers of bombs, guns, ships, and tanks. By 1944, aircraft capacity was twenty times what it had been in 1940, and annual output was over ninety-five thousand planes. In all, the government invested $23 billion in defense-

Camp Wallace, Texas, 1941. Courtesy U.S. Army Military History Institute.

Barracks under construction at Camp Edwards, Massachusetts, 1940. Courtesy National Archives. RG 69-N-23877.

Fort Leonard Wood, Missouri, 1941. Courtesy Office of History/Army Corps of Engineers.

Levitt and Sons' defense housing community, Norfolk, Virginia, n.d. Courtesy National Archives. RG 80-G-30821.

Aerial bombs fill a vault at Portage Ordnance Depot, Ravenna, Ohio, 1942. Courtesy National Archives. RG 111-SC-150456.

Opposite:
Poster, 1942. Courtesy National Archives.

related construction. America's productive capacity increased a staggering fifteen percent per year from 1940 to 1944, while successful war bond campaigns and the scarcity of consumer goods caused the savings rate to climb, putting wealth in people's postwar pockets.

By many accounts, 1943 was the pivotal year in this remarkable story. A little more than a year after the humiliation of Pearl Harbor, American forces captured Guadalcanal and began their island-hopping campaign to regain Japanese-controlled bases in the Pacific. The Allies invaded Sicily, the Germans surrendered to the Russians at Stalingrad, and the Teheran Conference launched plans for the Allied invasion of Normandy. At home, the Pentagon was completed, and Americans learned of great, morale-boosting production increases. Ford's Willow Run bomber plant outside Detroit went from producing thirty-one planes in January to one hundred ninety in June. By January 1944 the company was building more B-24s than anyone else, and by March an airplane rolled off the assembly line almost every hour. Willow Run, Charles Lindbergh proclaimed, was "a Grand Canyon of the Mechanized World."

With victory almost in sight, the country focused on peacetime conversion. Congress passed the G.I. Bill of Rights to ease the return to civilian life. The dream house would be central to postwar material comfort. That certainly expressed the hope of the Libbey-Owens-Ford glass company, whose model "kitchen of tomorrow" was covered by *Better Homes and Gardens* in July and later toured department stores across the nation. If the public longed for the day after war, they found the day before equally alluring, as evidenced by the popularity of Rodgers and Hammerstein's *Oklahoma,* which premiered that year on Broadway.

The publication of Wendell Willkie's 1943 best-selling book, *One World,* anticipated a postwar climate of expansive internationalism. English, the language of business, would replace French, the language of diplomacy, and the United Nations com-

Advertisement, 1943. Courtesy General Electric.

It's a promise!

JIM'S going away tomorrow . . . and there will be long, lonely days before he comes back.

But that little home sketched there in the sand is a symbol of faith and hope and courage. It's a promise, too. A promise of gloriously happy days to come . . . when Victory is won.

Victory Homes of tomorrow will make up in part at least for all the sacrifices of today . . . . *and that's our promise!*

They will have *better living built in* . . . electrical living with new comforts, new conveniences, new economies to make every day an adventure in happiness.

Plan for *your* Victory Home now . . . the one sure way is to buy War Bonds. Every Bond you buy is an investment in your future happiness and security . . . every dollar you put into Bonds helps bring our boys back sooner—*and safer.* Buy another Bond today.

↯ ↯ ↯

The General Electric Consumers Institute at Bridgeport, Conn., is devoted to research on wartime home problems such as: Nutrition · Food Preparation Food Preservation · Appliance Care Appliance Repair · Laundering · Home Heating and Air Conditioning. Helpful booklets are available from your G-E Appliance Dealer, or General Electric Consumers Institute, Dept. L5-3.

APPLIANCE AND MERCHANDISE DEPARTMENT, BRIDGEPORT, CONN.

GENERAL ⓖⓔ ELECTRIC

plex in New York would help establish an international style of architecture: sleek, steel-and-glass towers serving as ambassadors of multinational corporate culture.

In selected sites throughout the country, change was transforming the landscape. The city of Vanport, Oregon, a totally new town of approximately forty thousand people, was built to service Kaiser shipyards. Vanport illustrates the massive wartime migration of Americans in search of well-paid work at blossoming defense centers. Over half the fifteen million who relocated crossed state lines; at the time, only two states, Pennsylvania and New York, had populations over nine million. The West Coast with its vast aircraft and shipbuilding industries witnessed the most remarkable change. From 1940 to 1947, the combined population of California, Washington, and Oregon increased nearly forty percent. Between 1940 and 1944, over five hundred thousand people moved to the Los Angeles area alone, while the population of San Diego increased by nearly half. This migration resulted in economic and demographic shifts that permanently altered the nation's regional balance, giving the West Coast newfound status and independence.

The surge in defense home building brought on by wartime migration gave impetus to America's long-standing interest

Housing project under construction at Vallejo, California, ca. 1942. Courtesy National Archives. RG 208-EX-158B-44.

in prefabricated housing. Architects, engineers, and manufacturers responded by inventing unusual residential schemes: "bubble" houses constructed by spraying concrete over inflated rubber forms, "stressed-skin" construction that echoed advances in the aircraft industry, and even dwellings adapted from metal grain silos. It was a heady era of social problem solving, too, and gives evidence of what a nation can do by focusing its talents, energies, and resources. Defense towns were conceived and built as complete communities. In fact, the war acted as a catalyst for both postwar suburban development and modern architecture, incorporating the avant-garde into the mainstream. After the war, firms such as Skidmore, Owings & Merrill, architects of innumerable wartime projects, represented the best of a bureaucratic mode of architecture. They embraced the war's modernist aesthetics and functioned as big, corporate offices. On the other hand, architects like Louis I. Kahn, who designed war workers' housing, reacted to the postwar hegemony of modernism by tempering it with historicist and monumental impulses.[1]

The war forged other relationships as well, most notably among military, scientific, and academic interests. Corporate laboratories and individual inventors struggled to increase the development of new materials and techniques such as Styrofoam, Saran, and molded plywood, and the productive capacity of existing materials like fiberglass, aluminum, and acrylic sheeting rose dramatically. In those pre-environmentally-conscious days, every new synthetic garnered praise and enthusiastic acceptance. "Is this *really* the age of plastics?" Dow Chemical wondered in one of many wartime ads. And thus it happened that when the war was over, progressive designers explored the aesthetic possibilities of these materials, creating now-classic designs for modern living.

The war's scientific advances involved the talent of both government and industry. In pursuit of any technology that might have military applications, the United States created the Office of Scientific Research and Development to coordinate a nationwide program. The fruits of this effort included the world's most advanced aircraft wind tunnel at the California Institute of Technology, laboratories for the development of radar, and three top-secret cities for the production of atomic bombs. The bomb's strategic success in bringing the war to an end made America the world's preeminent global power. Nuclear warfare convinced the country's leaders that scientific advances would play a major role in future confrontations, and this framework established a permanent cooperative of military, scientific, and academic concerns. At the same time, and in a very profound way, the bomb changed forever our notion of space, time, and the American landscape; with total annihilation from the air just a push-button away, we could never again speak with conviction of an isolated Fortress America.

Modern, industrialized warfare also demanded a logistical infrastructure that eased the flow of men and material. During the summer of 1942, as the war threatened to interrupt coastal shipping routes, the Army Corps of Engineers oversaw the construction of the fifteen-hundred-mile ALCAN highway, the first overland transport between the mainland United States and Alaska. Within the continental United States, little highway construction occurred. However, sprawling road systems at some war plants were to become templates for the interstate highways that began to snake across the country in the 1950s.

The war's economic turnaround was not achieved without social costs. "Ordinary citizens were lost," novelist James Jones later recalled, "in the almost incomprehensible boom and mass movement, trying to pick their way uphill through the crush to some island of security, in a new world that seemed to have gone crazy with both destruction and a lavish prosperity. This wrenching social upheaval and realignment, as much as the fact of the war itself, accounted for an almost total breakdown of the moral standard of prewar U.S. living. And nothing would ever quite be the same again."

A host of urban problems were revealed by wartime migration. Richmond, California, a quiet and conservative city of twenty-three thousand, became the quintessential boomtown after the opening of four Maritime Commission shipyards. Labor and housing shortages propelled formerly "unacceptable" workers such as women and African Americans into the labor force. At some West Coast shipyards, Rosie the Riveters composed a quarter of the total work force by 1944. This wartime influx into traditional all-white male industries challenged conventional notions of gender and race. Chester Himes's novel *If He Hollers Let Him Go* conflates the two issues when a white female worker at a Los Angeles shipyard falsely accuses a successful black foreman of rape and hence precipitates his personal disintegration. Real-life incidents reinforced Himes's fictional account. In 1943, there were riots in Detroit, Los Angeles, and New York. The volatility of wartime employment and housing presaged radical upheavals to come. The working women of World War II, forced to return home or accept jobs that paid less, nevertheless anticipated their

Highway with tri-level overpass serving Willow Run bomber plant, Ypsilanti, Michigan, 1944, reportedly the first such overpass in the nation. Courtesy collections of Henry Ford Museum and Greenfield Village. P.833.80308.

feminist daughters of the 1960s, and it's no mere coincidence that Ralph Ellison began his epochal novel of African-American consciousness, *Invisible Man,* in 1945.

Patriotic publicity surrounding the construction program elevated the war into a symbol of American technological and organizational prowess. The greatly increased speed of modern, machine-age warfare gave a new resonance to the industrial design concept of planned obsolescence. With austerity and material shortages still in effect, manufacturers of prewar consumer goods kept their names before the public eye by publicizing the wonders awaiting veterans. Magazines, unable to publish stories of top-secret military developments, speculated on life after the war. As early as the fall of 1942, *Popular Mechanics* anticipated a post-war design culture of plug-in disposability, announcing that future home buyers would shop for residences "supplied by a mass-production corporation which turns out dwellings just as automobile companies rolled cars from the assembly line before the war."

Such optimistic media, reinforced by turbulent wartime change, enshrined a notion of accelerated progress in the nation's collective psyche. Annihilate the old, wartime rhetoric encouraged, and you hasten the new. Wartime achievements thus led the public to expect a new age of plenty after years of sacrifice and hardship, and an ever-expanding abundance seemed the just reward following a war fought to protect the American way of life.

The intention of *World War II and the American Dream: How Wartime Building Changed a Nation* is to interpret the multifaceted nature of the war on the occasion of its fiftieth anniversary. The ambiguities, complexities, and paradoxes of this most notable period in our nation's history have been analyzed from a different perspective by each essayist. The overall portrait conveys the all-consuming grip that the war had on American life in the 1940s and the repercussions that remain to this day. In the first essay, Peter S. Reed details the rise of modern architecture during the war. Virtually all wartime construction was influenced by the development of materials, a subject explored in depth by Robert Friedel. The third essay, by Margaret Crawford, investigates the perils and the promises of public wartime housing projects through five celebrated examples. Construction of large-scale private residential communities near defense plants prefigured postwar suburban and regional growth, which is Greg Hise's theme. In the next essay, Joel Davidson provides the economic and political history of the wartime building program, analyzing its impact on the postwar complex of military, industrial, and academic concerns. The final essay by Michael Sorkin functions as a coda—a personal and wide-ranging cultural reading of the war's lasting impact on the nation's psyche. In this first in-depth examination of World War II building, we grasp the shape of modern America, and our perception of it is forever changed.

Note

1. Henry-Russell Hitchcock proposed this postwar paradigm in "The Architecture of Bureaucracy and the Architecture of Genius," *Architectural Review* (January 1947): 3–6. I am indebted to Joan Ockman for bringing this to my attention.

Chronology

**Prepared by Heather Burnham
and Joel Davidson**

Architecture and Design Developments

The Army accepts the 700 Series as the standard building type for barracks and other mobilization camp structures. In less than a year, camp capacity quadruples to accommodate one and a half million men.

In Hawaii, the Navy begins construction of the Red Hill six-million-gallon fuel storage facility featuring twenty concrete tanks built inside a hill. Each tank is two hundred fifty feet tall and one hundred feet in diameter.

A program of over eighty fortified gun batteries is instituted to defend U.S. harbors.

Construction begins on the Detroit Tank Arsenal in Michigan, the first American plant devoted exclusively to tank production.

Henry J. Kaiser builds the first of seven West Coast shipyards. Employment reaches a peak of nearly two hundred thousand; by the war's end Kaiser's yards produce nearly fifteen hundred ships.

The Farm Security Administration architects design war workers' housing in Vallejo, California.

Karl K. Pabst designs the Jeep.

Seven-hundred Series Army barracks, Fort Bragg, North Carolina. Courtesy National Archives. RG 111-SC-117389.

Opposite top:
Underground access tunnel at Navy Red Hill fuel storage facility, Oahu, Hawaii. Courtesy NAVFAC Historical Program/Port Hueneme, California.

Opposite bottom:
Coastal defense battery #120, Fort Story, Virginia. Courtesy National Archives. RG 111-SC-564542.

OFFICIAL USN PHOTO
NAVY YARD, PEARL HARBOR
CONFIDENTIAL

16740   FOURTEENTH NAVAL DISTRICT, PEARL HARBOR, T.H.   4155-43
Noy-4173-344   UNDERGROUND FUEL STORAGE, RED HILL   8-9-43
PROJECT #16. BULKHEAD IN UPPER TUNNEL AT VAULTS #1 AND #2

Political and Social Events

The nation's first peacetime draft is instituted.

Foreign orders for military aircraft rise, and President Roosevelt urges U.S. industry to produce fifty thousand aircraft annually.

The German Army conquers France. The British Royal Air Force wins the Battle of Britain.

Congress triples the War Department's budget, appropriating $37 billion to build up the U.S. Army and Navy.

The Federal government forms the Defense Plant Corporation to finance construction of new war plants.

The Lanham Act, appropriating funds to create defense housing, is approved by Congress.

Roosevelt is elected President for an unprecedented third term.

Cultural Highlights

Ernest Hemingway's *For Whom the Bell Tolls* is published.

The film version of Steinbeck's *The Grapes of Wrath* opens.

Guernica is shown at New York's Museum of Modern Art in "Picasso: Forty Years of His Art."

Hit songs include *You Are My Sunshine*.

1941

Architecture and Design Developments

The War Department begins building large bomber assembly plants in Tulsa, Oklahoma; Fort Worth, Texas; Kansas City, Kansas; and Omaha, Nebraska.

The Radford Ordnance Plant, first of hundreds of munitions factories, opens in rural Virginia.

Army construction duties are consolidated under the Army Corps of Engineers.

The Army develops new, sturdier 800 Series buildings for mobilization camps.

Use of heavy bombers forces the Army to create improved runway designs.

The Quonset hut is designed at Quonset Point Naval Air Station, Rhode Island. By 1946, more than one hundred seventy thousand huts are erected throughout the world.

Wallace Neff and his Airform Construction Co. construct the first Bubble house. Twenty experimental houses are erected in Falls Church, Virginia, but the design is never mass-produced.

R. Buckminster Fuller's Dymaxion Deployment Unit is exhibited at New York's Museum of Modern Art.

William Stout's expansible trailer is demonstrated in a tourist camp in Washington, D.C.

The largest magnesium plant in the world is begun outside Las Vegas, Nevada.

The Division of Defense Housing commissions modern architects to design war workers' housing.

By July, the floor space of aircraft plants is more than double that of January 1940.

In San Diego, California, construction begins on Linda Vista, the world's largest modern planned community.

Architect Richard Neutra designs the Avion Village housing community for aircraft workers in Grand Prairie, Texas.

Six hundred houses using the Cemesto system are built in six months for aircraft workers at the Glenn L. Martin company outside of Baltimore, Maryland.

The Army designs Marston mat, a portable steel runway system that enables airfields to be erected quickly.

Corbetta beehive, an ammunition storage bunker, is designed—the elliptical dome requires only half the steel and two-thirds the concrete of the standard cylindrical bunker.

Production begins at Willow Run bomber plant, the largest factory to date.

Political and Social Events

The Lend-Lease act is approved, providing arms to Britain.

Hitler invades the U.S.S.R. Lend-Lease is extended to the Soviet Union.

Hitler orders systematic genocide of Jews in Europe.

December 7—Japan attacks Pearl Harbor. America declares war on Japan, Germany, and Italy.

Rubber rationing begins.

Plutonium is discovered; the Manhattan Project for atomic research is founded.

The government sets priorities for critical war materials.

The National Housing Act is amended to provide Federal mortgage insurance to private builders of emergency defense housing.

Cultural Highlights

The National Gallery of Art opens in Washington, D.C.

Noel Coward's *Blithe Spirit* opens.

Orson Welles's *Citizen Kane* premieres.

Hit songs include *Chattanooga Choo-Choo* and *Bewitched, Bothered, and Bewildered.*

1943

Architecture and Design Developments

All-wood Douglas Aircraft plant opens in Chicago with laminated-timber columns and trusses, which span one hundred fifty feet, thereby saving twenty thousand tons of steel.

The largest aircraft plant, the six-point-five-million-square-foot Dodge Chicago, opens.

Hughes Aircraft begins construction of an all-wood assembly plant for the Spruce Goose with seventy-two-foot-high laminated arches spanning one hundred twenty feet.

Midwest City, Oklahoma, a fully planned community consisting of fourteen hundred sixty-six homes, is built to serve Tinker Air Depot.

The Pentagon, the world's largest office building, is completed.

A prototype of Konrad Wachsmann and Walter Gropius's Packaged House is built in Somerville, Massachusetts, but the house never goes into production.

Libbey-Owens-Ford's "kitchen of tomorrow" is featured in *Better Homes and Gardens*.

The Federal government commissions architect Bertrand Goldberg and Westinghouse to design an air-conditioned, mobile penicillin laboratory for overseas use.

Opposite:
Drawing of buildings completed by Turner Construction Company during 1943. Two largest structures are Higgins Aircraft plant, New Orleans, Louisiana (left) and Pratt & Whitney Aircraft plant, Kansas City, Missouri (right). Courtesy National Building Museum/gift of Turner Corporation.

WORK COMPLETED IN THE ONE YEAR 1943
TURNER CONSTRUCTION COMPANY
FOUNDED 1902
BOSTON   NEW YORK   PHILADELPHIA

Preview of Your

Kitchen to Come

Smooth, colorful, clutter-free, designed as a
unit, everything inclosed, everything built-
in, your postwar servant is a magic package
that doesn't quit and doesn't talk back

By John Normile and Walter Adams

D-Day: Allies, led by Eisenhower, land at Normandy.

The Russian Army marches into Romania, Hungary, and Poland in pursuit of the Nazis.

Liberation of Rome and Paris.

The number of women in the labor force reaches nearly sixteen and a half million, a thirty-six-percent increase over December 1941.

Roosevelt is elected for a fourth term.

Cultural Highlights

Betty Comden, Adolph Green, and Leonard Bernstein's *On the Town* opens.

Kodacolor processing of photographs is introduced.

Hit songs include *Swinging on a Star*.

1944

Architecture and Design Developments

Aircraft factory floor space is twenty times its prewar level, and aircraft production is ninety-six thousand planes.

The Butler Manufacturing Company's portable airplane hangar is used in Pacific campaigns.

Black and Decker develops their plastic-encased power drill.

Erecting Butler portable airplane hangar, Espiritu, New Hebrides. Courtesy Butler Manufacturing Company.

Opposite:
Water tank used to test rocket-powered torpedos at the Jet Propulsion Lab in Pasadena, California. Courtesy Jet Propulsion Laboratory/ California Institute of Technology.

The Plexiglas Dream Suite. Courtesy Rohm and Haas.

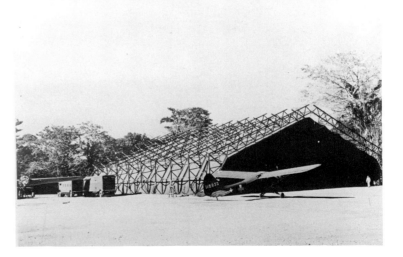

1945

Architecture and Design Developments

By 1945 the armed forces spend over $3 million on facilities at the Jet Propulsion Lab in Pasadena, California.

Fiberglass curtain doors for portable aircraft hangars are introduced by Butler Manufacturing Company of Kansas City, Missouri.

Torpedoes, flying boats, and larger and faster ships compel the Navy to begin an eighteen-hundred-foot addition to the David Taylor Model Basin near Washington, D.C.

The Case Study House Program is launched in Los Angeles by *Arts & Architecture* magazine.

The Plexiglas Dream Suite is designed to illustrate the domestic applications of Plexiglas as a postwar marketing tool by the Rohm and Haas Company in Philadelphia, Pennsylvania. The suite tours department stores and is featured in their 1947 promotional film *Looking Ahead through Rohm and Haas Plexiglas.*

Russel Wright designs plastic dinnerware for American Cyanamid.

Political and Social Events

Yalta Conference sets the stage for the beginning of the cold war.

Hitler commits suicide; Germany surrenders.

U.S. forces capture Iwo Jima and Okinawa.

United States drops an atomic bomb on Hiroshima. A second bomb is dropped on Nagasaki.

Japan surrenders.

The national debt stands at $247 billion, $199 billion more than in 1941.

Roosevelt dies. Truman takes office.

The United Nations Charter is signed in San Francisco.

Cultural Highlights

George Orwell's *The Animal Farm* is published.

Benjamin Britten's opera *Peter Grimes* premieres.

Popular songs include *It's Been a Long, Long Time.*

Political and Social Events

The War Assets Administration begins to dispose of surplus war plants.

The Kaiser Frazer Corporation purchases the Willow Run bomber plant from U.S. government to make automobiles.

British Prime Minister Winston Churchill calls domination of Eastern Europe by the U.S.S.R. an Iron Curtain.

Cultural Highlights

The bikini swimsuit debuts in Paris.

RCA's first postwar television receiver goes on sale.

The Common Sense Book of Baby and Child Care by Dr. Benjamin Spock is published.

William Wyler's *The Best Years of Our Lives* premieres.

Hit songs include (*Get Your Kicks on*) *Route 66* and *Come Rain or Come Shine.*

Architecture and Design Developments

Beech Aircraft announces production of R. Buckminster Fuller's Dymaxion Wichita house. Only two prototypes are built.

Eames molded-plywood furniture goes into production.

President Harry S. Truman appoints Wilson W. Wyatt Housing Expeditor, Veterans Emergency Housing Program.

Beech Aircraft workman atop Dymaxion Wichita house roof ventilator. © Allegra Fuller Snyder. Courtesy Buckminster Fuller Institute, Santa Barbara.

1947

Architecture and Design Developments

The prototype of a factory-built aluminum-panel house by Henry Dreyfuss and Edward Larrabee Barnes in collaboration with Consolidated Vultee Aircraft Corporation is unveiled. Only two are built.

Dreyfuss's flying automobile with a detachable wing and engine apparatus, designed for Consolidated Vultee, is test flown in San Diego.

Stran-Steel, wartime manufacturer of Quonset huts, markets low-cost metal houses.

Construction of Levittown begins.

Wallace K. Harrison and Associates designs the United Nations Secretariat in New York.

Convair Car test flight, 1947. Henry Dreyfuss, designer. Courtesy Henry Dreyfuss Archive/ Cooper-Hewitt Library/National Design Museum/Smithsonian Institution/Art Resource, NY/gift of Henry and Doris Dreyfuss.

Stran-Steel brochure, 1947. Courtesy Institute Archives and Special Collections/MIT Libraries.

1948

Architecture and Design Developments

Lustron houses, produced in a converted aircraft factory, are marketed and advertised in *Life* magazine.

Eero Saarinen begins the design of the General Motors Technical Center in Warren, Michigan.

Knoll International manufactures Eero Saarinen's "Womb" chair, the first fiberglass chair to be mass-produced in America.

Cadillac introduces tail fins inspired by Lockheed P-38 aircraft.

Wurlitzer introduces a juke box with an acrylic dome shaped like a bomber nose cone.

"Nuclear Bombing of New York." Chesley Bonestell, illustrator. Reproduced in *Collier's* in 1948. Courtesy Chesley Bonestell/Space Art International.

Levittown, New York. Courtesy National Building Museum/gift of Richard Wurts.

1949

Architecture and Design Developments

Henry Kaiser teams up with Fritz Burns to build Panorama City in the San Fernando Valley of Los Angeles.

The total number of homes built since January 1946 reaches five-point-one million.

Political and Social Events

NATO is formed with Canada and nine European nations. The Warsaw Pact alliance is formed of the Soviet Union and the Eastern European nations.

Germany is divided and separate governments are established.

The U.S.S.R. tests its first atomic bomb; the United States perfects the hydrogen bomb.

Cultural Highlights

Silly Putty, a failed attempt at synthetic rubber, is introduced as a toy.

Nineteen Eighty-four by George Orwell is published.

Death of a Salesman by Arthur Miller opens.

Rogers and Hammerstein's *South Pacific* premieres.

Publicity photograph for Kaiser dishwasher. Courtesy Bancroft Library/University of California at Berkeley.

Hutments at Fort Sill, Oklahoma, ca. 1942.
Courtesy Office of History/Army Corps of
Engineers.

Fuselage sections of B-29 Superfortress bombers awaiting final assembly, n.d. Courtesy National Archives. RG 208-PRA-8-1.

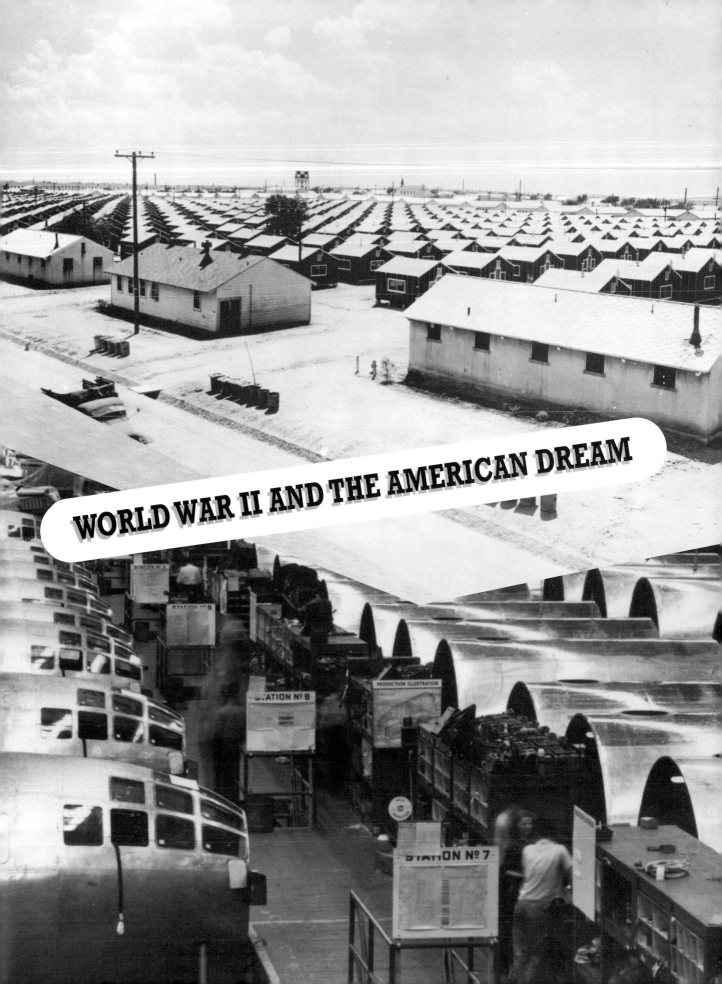

WORLD WAR II AND THE AMERICAN DREAM

Peter S. Reed

Enlisting Modernism

That everyday life would take place in modern architecture was a widespread cultural assumption at the end of World War II; a progressive optimism infused the pages of architectural journals, advertisements, and consumer-oriented pamphlets. In a 1943 brochure published by Revere Copper and Brass, for example, the dramatic juxtaposition of a fighter plane hovering over a suburban house, fabricated of aircraft materials, embodied the brave new world of modern architecture and industry. American enthusiasm for the modern movement had risen in the 1930s. The "Modern Architecture" exhibition at the Museum of Modern Art in 1932,[1] the arrival of such emigré architects as Walter Gropius and Ludwig Mies van der Rohe in 1937, and the publication of *The Modern House in America* by James and Katherine Ford in 1940 signaled modernism's growing acceptance.[2] The architectural triumphs and design innovations surrounding World War II, however, marked a turning point—thereafter modern architecture had come of age, emerging after the war as the hallmark of democracy, capitalism, and the Establishment.[3]

The wartime relationship between architects and industry was built largely on methods and processes of fabrication. The systematization, standardization, and speed of industrial production at which the United States excelled was most spectacularly captured in the factories designed by Albert Kahn, the world's foremost industrial architect. Known especially for his single-story automobile factories for Ford Motor Company after World War I, Kahn headed a company that at one time reached six hundred employees and built on five continents. In 1937, Albert Kahn Associated Architects and Engineers designed a factory for the Glenn L. Martin Company of Baltimore that was built in an astonishing eleven weeks. They adopted bridge-building methods and used three-hundred-foot steel trusses to create a light-filled, uninterrupted interior space that could house a squadron of planes.

Kahn's buildings impressed many (including Frank Lloyd Wright, who rarely acknowledged his admiration of a contemporary's work), but their impact was immediate and lasting on Mies van der Rohe. Awed by the impressive size of the overarching steel structure, Mies chose a photograph of the Martin plant with planes in the background as the setting for his 1942 concert hall proposal, which elevated Kahn's factory aesthetics to

Collage by Ludwig Mies van der Rohe of a proposed concert hall, 1942. Courtesy Mies van der Rohe Archive/Museum of Modern Art, New York/gift of Mary Callery.

House design by Pomerantz and Breines, featured in *Revere's Part in Better Living,* no. 10, 1943. Courtesy the architects.

Glenn L. Martin Company bomber plant, near Baltimore, Maryland, 1937, Albert Kahn Associated Architects and Engineers, designers. Courtesy Robert Damora.

Opposite:
Metallurgy Building, Illinois Institute of Technology, Chicago, Illinois, 1943, Ludwig Mies van der Rohe, architect. Hedrich-Blessing photograph/courtesy Chicago Historical Society. HB 07327I.

Detroit Tank Arsenal, Detroit, Michigan, ca. 1941. Albert Kahn Associated Architects and Engineers, designers. Hedrich-Blessing photograph/courtesy Chicago Historical Society. HB 06539C.

the realm of pure Miesian universal space.[4] The rhetorics of functionalism remained throughout Mies's career. The steel, glass, and brick buildings for the Illinois Institute of Technology (IIT) in Chicago (where Mies was Director of Architecture from 1938 to 1959) carry forward that early inspiration, brought to even richer expression in such masterpieces as IIT's Crown Hall (1956) and his 1954 proposal for a convention center in Chicago.

As the defense buildup continued, Kahn (who died in 1942) and his firm designed plants for tanks, trucks, and bombers. From the thirty-seven-acre Wright Aeronautical plant in Lockland, Ohio (1940), to the sixty-two-acre Willow Run bomber plant (1942) outside Detroit, Kahn's factories marked records for speed in concrete and steel construction.[5] As steel became a precious metal reserved for armaments, Kahn, like others, designed with alternative materials. Trusses built of reinforced concrete and laminated wood illustrated the capabilities of these materials on an enormous scale that could be applied to smaller wartime structures, such as Skidmore, Owings & Merrill's 1942 Reception Building at the Great Lakes Naval Training Station.

With the industrial defense expansion came a concomitant need for housing the workers and their families who were drawn to production centers. Prior to World War II the government had been a reluctant client with regard to housing; however, during the national defense emergency it had no choice. Initially, the government agency chiefly involved in defense housing was the Farm Security Administration (FSA). Established in 1937, the FSA had taken over the functions of the Division of Subsistence Homesteads and Resettlement Administration and several other agencies, constructing houses in nearly forty-eight states.[6] The FSA was the agency most experienced and effective in building minimum-standard houses for thousands of families living in squatters' camps amid substandard conditions, whose plight was immortalized in John Steinbeck's *The Grapes of Wrath* and in Dorothea Lange's photographs. A fine example of prewar

Reception center at the Great Lakes Naval Facility, Chicago, Illinois, 1942. Skidmore, Owings & Merrill, architects. Courtesy National Archives. RG 208-NS-3558-G7C-22.

FSA design was a farm workers' community at Yuba City, California (1940), one of many designed by Vernon DeMars, district architect for the western states. In the two-story, multifamily units, DeMars varied the spare design of unbroken horizontal lines both chromatically and in the arrangement of windows. Redwood sheathed the lower floor, which contained the living room and kitchen. The upper bedroom floor was clad in light-colored Cemesto, a newly invented, one-and-one-half-inch-thick sandwich panel consisting of layers of asbestos-filled cement on a fiber core.[7] Rows of windows provided ample cross-ventilation. Parallel rows of uniform buildings were arranged in staggered formation, comfortably fitting the site.

With its proven track record, the FSA was the logical choice to create planned communities for war workers. This was especially true because the government had decided to build in outlying areas adjacent to decentralized factories rather than implement a slum clearance program in the cities. In 1940, DeMars designed dormitories, cabins, and community buildings for several thousand workers and their families in Vallejo, California, near the shipyards of San Francisco Bay. Among the first prefabricated houses of the war, they employed stressed-skin, glued ply-

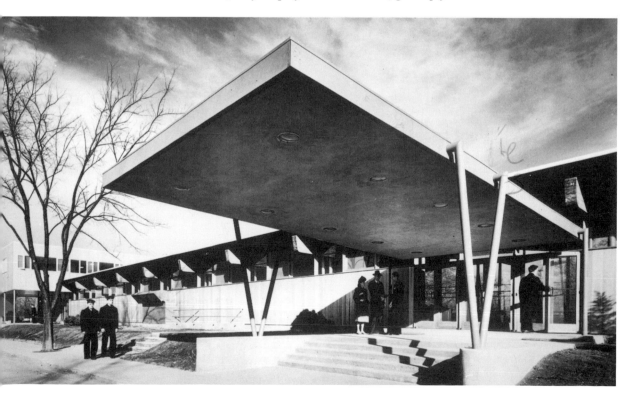

wood panels made in a factory by assembly-line production, using a system pioneered in aircraft construction. Panels were trucked to the site; entire walls were assembled on the floor and then raised into place. Many prefabricated structures such as those at Vallejo were demountable so they could be reused after the war, thus preventing ghost towns from resulting when the shipbuilding industry dried up.[8]

FSA architects took pride in creating sensitive and imaginative site plans for these instant communities. Although time was limited, contours were considered carefully, eliminating the need for extensive grading, and the buildings themselves were oriented for sun and breezes. Site plans were often picturesque arrangements that avoided monotony. Landscaping and colors such as blue, yellow, buff, and mulberry provided external variety.

The FSA was not the only government agency to build wartime housing. The Federal Works Agency, established in 1939 and headed by John M. Carmody, was responsible for the complex administrative task of organizing its affiliated agencies dealing with public works, including the United States Housing Authority (USHA) and the Public Buildings Administration (PBA). Neither was very effective, and by the spring of 1941 the housing program was the furthest behind schedule of all defense building efforts. In response, on April 5, 1941, Carmody announced the formation of the new Division of Defense Housing. For a short but significant period, the division's director, Clark Foreman, aided by Talbot Wegg, who headed the Special Operation Section, hired independent, practicing architects to solve the nation's acute housing shortage.[9] Foreman sought to make the program a contribution not only to defense but to architecture as well, convinced that by employing leading modern architects, the stigma attached to most public housing in the United States might be eliminated.[10] Within the next seven months, at least eleven new housing projects were designed and built. Widely acclaimed in the architectural press, the program enlisted, among others, William

Yuba City, California, ca. 1940. Vernon DeMars, regional FSA architect. Courtesy National Archives. RG 208-EX-156-A-35.

Housing unit at Yuba City, California, 1940. Courtesy National Archives. RG 208-EX-158-A-37.

W. Wurster, Walter Gropius, Marcel Breuer, George Howe, Louis I. Kahn, Alfred Kastner, Hugh Stubbins, Jr., Antonin Raymond, and Frank Lloyd Wright.

Architects were issued strict guidelines in accordance with the Lanham Act, which in 1940 allocated $150 million to the Federal Works Agency for housing defense workers. (By July 1943, the government expanded Lanham Act funding to $1.3 billion.)[11] Average construction costs were limited to $3,000 per dwelling unit, raised to $3,750 in 1942.[12] Although the requirements for these minimal dwellings offered little latitude, architects nonetheless produced innovative designs.

William W. Wurster, the established San Francisco architect, designed almost seventeen hundred demountable one-story houses in Vallejo, half of which were constructed of plywood, the remaining half of Homasote, a new wallboard made of wood pulp and ground newspaper, bound with resin.[13] Wurster insisted that the government give him the opportunity to experiment with different construction methods on twenty-five houses. With the assistance of Fred Langhorst, a former apprentice of Frank Lloyd Wright, he designed three types: masonry walls, bent-wood frames, and wood-skeleton frames. The bent-wood frame system adapted factory methods: workers joined columns and roof trusses on the ground then raised them into place. The wood-skeleton system combined widely spaced post-and-beam construction with infill panels. All three systems eliminated load-bearing partitions, thus creating open interior plans. Large expanses of glass filled the interiors with light. While the results were attractive and the costs low, Langhorst realized as early as 1942 that a major impediment of peacetime application of these standardized designs was the proliferation of building codes in the United States. "Without a streamlining of the local building ordinances for low-cost work," he claimed, "it seems unlikely that private work will be able to achieve the savings possible in government work." [14]

Walter Gropius and Marcel Breuer were probably the best-known modernists practicing at the time in America, bringing to this country the legacy of the German Bauhaus. After emigrating to the United States, they began a long association with Harvard's School of Design and revolutionized its program at the invitation of Dean Joseph Hudnut, a leading advocate of modern architecture in America. Gropius especially had much experience in building low-cost housing in Germany. Under Foreman's program, he and Breuer were commissioned to design Aluminum City Terrace in New Kensington, Pennsylvania (near Pittsburgh), for workers at the nearby ALCOA plant. The project's designs featured many hallmarks of European modernism: ribbon windows, flat roofs, gangplank walkways to the entrances, and open plans. For a brief period, the project was caught in the center of a political dispute, and predictably one mayoral candidate criticized the novel designs as "chicken coops." [15] While some tenants did find the exteriors severe, most were happy with the large windows and the openness of the interiors, created by the architects' use of a low partition between the kitchen and dining area. In 1944, *Architectural Forum* reported that eighty-nine percent of the resi-

DEFENSE HOUSES AT VALLEJO, CALIF.*   WILLIAM WILSON WURSTER, ARCHITECT

Peter S. Reed

1. **2.** **3.**

Picture **1** shows Homasote sheets being wet down before use, in order to swell sheets so that subsequent shrinkage will stretch material on frames. **2** shows precutting of openings for electric outlet boxes, **3** precutting of studs and other framing lumber outside the plant.

4. **5.** **6.**

4, 5, and **6,** show assembly of a typical, room size wall panel on a "jig table" marked off in modular units. Door opening is cut after the sheet is applied, using plywood template and skill saw; sheets are glued and nailed to 2 x 3 studs, using mechanical glue spreaders.

7. **8.** **9.**

7, 8, and **9** show fabrication of a roof panel, complete with overhang and screened vent. Homasote ceilings are applied to furring strips on the bottom of the rafters, tops of rafters canted to receive sloping roof at job. Four such panels, plus seven smaller units, roof one house.

10. **11.** **12.**

10. Trailer-truck loaded with three complete houses ready for 29 mile trip to the site.

SITE PREPARATION. Picture **11** shows form for casting foundation piers in batches of 84 piers. **12** shows hole-boring apparatus for drilling foundation holes, and operation of setting piers.

*Constructing Agency: FWA Division of Defense Housing

227

fourteen

WILLIAM WILSON WURSTER, ARCHITECT

13.   14.   15.

Pictures **13** and **14** show site-assembly (on a special jig table) of floor framing panels and erection on post foundations. Single thickness flooring is laid in the conventional way. Picture **15** shows traveling crane unloading wall panels from trailer truck.

16.   17.   18.

16, 17, and **18** show successive stages in the erection of wall panels on the floor platform. Assembly is handled in two stages, with a fifteen minute intermission (during which the crew shifts to the next house in the row) for the installation of prefabricated plumbing.

19.   20.   21.

19 shows completed walls, ready to receive roof panels, which are lifted into place by a light traveling crane (**20** and **21**), covered with roofers in the conventional way, and surfaced with roll roofing (**22**). **23** shows application of trim, the larger picture below completed houses.

Gabriel Moulin

22.   23.

dents liked the houses.[16] Today, Aluminum City Terrace remains a successful resident-owned cooperative.

Philadelphia architects George Howe and Louis I. Kahn formed an association in 1941. Howe, in collaboration with William Lescaze, had designed the first International Style skyscraper in America, the Philadelphia Savings Fund Society Building (1932). The first project designed by Howe and Kahn for the Division of Defense Housing was Pine Ford Acres in Middletown, Pennsylvania, consisting of four hundred fifty units of multifamily dwellings. In subsequent projects Howe, Kahn, and Oscar Stonorov, who worked for Le Corbusier, introduced several unique aspects that distinguished their projects from ordinary government housing. At Pennypack Woods in Philadelphia, and at Carver Court, a housing project for black steelworkers in Coatesville, Pennsylvania, the plans of the houses were varied. The architects placed living spaces on the second floor, thereby freeing the ground floor for services. They noted that while modern architects had succeeded in developing closely knit areas for living, this very space often became "bedlam when the bicycle and the baby carriage must be stored in the living room, the laundry washed in the kitchen, and the chair repaired in the bedroom."[17] At Carver Court the open ground floor served as a carport, an outdoor living space, and an entrance shelter with utility and storage areas. Most housing projects also included community centers, which were larger showpieces for modern design. Carver Court was one of several wartime projects included in the Museum of Modern Art's exhibition "Built in USA 1932–1944."[18]

Chabot Terrace housing project, Vallejo, California, ca. 1943. William W. Wurster, architect. Courtesy Roger Sturtevant Collection/ Oakland Museum/City of Oakland/gift of the artist.

Aluminum City Terrace, New Kensington, Pennsylvania, ca. 1942. Walter Gropius and Marcel Breuer, architects. Courtesy National Archives. RG 208-EX-158-C-143.

Carver Court housing project, Coatesville, Pennsylvania, ca. 1942. George Howe, Oscar Stonorov, and Louis I. Kahn, architects. Courtesy National Archives. RG 208-EX-158-C-133.

Community center at Carver Court, ca. 1942. Courtesy National Archives. RG 208-EX-158-C-132.

Peter S. Reed

In 1941, Frank Lloyd Wright received one of the last commissions of the Division of Defense Housing. The seventy-four-year-old Wright had never received a government commission, and his assignment was to design a one-hundred-unit housing project in Pittsfield, Massachusetts, in conjunction with a rifle factory. Throughout his career, Wright had addressed the problem of the low-cost house and, in particular, the paradoxical problem of how individuality of design could be reconciled with standardized production methods that tended to create uniformity. "Cracker boxes without spirit or sense laid out like the skyscraper laid down on its side do not seem the right thing—to me," Wright wrote to Foreman at the start of the project."[19] For Pittsfield, Wright proposed a quadruple house type, a cloverleaf of four houses arranged in a pinwheel cluster and sharing party-walls, each facing a different direction onto petal-shaped yards. The design followed Wright's Suntop homes in Ardmore, Pennsylvania, where in 1939 one such quatrefoil cluster was built for a private developer. At the Cloverleaf project, Wright decided to build floors and shared walls of precast concrete slabs with contrasting wood sun decks. Each house included a mezzanine-level kitchen, overlooking a two-story living room and offering views of a rooftop play area and the yard. Wright described the design as "standardization complete without stultification or loss of individual freedom . . . privacy complete."[20] In keeping with requirements,

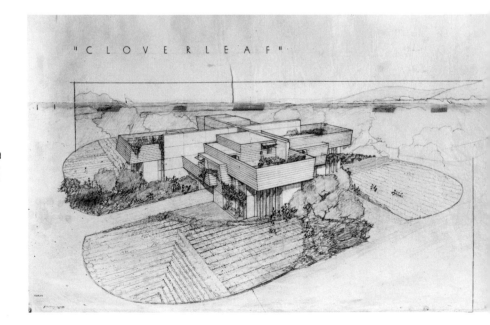

Sketch by Frank Lloyd Wright of the proposed Cloverleaf housing project, Pittsfield, Massachusetts, ca. 1941. Courtesy the Frank Lloyd Wright Foundation, Scottsdale, Arizona ©.

the $3,500 house was within the limitations imposed by the Lanham Act.

As Wright completed the Cloverleaf construction documents in January 1942, the Division of Defense Housing was abruptly terminated. Unwittingly at the center of a political controversy, Cloverleaf was never implemented. Foreman had angered John W. McCormack, Majority Leader of the U.S. House of Representatives, by hiring out-of-state architects, especially for a project in McCormack's home state. This must have struck Foreman as ludicrous—why would anyone pigeonhole Wright as a "Wisconsin" architect? In any event, Foreman was branded a radical, and all subsequent defense housing was handled by the Public Buildings Administration. In February 1942, George Howe left his partnership with Stonorov and Kahn to become supervising architect of the PBA, the highest architectural post in the government. Howe's appointment guaranteed an ally of modern architects in Washington.[21]

Wright's criticism of government housing as "cracker boxes" seems more applicable to European *Zeilenbau* than to wartime housing projects designed by modern architects. Richard Neutra, the leading Los Angeles modernist, demonstrated a special sensitivity to site planning in his 1942 design of the Channel Heights housing project near the city's San Pedro shipyards.[22] A dramatic, one-hundred-sixty-five-acre site oriented toward the Pacific Ocean, the project was elegantly adapted to the irregular contours of hills, canyons, and ravines. Neutra arranged two hundred twenty buildings to house six hundred families along short, cul-de-sac streets, grouped in superblocks. The project featured a meandering main road and a continuous central park with pedestrian paths that tunneled under the road and extended through the project, recalling Clarence Stein and Henry Wright's famous 1928 plan for Radburn, New Jersey.[23]

As many of the previous examples attest, the war's unprecedented building demands fueled an increased interest in pre-

fabrication. The government, in a state of emergency, provided
virtually risk-free financing to investors and developers, and at
least two hundred thousand housing units, or about ten percent
of the total, were constructed by prefabrication methods. Some
seventy firms were active in producing such homes.[24] In the forefront was Foster Gunnison, whose New Albany, Indiana, plant
produced standardized house parts along conveyor belts, supporting the firm's slogan, "Press a Button, and You Get a Home."

Architects also tried their hand at prefabrication. In the
fall of 1941, Konrad Wachsmann came to the United States from
Germany and lived with Walter and Ise Gropius in Lincoln, Massachusetts. Gropius and Wachsmann had experimented with prefabrication as early as the 1920s; a demonstration house by
Gropius was built in 1927 at the Weissenhof Siedlungen in Stutt-
gart. Following Pearl Harbor, Gropius and Wachsmann developed
a system of plywood panels connected by four-way metal wedges
that were eventually patented. The General Panel Corporation
was set up to produce and market the Packaged house, and on
February 23, 1943, a prototype was erected and demounted in
Somerville, Massachusetts, in one day.[25] Announced with much
fanfare, this conceptually rigorous scheme never went into production. Gropius eventually assigned his Harvard design students an
exercise using the panel system. The adaptability of the forty-
inch modular units was further demonstrated by such leading
architects as Richard Neutra, whose designs for various two-story
buildings were published in architectural journals.[26] Two more
test houses were constructed in New York, and a Lockheed Aircraft engine factory was acquired in Burbank—but by 1947 when
the company was ready to produce, government insurance of such
projects had died, and the company soon folded.

R. Buckminster Fuller's steel Dymaxion Deployment
Unit, designed to take advantage of existing industrial processes,
was expected by many to do for the house what Henry Ford had
done for the automobile. Adapted from round grain bins, the de-

Model of Channel Heights, ca. 1941. Richard
Neutra, architect. Courtesy Julius Shulman.

Channel Heights, ca. 1942. Richard Neutra,
architect. Courtesy Julius Shulman.

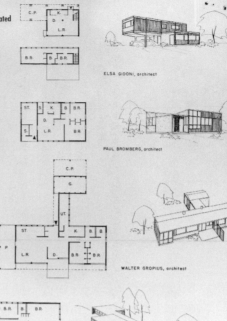

ADAPTABILITY of General Panel's system to a wide range of plan problems is demonstrated by designs of well known architects.

The designs on this page illustrate one of the most important characteristics of the General Panel line—what Wachsmann terms its "universality." Any architect or consumer who is willing to use a 3 ft. 4 in. module as the basic unit of measurement can easily build any sort of house he chooses from the system. In reality, this is no great limitation for it easily provides for such minimum dimensions as doors, passages, built-in storage, etc. Clear spans of up to 13 ft. 4 in. are possible, ceiling heights may be varied and—by an ingenious detailing of the roof framing—any desired slope may be had without modification of the panel. Nor is the system restricted to residential work: on the contrary, Wachsmann sees a wide application for it in nurseries, schools, hospitals—in fact, almost any single or two-story building type.

As presently manufactured by the California company, the system has, of course, certain limitations. Curves are impossible in it, as are wall intersections at any angle other than 90°. Heating must necessarily be by hot air (although General Panel engineers are already at work on a system of built-in radiant coils). Like any system fabricated of wood, the system is not 100 per cent fire- or termite-proof. However, in the real context of America's present housing shortage, these are rather far-fetched considerations. As of today, no manufacturer of industrial houses can lay a better claim to a "universal" system than General Panel's Konrad Wachsmann.

ELSA GIDONI, architect

PAUL BROMBERG, architect

WALTER GROPIUS, architect

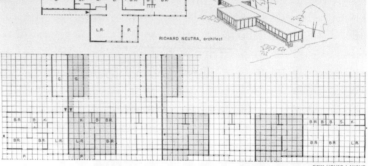

RICHARD NEUTRA, architect

ROW HOUSE LAYOUT

Peter S Reed

Architectural Forum, February 1947.

Working on house panels at the Gunnison Housing Corporation, New Albany, Indiana, n.d. Courtesy National Archives. RG 208-EX-158-D-L-203.

twenty-two

BUILDING FOR DEFENSE ... 1,000 HOUSES A DAY AT $1,200 EACH

promised by biggest sheet steel fabricator. Buckminster Fuller dresses up a grain bin, invents a trim three-room defense house, a six-man steel tent. The "Dymaxion" is totally demountable.

Ernest Weissmann

This spring Federal Works Administrator John M. Carmody, high mogul of defense construction, skeptically asked THE FORUM *to point to houses in the $2,000-$3,000 price range which are demountable (*ARCH. FORUM, *March 1941, p. 54-56). Herewith,* THE FORUM *presents such a house—priced not at $3,000, but less than half that amount; not 80 or 90 per cent demountable, but completely so.*

During the past two years, the Butler Manufacturing Co. sold the Government 36,000 steel grain bins like the one reproduced from a catalogue page above. Today, Butler stands ready to supply up to 1,000 steel houses a day like the one which went up in a Washington, D. C. trailer camp last month (right). A dressed-up adaptation of the lowly grain bin, the cylindrical dwelling is aimed at the defense housing market and hopes to make a bull's-eye by virtue of its complete demountability, its availability in quantities and its newsworthy price—$1,200 complete with utilities and furniture.

Inventor. Spark behind the metamorphosis which has taken place in Butler's Kansas City plant is Richard Buckminster Fuller, inventor-designer-writer of wide repute. A past master at astounding the public by altering sacredly traditional forms, Fuller has concentrated his inventions in the field of shelter, for Fuller believes that environment is "95 per cent a shelter problem." Most memorable are his Dymaxion house whose light walls and floors were suspended by steel guys from a central utility tower, his Dymaxion bathroom whose compactly integrated fixtures gave it the appearance of sculptured metal and his streamlined Dymaxion automobile whose motor was mounted at the rear of a three-wheeled chassis. More successful than any of these, a subsequent Fuller invention, his book entitled "Nine Chains to the Moon," has sold by the thousands.

Besides discussing everything from Einstein's theories to death in its XLIV chapters, this book makes a score of startling technical prophecies, amply justifies the phrases which various writers have used to describe the rotund, little, white-haired man who is Richard Buckminster Fuller (see photograph, p. 381): "prophet of civilization" . . . "arch-theorist of housing" . . . "genius in a business suit" . . . "prefabrication's liveliest intelligence."

Through a car window one day last November Fuller noticed a number of Butler's bins on the Illinois countryside, immediately saw in them the basis for a solution to the defense housing problem of speed and low cost. Forthwith he visited Butler's Kansas City, Mo. plant, noted production methods and limitations, returned to his New York City home with an armful of catalogues and a brainful of ideas. A group of young friends was invited to help put the ideas on paper—notably Architect-Partners Walter Sanders and John Breck, Architect Ernest Weissman and Designer-Partners Rex Allen, Arthur Malsin and Edward Toole.

By year-end the preliminary presentation of his grain-bin house was ready for submission to Government officials and potential backers. Without committing themselves, Government housers looked kindly on the proposal, prompted Investor Robert Colgate to underwrite the cost of developing the house. (Since the design permitted Butler to use only existing dies and required no retooling, this development cost was comparatively small.) During the next three months, inventor, manufacturer and designers perfected and produced a full-size experimental model, demounted it, re-erected it, tested it and finally named it "Dymaxion Deployment Unit."

Embodying several improvements over the experimental unit, the second house last month was loaded in a railroad box car (with room for fourteen additional houses to spare) and shipped to Washington for official inspection. Freight charge: $14.

House. In six man-days two unskilled laborers earning 45 cents an hour stripped the crating off a half-dozen packages of tightly nested parts, completed their erec-

sign was made by the Butler Manufacturing Company of Kansas City, Missouri, the largest general steel-sheet fabricator in the country. Constructed in six days by two men, an experimental unit was displayed in Washington, D.C., and another at the Museum of Modern Art in the fall of 1941. The minimal three-hundred-fourteen-square-foot units were lightweight, mobile, and cost only $1,200, including furnishings and prefabricated kitchen and bath. A thousand could be manufactured in a day, but only a few hundred were built before restrictions on strategic materials were imposed.

Prefabrication seems to have been especially well suited to mobile structures such as trailers. The wartime demand for housing had revived the slumping house trailer industry. War trailers were usually wood-framed structures with Homasote walls, measuring only seven by eighteen feet. To provide more spacious accommodations, the government adopted an innovative folding system for convenience. Designed by William Stout in the 1930s, the system was not produced until the war put a premium on cheap movable housing. Only eight feet wide in travel configuration, the Stout expansible trailer unfolded to a width of nineteen and one-half feet. Mobile houses that consisted of two or three sections were developed by the Tennessee Valley Authority.

Demonstration of Stout expansible trailer, ca. 1942. Courtesy National Archives. RG 208-EX-158-D-L-250.

Transported in pieces and joined at the site, these sectional homes anticipated the postwar "double-wide" trailer, used as permanent housing.

Interest in prefabrication continued because of speculation about the postwar building boom. In January 1946, President Harry S. Truman appointed Wilson W. Wyatt head of the Veterans Emergency Housing Program, which targeted the construction of over a million houses in 1946 and an even greater number in 1947.

Demountable, prefabricated Quonset huts, one of the most pervasive World War II building types, were available because they were so easily transported from abroad. The Quonset hut had been the archetypical military building type of the war. Designed in 1941 at Quonset Point Naval Air Station, Rhode Island, by a team of architects working for the U.S. Navy, Quonsets featured steel arched-rib frame supports, a pressed-wood lining, an insulation layer, and an outer skin of curved corrugated-steel sheets. Quonsets came in a variety of sizes and could be adapted to eighty-six different interior layouts ranging from barracks to hospitals and chapels. By 1946, an estimated one hundred seventy thousand had been produced and erected around the world, many to return to the home front as dormitory

Chapel, Camp Parks, California, 1945. Bruce Goff, architect. Courtesy Art Institute of Chicago.

Dymaxion Wichita house prototype, 1946. Dis-
assembled house was shipped in tube at left.
R. Buckminster Fuller, architect. © Allegra Fuller Snyder. Courtesy Buckminster Fuller Institute, Santa Barbara.

Publicity photograph, bedroom of Dymaxion
Wichita house prototype, 1946.

housing on college campuses. Although attempts by manufacturers to sell the idea of Quonset huts as civilian housing failed, the huts' kit-of-parts aesthetics attracted some architects. In 1947, Pierre Chareau, the architect of the *Maison de Verre* (1932) in Paris, modified a Quonset hut to serve as artist Robert Motherwell's Long Island studio. Bruce Goff, who served in a Navy Construction Battalion, combined three huts for his 1945 Camp Parks Chapel. In the Ruth Ford house of Aurora, Illinois, Goff inventively reassembled the hut's ribs in a spherical composition, combining them with an amalgam of wood, coal, and such found industrial detritus as acrylic domes salvaged from aircraft.[27]

Idle defense factories could potentially be converted to produce houses as well. Richard Neutra spoke of the dichotomy between the sleek, mass-produced "modern instruments of war" and the "obsolete, unplanned turmoil of slums and substandard structural accommodations, which . . . fill . . . our current cities."[28] The questions universally pondered during the war were whether buying a house would become like purchasing a car and whether World War II would do for prefabricated housing what World War I did for the airplane. For a time, the optimistic view that industry and machine production would fulfill housing needs inspired much experimentation. Quick and cheap production would bring what one advertisement called a new standard of living in homes of "cheerful convenience."[29] Anticipating a peacetime conversion of its bomber assembly plant, Beech Aircraft of Wichita, Kansas, manufactured the famous Dymaxion Wichita house, designed by R. Buckminster Fuller. Larger than the Dymaxion Deployment Unit, it cost $6,500, but despite efforts to domesticate the grain bin with frilly curtains, this aero-house never got off the ground.

A similar experiment by the Consolidated Vultee Aircraft Corporation, one of the largest airplane manufacturers in the world, also attempted to produce the modern house in an airplane factory near Los Angeles. Designed by Henry Dreyfuss and Edward Larrabee Barnes in 1946, the Vultee house was con-

Assembling Vultee house wall panel in Consolidated Vultee Aircraft factory, Los Angeles, California, 1947. Henry Dreyfuss, designer, and Edward Larrabee Barnes, architect. Courtesy Julius Shulman.

Vultee house built for Mr. and Mrs. Reginald S. Fleet, Los Angeles, California, ca. 1948. Henry Dreyfuss, designer, and Edward Larrabee Barnes, architect. Courtesy Julius Shulman.

structed of high-strength, lightweight aircraft panels made up of thin sheets of aluminum glued and bonded to a cellular paper core.[30] Three-inch-thick panels measuring up to eighteen feet long and eight feet high could be shipped flat and joined at the site. Joints were precise, surfaces smooth and true, and thin sections expressed the lightness of the material.[31] The fully furnished demonstration house with its open spaces and large expanses of glass between the interior and patio conveyed a modern approach to comfort and convenience, clearly distinct from mere "housing." Only two were ever built.

A fascinating, though unsuccessful, attempt at postwar prefabrication was architect Bertrand Goldberg's Unishelter housing unit of 1953. Inspired by the architect's wartime proposal for a molded-plywood mobile penicillin laboratory for the military, the Unishelter was promoted as mass-produced, low-cost housing. Each shelter could be packed with materials and equipment, thereby serving as both carrier and house.[32]

Neither design nor quality was to blame for the failure of the factory-produced house. Rather, the problems of economics and production coupled with revised mortgage-lending policies in 1948 limited the possibilities inherent in prefabrication.[33] The problem of distribution and the need for enormous quantity to make start-up feasible prevented production from going forward. Local building codes and zoning laws often worked against modern, standardized design, as did vehement opposition from building trade unions, the reluctance of banks to finance experimental houses, and the psychological resistance of consumers. Although prefabrication was given an enormous impetus during the war, opinion polls suggested that the public found it less than desirable.[34] Because of its use in the construction of temporary wartime housing, prefabrication became associated with impermanence. Public reaction to the Museum of Modern Art's 1945 exhibition "Tomorrow's Small House" confirmed this sentiment.[35] The museum compiled an audience survey, concluding that if prefabrication were to succeed, the public must be convinced that it was "an evolving phenomenon, and that various parts of buildings have been more or less prefabricated for years . . . and that in these houses the prefabricated walls, roof and closet sections are but the logical extension of the prefabricated parts in the conventional house."[36]

If success is measured by the number of houses sold, perhaps the most impressive results were achieved by Levitt and Sons, the largest private builder of housing communities in the eastern United States. Between 1934 and 1941, the Levitts had constructed only about two thousand upper-income houses on Long Island. But taking advantage of wartime programs, they financed and built Oakdale Farms in Norfolk, Virginia, in 1942. With its seven hundred fifty permanent homes on a two-hundred-acre site, the project was their first venture into mass-produced houses for moderate-income residents.[37] Like other private wartime home builders, the Levitts exploited the potential of streamlined production methods.[38] The houses were not prefabricated, but by producing enormous quantities, prices were kept low. Levitt reduced the construction of a house to twenty-seven basic tasks.[39] With factory-cut lumber, the houses could be assembled with minimal on-site construction, a process recalling Frank Lloyd Wright's American System-Built houses developed during World War I. Their wartime experience was successfully applied to the famous postwar Levittowns in New York and Pennsylva-

Proposed Unishelter cargo carrier and prefabricated house, 1953. Bertrand Goldberg, architect. Courtesy the architect.

nia. The Levitts knew their consumers' tastes from their own market research: at Oakdale Farms and in the Levittowns, the "Cape Cod" houses looked like traditional American homes, and they offered built-in features that were certain to seduce prospective buyers.

Although buyers were pleased, critics were not. "The little Levitt house," Eric Larrabee scornfully noted in *Harper's,* "is American suburbia reduced to its logical absurdity."[40] Leading architects shared Larrabee's criticisms. Harvard University's Dean Joseph Hudnut, for example, cautioned against the overly functional aspects of the wartime housing industry. In his important 1945 essay "The Post-Modern House," he summed up his position: "I have been thinking about the cloudburst of new houses which as soon as the war is ended is going to cover the hills and valleys of New England with so many square miles of prefabricated happiness."[41] Although Hudnut was progressive and intrigued by the new inventions of industry, he found prefabricated houses cold and heartless and generally devoid of the emotion, texture, and richness necessary for good architecture. "We are too ready to mistake novelty for progress and progress for art. I tell my students that there were noble buildings before the invention of plywood."[42]

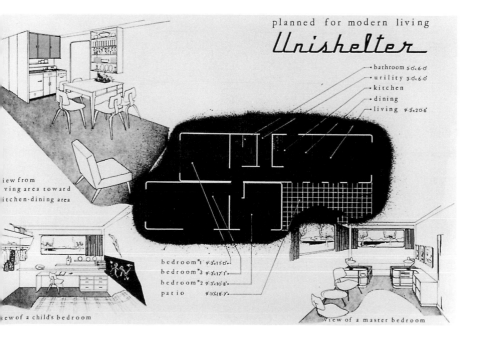

Proposed Unishelter prefabricated house, 1953. Bertrand Goldberg, architect. Courtesy the architect.

If Hudnut feared the worst for the New England landscape, the prospect of Cape Cod happiness covering the valleys of California inspired John Entenza, editor of *Arts and Architecture* magazine, to launch the ambitious Case Study House Program in January 1945.[43] During the war, the magazine had enthusiastically covered new aircraft plants, military facilities, and community projects, which Entenza hoped would provide models for postwar industrialized housing.[44] Through the Case Study Program, he commissioned modern architects, many of whom had been involved in the war, to design and build furnished prototypes of good design.[45] Case Study house #8 of 1949, designed by Charles and Ray Eames for a site overlooking the Pacific Ocean, epitomized the program's goals. Its lightweight steel frame was erected by five men in sixteen hours, and the frame had infill panels of Cemesto. The Eameses used exposed, ribbed Ferroboard as the ceiling of the main space; its industrial aesthetics recalled the appearance of the war's great aircraft factories. Fiberglass cloth and plastic resin material, which they found in war-surplus stores, were employed as screens; other furnishings included the molded-plywood chairs that grew out of their wartime experiments making leg splints for the U.S. Navy.

While many architects focused on housing, others were anxious to design more ambitious, public projects. Certainly one of the most notable was the United Nations complex in New York, an architectural symbol of the globalization of American prestige

Ranch-style house, Levittown, New York, ca. 1949. Courtesy the National Building Museum/gift of Richard Wurts.

Opposite:
Eames house living room, Pacific Palisades, California, ca. 1949. Charles and Ray Eames, architects. Courtesy Julius Shulman.

and power. As various sites around the country were considered, many architects, under the aegis of the short-lived American Society of Planners and Architects whose members included Breuer, DeMars, Gropius, Howe, Hudnut, Louis I. Kahn, Stonorov, and Wurster, lobbied for a modern design.[46] In their opinion none of the architectural styles of the past would be appropriate to express the far-reaching goals of the United Nations. Moreover, the architecture had to transcend national traditions and prejudices. Although many architects felt the final design fell far short of its monumental potential, the aluminum curtain wall of the Secretariat (1950) remains the apotheosis of the war's functionalist aesthetics. The steel-framed office building with glass facade soon became the preferred language of the corporate Establishment. Eero Saarinen's General Motors Technical Center in Warren, Michigan, begun after the war and completed in 1956, was a massive campus of clean, rectangular forms, somewhat in the manner of Mies. Skidmore, Owings & Merrill adapted a similar vocabulary for Lever House in New York (1952).

United Nations complex, New York, New York, ca. 1952. Le Corbusier (main idea), Wallace K. Harrison, and Max Abramovitz, architects. Courtesy Ezra Stoller/ESTO.

The war-propelled victory of modernism was observed by Alfred H. Barr, Jr., director of the Museum of Modern Art, at an architectural symposium held at the museum in 1948. "Our best architects," Barr claimed, "take the style for granted so far as large buildings are concerned."[47] No sooner was such a pronouncement made than the orthodoxy of the new International Style began to unravel, now called into question as meaningless and dispirited. One by one, modern architects turned against the style they had once so energetically supported. Wurster, for example, became an exponent of a new Bay Region style with its preference for redwood and stone in an effort to create a more humane environment. Following the General Motors center, Saarinen de-

Lever House, New York, New York, ca. 1952. Skidmore, Owings & Merrill, architects. Courtesy Ezra Stoller/ESTO.

Illustration from *Revere's Part in Better Living*,
no. 10, 1943.

veloped a dramatic, expressive mode in such buildings as the Trans World Airlines Terminal at New York's Kennedy Airport (1962), while others espoused a renewed interest in monumentality and history, two themes that became central to the subsequent work of Louis I. Kahn. The crosscurrents in architectural thought expressed throughout the symposium were the issues modernists developed over the following decades as the war's functionalist grip loosened and architects could pursue more personal directions. Like returning veterans, they had won their battle, and were anxious to start living.

Notes

My sincere appreciation to Curator and Editor Donald Albrecht for sharing research and insights into the history of wartime building. Heather Burnham, Curatorial Assistant at the National Building Museum, also generously assisted with research and photo files. I would also like to thank James Dart for his comments on an earlier draft.

1. On the exhibition and related publications see Terence Riley, *The International Style: Exhibition 15 and The Museum of Modern Art* (New York: Rizzoli, 1992).

2. James Ford and Katherine Morrow Ford, *The Modern House in America* (New York: Architectural Book Publishing Co., Inc., 1940).

3. In the period under discussion, the program in many architecture schools in the United States was also transformed from one based on the Ecole des Beaux Arts to one that dealt more relevantly with materials, techniques, style, planning, and social concerns.

4. The connection between Kahn and Mies has been noted by such sources as Franz Schulze, *Mies van der Rohe: A Critical Biography* (Chicago and London: University of Chicago Press, 1985), and Oswald W. Grube, *Industrial Buildings and Factories* (New York: Praeger Publishers, Inc., 1971).

5. "Architects and Defense," *Pencil Points* 22 (October 1941): 660–661.

6. "Farm Security Administration," *Architectural Forum* 74 (January 1941): 2–16.

7. Cemesto was invented by George Swenson in 1936 and was developed with the John B. Pierce Foundation, New York.

8. A good summary for the enormous amount of wartime building that took place in the Vallejo area is "Vallejo Housing Authority Supplement," *California Arts and Architecture* 60 (June 1943): 33–50.

9. "Building for Defense," *Architectural Forum* 75 (July 1941): 8–9.

10. Talbot Wegg, "FLLW versus the USA," *AIA Journal* 53 (February 1970): 48–52.

11. Miles L. Colean, *American Housing: Problems and Prospects* (New York: The Twentieth Century Fund, 1944), 286.

12. Ibid.

13. "Houses for Defense," *Architectural Forum* 75 (October 1941), 226–228.

14. Fred Langhorst, "A New Approach to Large Scale Housing," *California Arts and Architecture* 59 (April 1942): 27–31.

15. "New Kensington Housing Project," *Architectural Forum* 81 (July 1944): 67 and 76.

16. Ibid., 69.

17. "'Standards' versus Essential Space," *Architectural Forum* 76 (May 1942): 309.

18. Elizabeth Mock, ed., *Built in USA 1932–1944* (New York: The Museum of Modern Art, 1944).

19. Letter from Frank Lloyd Wright to Clark Foreman, October 17, 1941. Copyright © The Frank Lloyd Wright Foundation 1995, courtesy The Frank Lloyd Wright Archives, Scottsdale, Arizona.

20. This is inscribed on a drawing among the Cloverleaf series (4203.045) in the Frank Lloyd Wright Foundation Archives, Scottsdale, Arizona.

21. Of the Division of Defense Housing projects discussed here, Aluminum City Terrace, Pine Ford Acres, Pennypack Woods, and Carver Court exist. The others have been demolished.

22. On Channel Heights and Neutra's other community plans, see Thomas S. Hines, *Richard Neutra and the Search for Modern Architecture* (New York: Oxford University Press, 1982), 161–191.

23. Channel Heights has been demolished.

24. Gilbert Herbert, *The Dream of the Factory-Made House: Walter Gropius and Konrad Wachsmann* (Cambridge, Mass.: The MIT Press, 1984), 276.

25. For an in-depth study of this project see Herbert, *The Dream of the Factory-Made House*.

26. "The Industrialized House," *Architectural Forum* 86 (February 1947): 120.

27. See chapters two and three in David G. De Long, *Bruce Goff: Toward Absolute Architecture* (New York: The Architectural History Foundation, and Cambridge, Mass.: The MIT Press, 1988).

28. Richard J. Neutra, "Governmental Architecture in California" *California Arts and Architecture* 58 (August 1941): 22.

29. Lustron advertisement, *Life* (April 19, 1949).

30. Walter Gropius, under whom Barnes had studied at Harvard, recommended the young architect to Dreyfuss. The Vultee House was one of

many conversion projects that Dreyfuss developed for Consolidated Vultee.

31. "House in a Factory by Henry Dreyfuss, Designer, and Edward L. Barnes, Architect," *Arts and Architecture* 64 (September 1947).

32. Taped interview with Bertrand Goldberg by Donald Albrecht, April 1, 1994. See also Michel Ragon, *Goldberg on the City* (Paris: Paris Art Center, 1985). During this interview, Goldberg noted that his interest in molded plywood as a form of thin-shell construction ultimately led him to design structures of thin-shell concrete. His 1964 Marina City Towers in Chicago is a famous example.

33. Burnham Kelly, *The Prefabrication of Houses: A Study by the Albert Farwell Bemis Foundation of the Prefabrication Industry in the United States* (Cambridge, Mass.: The MIT Press, 1951, reprint 1964), 73.

34. Ibid., 62–63.

35. "Tomorrow's Small House," *Bulletin of the Museum of Modern Art* 12 (Summer 1945). The houses on exhibit were originally designed for *Ladies' Home Journal* and had appeared in the magazine beginning in January 1944.

36. Roslyn Ittelson, "Report on the Reaction of the Public to the Exhibition of Small Houses at the Museum of Modern Art" (Department of Architecture and Design, the Museum of Modern Art, New York, 1945).

37. A good recent study on Levitt's wartime building is an unpublished paper by Marguerite C. Rodney, "Oakdale Farms: Levitt's Prototype for Postwar Suburban Housing" (George Washington University, April 1993).

38. Greg Hise, "Home Building and Industrial Decentralization in Los Angeles: The Roots of the Postwar Urban Region," *Journal of Urban History* 19, no. 2 (February 1993): 95–125.

39. Joseph B. Mason, "Levitt & Sons of Virginia Set New Standards in Title VI War Homes," *American Builder* (Chicago, June 1942): 48–53, 84–85.

40. Eric Larrabee, "The Six Thousand Houses That Levitt Built," *Harper's Magazine* 197 (September 1948): 88.

41. Joseph Hudnut, "The Post-Modern House," *Architectural Record* 97 (May 1945): 70.

42. Ibid., 73.

43. For an excellent study see the catalog that accompanied an exhibition at the Museum of Contemporary Art, Los Angeles, edited by Elizabeth A. T. Smith and entitled *Blueprints for Modern Living: History and Legacy of the Case Study Houses* (Cambridge, Mass.: The MIT Press, 1990).

44. Entenza's intentions were noted by Ralph Rapson in a telephone conversation with Donald Albrecht on September 22, 1993.

45. Examples include Whitney R. Smith, co-designer of the commercial center at the Linda Vista war workers' housing project in San Diego, and Ralph Rapson, who worked on defense housing in the office of Saarinen, Swanson, and Saarinen.

46. In a letter from Louis I. Kahn to Frederick Gutheim, Kahn feared that a tired architectural symbolism would inevitably represent the new institution, "a dome flanked by two legislative palaces, and possibly a reflecting pool." Kahn to Gutheim, March 12, 1946, Box 63, Louis I. Kahn Collection, University of Pennsylvania, Philadelphia, and Pennsylvania Historical and Museum Commission.

47. "Symposium at MOMA, February 11, 1948," *The Museum of Modern Art Bulletin* 15, no. 3 (Spring 1948).

Robert Friedel

Scarcity and Promise: Materials
and American Domestic Culture
during World War II

In the summer of 1943, my mother and father moved into a four-room brick house in the town of Pryor, in the northeastern corner of Oklahoma. They had waited a year for that house. My father, along with many others, had been making the twenty-five-mile drive from Tulsa each day to work in Pryor's munitions plant, while my mother cared for their first child, less than a year old. The house in Pryor was better than most; its brick set it off from the more common ones made, as my mother put it, of "that asbestos stuff." And in its front yard was the only tree in the neighborhood.

That little house in Pryor was a large part of my parents' lives: it was their first new home, the first real place for raising a new family. In its many manifestations across America, that house and the hundreds of thousands raised in those war years

Robert Friedel

ICE CUBES FOR JAPAN !

Listen, Tojo—when you hear that *kar-rump* some night and the factory walls start sliding into the sea—look out, it's one of those new "ice cubes" from Nash-Kelvinator!

We are building *plenty* of them just for you—huge Kelvinators that fly and ice cubes that hurt.

Monster metal-bellied flying boats—growing on Nash-Kelvinator assembly lines—to whisk the Navy's men and material to any spot you raise your head! Giant Vought-Sikorsky cargo carriers built *complete*—and not in ones or twos, but in fleet upon fleet!

Want to hear some more?

Then listen—that angry hum coming out of the East—

They are the propellers built by Nash-Kelvinator, built by the many thousands!

And that mighty roar you'll soon be hearing is the voice of the most powerful engine ever placed in a pursuit ship. It will take the Navy's new *Corsair* higher, faster than any "Zero" in your stable.

They're coming, Tojo—coming from men who, in building last year's refrigerators and automobiles, thought only of a nation's health and happiness.

But now, it's hate and vengeance and the remembrance of a thousand Axis wrongs that are guiding their hands . . . beating every production record in Nash-Kelvinator history by two and three.

Look out, Tojo, *the nights are growing longer.*   •   •   •

NASH-KELVINATOR CORPORATION

NASH KELVINATOR

PRATT & WHITNEY HIGH-ALTITUDE ENGINES   VOUGHT-SIKORSKY FLYING BOATS   HAMILTON STANDARD PROPELLERS

forty-four

loomed large in the American domestic landscape, for they were the visible sign of a great economic and demographic upheaval, an explosion of productive activity that made the country truly what its President had promised it would be, an "arsenal of democracy," and brought a massive moving of people to serve the needs of that gigantic arsenal, as well as their own dreams.

Those dreams—and the country's own great economic drama—were played out against the backdrop of the most horrifying war in history. But they were also pursued in the midst of a dramatic recovery from the nation's longest and deepest Depression. In Pryor, Oklahoma, and all across the land, contradictory forces were in the air. Great patriotic fervor moved men and women to make sacrifices, both overseas and on the home front, and the government, awed and sometimes overwhelmed by its great responsibilities, ensured that those sacrifices were made even when fervor flagged. But long-awaited boom times, and the desperately needed paychecks that made them palpable, gave impetus to making life as good as circumstances would allow and to casting the future in ever more glowing terms.

The contradictions of sacrifice and prosperity left their permanent mark on American life. The experience of total mobilization forever changed the relationship of the people to their government. The new burdens of global responsibility shattered the comfortable naiveté of isolationism. In the dreams of ordinary life, too, there were changes. The conflicting forces of the war years reshaped the material and domestic culture that both reflected and reformed the most basic aspirations of women and men—to be at home, to feel comfort, to experience a measure of well-being.

It is reasonable, then, to ask ourselves what we can make of the tangible, material manifestations of these changes and of the forces that caused them. By looking at the ways in which Americans' dreams of their domestic future intersected with the enormous forces of war and statecraft, we can catch a

Advertisement, *Life,* October 12, 1942. Courtesy Senior Trademark Council.

glimpse of how the transformation of life grew out of the ungodly mix of war, economics, and technology.

The home is a natural repository of people's dreams. So it is not surprising that during the Great Depression, when dreams were nearly all there was to sell and show, houses and the possibilities the future held for them attracted attention. At the great world's fairs that flanked the decade—Chicago's "Century of Progress," in 1933–34, and the New York World's Fair, in 1939–40—the "House of Tomorrow" was conspicuously promised to a Depression-weary audience. Although the architectural experiments of European modernism and the construction techniques promised by adapting an assembly-line philosophy to housing were of interest to many, perhaps novel materials were the most striking of the marvels promised for future domestic life, especially those in the "World of Tomorrow" exhibit at the 1939 Fair in New York's Flushing Meadow. The November 1939 issue of *National Geographic* magazine offered a summary of these material promises, including more than two dozen color photographs and an article titled "Chemists Make a New World," with examples from the Fair and elsewhere. One of the pictures featured a young model outfitted in dress, hat, gloves, and high heels, every bit of whose ensemble, the reader was told, came from the chemist's laboratory, from the cellophane hat to the plastic parasol handle and nylon stockings.[1]

The world was indeed poised at the edge of new material wonders. Nylon had been announced in a meeting on the Flushing Fair grounds in October 1938, and its virtues were not understated. The *New York Times,* in reporting the Du Pont company announcement, headlined it "New Hosiery Strong as Steel." A second piece ran in the business section of the paper, touting another key aspect of the new material's image, that it came, according to company publicity, from "coal, air, and water." Nylon was unambiguously introduced to the public as a replacement for and improvement on silk, particularly in women's stockings.[2]

If the "House of Tomorrow" did not quite arrive in the Depression decade, there were other, more modest changes in the structures in which Americans lived and worked, changes that were also to set the stage for the following decade's buildings. Economic difficulties themselves sometimes altered tastes; "knotty pine," a cheap, low-class material, found favor under Depression conditions and achieved a lasting stylistic niche. Chemical preservatives and artificial resins made possible the wider use of woods and plywood. Concrete expanded its domain in building and was shown off to great effect at the "Century of Progress" exhibition. Glass brick provided a briefly popular alternative for walls where rooms needed to offer more light. Bright new metals, such as stainless steel and aluminum, gave architects new effects, shown off most spectacularly in great skyscrapers such as New York's Chrysler and Empire State buildings. The plastics attracting the attention of *National Geographic* were even more novel, but their place in the home, office, or factory building was still quite modest. The most important for the builder were the artificial resins, such as Bakelite. By the 1930s, builders used these resins not only for molded products such as telephones and radio cabinets but also in laminates of paper, cloth, and wood. Favorable, as well, for countertops, tables, cabinets, and other furnishings, they had become prized materials for designers of the period. Plywood gained in quality and reliability owing to the new resins, as well. Perhaps the most radically new design possibilities were presented by the crystal-clear acrylic resins, notably Plexiglas (methyl metacrylate sheet), which had been introduced by the firm of Rohm and Haas in 1936, although the cost and difficulty of shaping it slowed widespread application.[3]

The long Depression had left many Americans with little confidence that tomorrow would in fact bring them new homes or better lives, and the state of the world at the decade's end did nothing to inspire them further. By early 1939, the likelihood of a general war in Europe was widely acknowledged, although the belief that America could stay out prevailed. When Nazi forces crossed the Polish border on the morning of September 1, American sentiment quickly (though not universally) swung behind the Allies. President Roosevelt declared a "Limited National Emergency" a week later, but with the quick collapse of Poland and the ensuing six-month "phony war" in Europe, little action followed. At first the effects of the war on the American economy were negligible. Popular sentiment and the law were behind the maintenance of neutrality. Until November 1939 the Neutrality Acts prevented any of the combatants, Allies or Axis, from purchasing matériel from the United States. The Roosevelt administration moved quickly to change this, and by the end of the year, both the British and the French were beginning to move massive amounts of cash into the American economy. After the German *Blitzkrieg* crashed across the Low Countries and France in May 1940, the effects on American industry and workers became more direct. The Army began a large-scale draft, the Navy began to prepare for a two-ocean war, and the Roosevelt administration did what it could to help the beleaguered British without breaching neutrality completely.[4]

The deeper involvement with the British plight, increased concern over the activities of the Japanese in Asia (Roosevelt cut off supplies of iron and steel scrap to them in the summer of 1940), and the drive for preparedness at home caused both a change in attitude among the American people and a revival of their economic fortunes. Slowly but inexorably the economy moved to a war footing. As early as one week after the invasion of France, Roosevelt warned Congress of what was coming and began to push military purchases and priorities. A series of agencies struggled to make the transition work. The National Defense Advisory Commission (NDAC), and later the Office of Production Management (OPM), operating largely under World War I legislation, tried to rationalize the organizing of the American economy for defense, with generally poor results. Nonetheless, this so-called Defense Production Period saw the groundwork laid for the wartime economy to come.[5]

Very early in this period, the control of materials was recognized as a key problem. In June 1940, the White House established the Office of the Coordinator of National Defense Purchases, and the President gave the order for it to "investigate the necessity for and make recommendations . . . relative to the granting of priority to all orders for material essential to the national defense over deliveries for private account or export." A couple of months later the Army and Navy Munitions Board was authorized to institute a system of priorities for "critical and essential items," and the first so-called Priorities Critical List was drawn up. At this point the system was mostly voluntary, but warnings were soon issued that its success depended on widespread compliance and that, if needed, more forceful measures would be forthcoming. The A-1 rating that put a product at the top of the list did in fact have clout. The manufacture of machine tools, for example, was quickly singled out as high priority, and orders flowed from Washington to assure that machine shops got needed equipment, materials, and workers. By mid-autumn, it became clear that the current system could not prevent disruptive shortages of materials: some aluminum alloys had become scarce, and it was growing difficult to acquire metals such as magnesium, tin, copper, and chromium. Despite the conscientious efforts of the Munitions Board, it was evident that the controls required to manage the economy's ability to supply the rapidly expanding war machine would require a stronger administrative entity.[6]

In January 1941, the President issued an Executive Order establishing the Office of Production Management (OPM). Operating under White House supervision, it was more visible than the earlier agencies had been, especially the NDAC, but it still lacked the unquestioned authority to shape the economy to national needs. In August, the Supply Priorities and Allocations Board (SPAB) was established to ensure that OPM priorities actu-

Robert Friedel

ally matched military needs and that procurement fit these priorities. This mechanism, too, was not sufficient.[7]

By December 7, 1941, when the Japanese attacked Pearl Harbor, many Americans wanted a much more vigorous and centrally controlled system for converting to a wartime economy. The official declaration of war on Japan on December 8 and on Germany three days later equipped the government with the moral force it needed to construct this system. In mid-January of 1942, both the OPM and the SPAB gave way to the War Production Board (WPB), guided by Donald Nelson, a former executive of Sears, Roebuck, the Chicago catalog-merchandising company. By springtime, the War Powers Act gave the Production Board the authority to shut down production of low-priority items, reallocate materials and machines, and generally take control of the economy. Automobile production lines were to be converted to turning out tanks and other needs of war. By the summer of 1942, close to three hundred L (limitation) and M (materials conservation) orders had been filed, halting or limiting the production of everything from household thermometers to refrigerators. The most sweeping was M-126, issued on May 5, 1942, to halt pro-

A-20 acrylic nose cones in Douglas Aircraft factory in California, n.d. Courtesy National Archives. RG 208-EX-165-18.

duction of more than four hundred products using iron and steel. Or rather, in the arcane way of these directives, the order actually limited substitution for the needed steel to gold or silver. One of the key limitation orders was L-41 of April 9, which placed severe restrictions on any sort of private or commercial construction. Any residential remodeling or building project costing more than $500 required a permit; for farms the limit was $1,000, and for businesses $5,000.[8]

Even before the L and M orders of the Production Board began to take their bite, and before Pearl Harbor and the establishment of the WPB itself, the building industry had begun to feel the effects of supply constraints and government controls. By mid-October 1941, copper was in short supply, and the OPM forbade its use in almost all nonpriority construction (maintenance was the sole significant exception). Other metals were not far behind. Aluminum allocations were already controlled; the production of aluminum hardware items had been stopped in early 1941. The makers of plastics also had to adjust fairly early. Supplies of methanol—a key predecessor of formaldehyde, which in turn was indispensable to most artificial resins (like Bakelite)—were getting scarce. Because the plastics industry was then being called on to help replace light metals such as aluminum and magnesium, these shortages were viewed as a failure on Washington's part to comprehend fully the complexity of the task it had set itself. Furthermore, the armed services had commandeered certain plastics. The Navy, for example, laid claim to vinyl as the most trusted material for insulation on seagoing ships. In the case of acrylic sheeting, the explosion of demand was simply impossible to keep up with, as the clarity of the material and its ability to be molded made it the material of choice for bomber nose cones and fighter-plane canopies. The proposal to manufacture eighty million gas masks for civilians threatened to claim a large part of the supply of cellulose acetate. And, as if the basic supply problems were not enough for the plastics industry, the molders were

Molding an acrylic aircraft canopy, n.d. Courtesy National Archives. RG 208-SA1-28-13.

For vision

Lumarith

A CELANESE* PLASTIC

For dials and sight gauges

For aircraft

For gas masks

"How about using plastics?" Sooner or later
it comes up in 'most every production conference. . . .
As founder of the plastics industry and as producer
of the complete range of Lumarith
plastics, we can help you very directly.
Celanese Celluloid Corporation,
THE FIRST NAME IN PLASTICS,
180 Madison Avenue, New York City,
a division of
Celanese Corporation of America.

*Trade Marks Reg. U.S. Pat. Off.

Advertisement, *Fortune*, September 1943.

caught in the same bind that plagued users of machine tools and other large machines everywhere: tool-and-dye manufacturers were still playing catch-up.[9]

Shortly after Pearl Harbor, the construction industry began to take stock of its situation. In early 1942, Herbert Whittemore of the National Bureau of Standards, a key figure in the establishment and promotion of structural safety codes, concluded, "Unusual materials, designs, and methods of fabrication not used in normal times are entirely justified under prevailing conditions." He made the point that shortages should be dealt with not merely by substitution but also by careful design and analysis. If structures were better understood from a theoretical standpoint, he argued, then margins of safety could be narrowed with little danger. He pointed to the European tradition of "scientific design by theoretical studies and laboratory investigations," which resulted in structures considered "daring" in terms of Amer-

Robert Friedel

Douglas Aircraft assembly plant, Chicago, Illinois, 1943. The Austin Company, designers and builders. Hedrich-Blessing photograph/ courtesy Chicago Historical Society. HB 075 11 C.

ican practice. This could prove a key means for saving materials. Advanced treatment and handling of materials could also conserve resources; for example, attempts to increase the strength of steel by heat treatment or by using welds rather than rivets were now justified. Whittemore also suggested that alternative materials such as masonry and concrete, which were available, should be put into service to conserve metals. Even wood, which had fallen out of favor with engineers for structures such as bridges and factories, should now be pressed into extended service, using advanced techniques and preservatives.[10]

The squeeze on building supplies in late 1941 and early 1942 coincided with increasing concern for the availability of housing for defense workers. In April 1941 President Roosevelt specified those areas of the country adjudged to be experiencing "an acute shortage of housing" and directed that priorities be set for filling a shortage that threatened "to impede national defense activities." By the end of 1941, about sixty thousand units had been completed, with many more under construction, but the pressure on housing supply still overwhelmed the best efforts. The Priorities and Allocations system attempted to cope with the housing shortage, at least as far as could be justified for defense workers. Building Limitation Order L-41, for example, encouraged home remodeling to increase available living space for those residing in designated defense areas, which at one point encompassed two-thirds of the U.S. population. But such exemptions were more apparent than real in many cases; the higher priorities for direct defense manufacture made everything from nails to insulation to piping extremely scarce and therefore unavailable to builders. It was quickly recognized that this situation posed particular problems for small contractors not located in priority areas. Indeed, they shared the fate of small businesses everywhere, which were particularly vulnerable to the bite of the Priorities and Allocations system, especially since they were less likely to be able to convert their skills, tools, and workers to alternative, defense production. In early 1942, *Fortune* profiled Ray Elliott, a successful building contractor with a small company in White River Junction, Vermont. Elliott's travails with the housing and OPM bureaucracy and his uncertainty about the very survival of his business mirrored the experience of thousands across the country. While the Office of Production Management and later the War Production Board attempted to make provisions for the special problems of small business, the war effort clearly left losers as well as winners in its wake.[11]

The most extraordinary architectural emergency in the country's history—combining urgent building needs with scarcity caused by both military requirements and the cutoff of foreign supplies—yielded an extraordinary building effort. The adjustment to the emergency required accommodation on many fronts: Federal, state, and local governments adjusted their standards and expectations; architects and engineers came up with in-

Advertisement, *Fortune*, June 1944. Courtesy Libbey-Owens-Ford Company.

genious designs and practical solutions; manufacturers and suppliers altered familiar habits of fabrication or devised suitable substitute materials; and the public—perhaps because there was no choice, but also because it was the patriotic thing to do—went along. The shortage of materials was the primary reason that buildings raised for the war effort were different from what had gone before. By mid-1942, stocks of traditional materials and building elements had been largely exhausted, and substitutes were the order of the day. Timber widely replaced steel in building frames; laminated-timber columns and heavy wood supporting trusses supplanted structural steel in the vast Douglas Aircraft assembly plant built in Chicago in 1942–43. During this period metal supports, reinforcements, and joining elements were minimized by design and replaced by alternative materials. Buildings were designed a little closer to the margin of safety, or were a little less permanent or a little bit swifter to erect.[12]

Advertisement, *Fortune*, September 1943.

Robert Friedel

Machine gunner in molded-plywood gun turret on Navy P.T. boat, n.d. Courtesy P.T. Boats, Incorporated.

Cranes hoisting a wing of the Hughes cargo flying boat, the Spruce Goose, in the company's assembly plant, Culver City, California, ca. 1944. Courtesy Hughes Aircraft Company.

With the war years came a turning point in the status of plywood as a material for design and construction. Thanks in large part to the new synthetic resins such as Plaskon (the trade name for a tightly bonding resin glue made from urea-formaldehyde) and new processes such as the "rubber bag" technique in which veneers and resin could be vacuum-molded over large forms (dubbed Plymold by Haskelite Manufacturing Company), it became possible to make fine-quality plywood in sizes and shapes that were hitherto unthinkable. The new "plastic" wood beckoned architects, engineers, and product designers. Aircraft wings and fuselages, PT boat hulls and gun turrets, radio signal towers, and similar military constructions that would otherwise have used scarce metals were made of plywood. (The famous RAF Mosquito fighter-bomber was made entirely of artificial-resin-bonded plywood; the bonding agent was Beetle Cement, also a form of urea-formaldehyde). The roof of Hughes Aircraft in Culver City, California, Howard Hughes's Spruce Goose facility, was, like some other large factories, spanned with the help of laminated-wood joints and supported with laminated-timber columns. On the eve of war, the young Cranbrook Academy of Art designers Charles Eames and Eero Saarinen had discovered the artistic capabilities of the new plywood, winning a furnishing competition at New York's Museum of Modern Art in 1940. Initially their furniture was not economical to produce, but during the war Charles Eames and his wife Ray applied their expertise to the shaping of stretchers and splints for wounded servicemen, and this experience was crucial to the production of Eames's molded-plywood furniture, which broke new ground for furniture design in the postwar years.[13]

Concrete, too, came to be viewed quite differently as a result of wartime experience. The need to stretch the capabilities of materials to their limits, to speed up construction even as the work force was reduced, and to cover large spaces with the minimum of support encouraged the use of concrete in ways that had

Eames plywood leg splint in use. Courtesy
Lucia Eames Demetrios dba Eames Office
© 1994 Library of Congress, the work of
Charles and Ray Eames.

Plywood sheet being molded for an aircraft
tail section at the Eames workshop in Los
Angeles, California, 1943. Courtesy Lucia
Eames Demetrios dba Eames Office © 1994
Library of Congress, the work of Charles and
Ray Eames.

Opposite:
Eames molded-plywood chairs, 1947. Courtesy
Lucia Eames Demetrios dba Eames Office ©
1994 Library of Congress, the work of Charles
and Ray Eames.

Dodge Chicago aircraft engine plant, Chicago, Illinois, ca. 1943, Albert Kahn Associated Architects and Engineers, designers. Hedrich-Blessing photograph/courtesy Chicago Historical Society. HB 07595D.

generally been avoided before the war. The first decades of the twentieth century had seen considerable experimentation with both reinforced and prestressed concrete structures, primarily in Europe. French engineer Eugène Freyssinet's bold parabolic twin airship hangars built at Orly near Paris in the mid-1920s demonstrated the strength and lightness of thin, prestressed concrete shells (the maximum thickness was three and one-half inches); this was just the kind of "scientific design" that Whittemore had in mind and that had been notably absent in America in normal times. These daring designs, it was discovered, could save precious steel (prestressed concrete is far more economical in this regard than reinforced) and construction time. In 1943 Albert Kahn Associated Architects and Engineers proved as daring in designing the vast, eighty-acre Dodge Chicago aircraft plant, finding an innovative way of constructing the roof. Replacing structural steel with multiple vaulted-concrete roofs, the firm used thin-slab concrete sections put in place by movable wood forms, simultaneously speeding production and reducing the thickness of the concrete slabs from eight to three inches.[14]

The results of wartime building needs and the conditions under which they were met were remarkable in both scope and kind. Building activity in 1942 exceeded the record high level of 1941 by thirty-seven percent, totaling almost $6.2 billion. Of this, less than one-quarter was spent for housing (including military), $2 billion was spent on military construction (excluding housing), and the remainder was devoted to building factories and other industrial structures. Commercial building, either private (office buildings, for example) or public (such as post offices), plunged to twenty-eight percent of the previous year's level, further evidence of the massive shift in focus of construction. Carried out under the pressure for speed and the constraints of materials shortages, the effort yielded some novel structures.[15]

The substitution of concrete and wood for steel was the most visible and in some ways the most influential change in

building. In late 1942, the chief chronicler of the building industry, the *Engineering News-Record,* reported on several remarkable examples. A large machine shop in Wisconsin was built of
concrete and laminated wood to save both time and materials. Following customary designs, the eighty-six-thousand-square-foot
building ordinarily would have required about six hundred tons
of steel. But by using reinforced concrete for all columns and the
shop-crane rails, as well as laminated wood for the roof girders,
the amount of steel used was reduced to one hundred seventy-five
tons. In addition, it was estimated that about five weeks had
been shaved off the building's construction time. At an eastern
Navy Yard (the journal was consistently vague about locations),
another shop was constructed with wood largely replacing steel.
This facility was distinctive for being three rather tall stories
high (a total of one hundred twenty-five feet), in which columns
were made of timber and the floors were separated by wood
trusses. Equally remarkable was the fact that no large pieces of
wood were required; the building was designed to make use of
members no larger than four by sixteen inches and no longer
than twenty-four feet. Asbestos-cement siding sheathed the build-

Timber Navy blimp hangar, Richmond, Florida,
ca. 1944. Courtesy Kidder-Smith Collection/
NAVFAC Historical Program/Port Hueneme,
California.

Opposite:
Timber Navy blimp hangar, South Weymouth,
Massachusetts, ca. 1944. Courtesy Kidder-
Smith Collection/NAVFAC Historical Program/
Port Hueneme, California.

ing; all framing, lintels, and window sashes were wood, as were the doors (except for interior fireproof ones in stairwells). The whole was designed around prefabricated units to enable rapid on-site assembly. Perhaps the most striking example of wood replacing steel was in hangars built for the Navy's blimp fleet. For these, timber arches spanning two hundred forty-six feet—almost fifty feet more than the previously recorded span for timber— were designed to rest on concrete A-frames. Structural steel was entirely eliminated, except for the huge vertical doors at the ends of the buildings. Although a larger span would have been possible had steel been used for the arches, this successful design allowed the Navy to accommodate its new fleet of one hundred sixty-six airships, while avoiding the use of the sixty-eight thousand tons of steel required in conventional construction.[16]

Cement and reinforced concrete were pressed into service in other unprecedented ways. Where concrete would once have been used only in conjunction with metal framing, joining, and reinforcing, now the drive to save iron and steel led to structures in which thicker pourings of the material made up for the decrease in metal. Smaller reinforcing elements (wire or cable instead of bars, for example), saved steel. California architect Wal-

Concrete Bubble house, Falls Church, Virginia, ca. 1941. Wallace Neff, architect. Courtesy National Archives. RG 208-EX-158-D-L-288.

lace Neff took a more novel approach in his experiments with the material, creating the sprayed-concrete Bubble house. Beginning with an inflated rubber or fabric balloon overlayed with reinforcing mesh, Neff sprayed the hemispheric form with an inch-thick layer of concrete. When the eleven-foot-high concrete shell had dried, the balloon could be deflated, removed, and used again, "up to a thousand times," Neff claimed. He created an outer shell by covering the surface of the sphere with insulation, adding mesh, and repeating the spraying operation. A few houses were built in Virginia and Arizona using this approach, but they did not prove popular. Floor slabs of plain concrete became more common, and sometimes led to interesting innovations. In one bomber assembly plant, for example, the concrete floor slab was topped with a layer of bright white cement, its light-reflecting surface measurably improving visibility beneath the plane assemblies. Improved lighting was also the reason for the expanded use of glass block. A new form of block directed incoming sunlight to the ceiling of rooms, from which it was reflected and diffused. Such innovations were ingenious ways of applying the properties of the available, often substitute, materials and using them to their best advantage.[17]

The difficulties of expanding production while experimenting with substitutes challenged the ingenuity of the producers of building materials, fixtures, or the articles of domestic life. In items ranging from candy wrappers to oil cans, paper and paperboard were made to do where aluminum foil and tin had been common. Plastic came to be used for bottles, tool handles, window screens, and even plumbing. According to an advertisement for the Sloan Valve Company, its plastic "Victory-Type" flush valve reduced the amount of copper needed "to less than four ounces." New plastics with useful new combinations of properties were introduced. The Dow Chemical Company made a version of vinylidene chloride and introduced it as Saran, particularly desirable for its imperviousness to water, air, gasoline, and acid. Urea-formaldehyde, the synthetic resin that had seen slowly expanding applications in the 1930s, now had a vast range of new uses. Melamine formaldehyde, another relatively unexploited plastic, emerged in new identities in the 1940s; the Army used it for helmet liners, and the Navy, as modern gunnery practices subjected ships to much more violent recoils than before, replaced its breakable dishes and trays with melamine tableware. At war's end American Cyanamid, melamine's manufacturer, approached designer Russel Wright to produce dinnerware for the domestic market. *Meladur,* introduced in 1949, imitated glazed ceramic in finish and thickness and gained popularity in restaurants. Wright refined his design over the next several years, and in 1953 he introduced the *Residential* line of dinnerware, the first plastic tableware to come into widespread use in the home.[18]

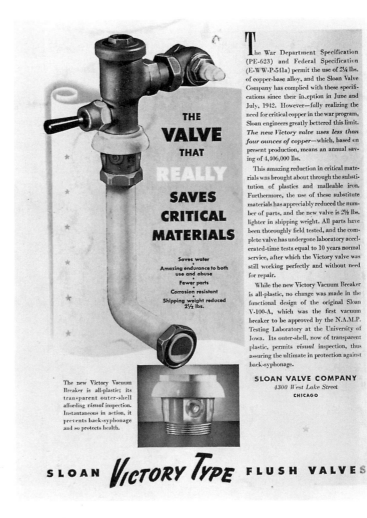

Advertisement, *Architectural Record,* April 1943. Courtesy Sloan Valve Company.

Lists of critical materials and descriptions of important building innovations of the time emphasized the importance of substituting wood for iron, steel, or other metals. Baseboards, doors, gutters, light poles, and shelving—almost every conceivable metal object or fitting—were to be made of wood. Thus in 1942, when a timber shortage threatened to halt a wide range of urgently needed building projects, from dry docks to military housing, there was widespread alarm. The United States had always viewed itself as a forest-rich nation, whose timber supplies were limitless. The experience of 1942, however, revealed how simplistic this thinking had been. At the beginning of the year, when the building industry began to take stock of the implications of the war emergency, there was no hint that wood might be in short supply. As late as March, timber found no place in the discussions of spreading shortages of other building materials.

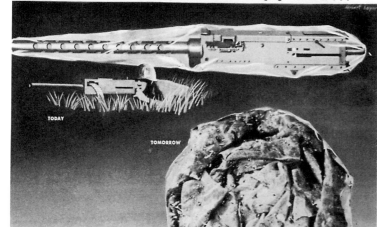

Dow Announces a Revolutionary Advance in Packaging Materials . . .

SARAN FILM

Keeps Moisture in its place!

Guns—spare parts for aircraft, tanks and jeeps—these and other essential supplies can now be shipped to our far-flung battle fronts adequately protected from their common enemy —moisture. By developing *Saran Film*, Dow has made a revolutionary advance in packaging materials.

Saran Film provides a degree of protection hitherto impossible to obtain. It is three times more impervious to moisture than any other comparable material.

Its high resistance to chemicals is important in packaging food and chemical products. Extreme flexibility at low temperatures increases its serviceability. As for moisture, it keeps it in its place—in or out, as the case may be.

Distinguished by these remarkable advantages, an infinite variety of uses—the packaging of fruits, vegetables and many other products— await *Saran Film* on the home front when Victory is won.

THE DOW CHEMICAL COMPANY
MIDLAND, MICHIGAN

New York · St. Louis · Chicago · Houston
San Francisco · Los Angeles · Seattle

Saran film

DOW PLASTICS

ETHOCEL · STYRON

DOW

CHEMICALS INDISPENSABLE
TO INDUSTRY AND VICTORY

Advertisement, 1943. Courtesy Dow Chemical Company.

But in April, the enormous increase in demand not only for building materials but also for crates, planking, and lend-lease supplies coincided with a decline in production. The military draft, along with rapidly expanding employment in industry, caused a shortage of labor in the forests. Added to the difficulties plaguing the economy in transportation and machinery, the timber and wood products industry entered a period of crisis. Even the Army Corps of Engineers, whose procurement system was the most successful in the military, felt the crunch, and similar difficulties were to be felt throughout the economy. Orders went out to conserve timber wherever possible, even if it meant changes in a design that reduced safety margins to the limit. Thus barracks and other quickly constructed buildings were put up that would in ordinary times have been judged too hazardous for occupancy. Substitutes for wood—that supposedly ultimate substitute for everything else—were ordered, with increasing reliance on con-

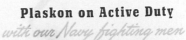

Advertisement, ca. 1943. Courtesy Libbey-Owens-Ford Company.

Meladur plastic dinnerware. Russel Wright, designer. Courtesy William H. Straus/Helburn Associates. Photograph by Rick McCleary.

Residential plastic dinnerware. Russel Wright, designer. Courtesy William H. Straus/Helburn. Photograph by Rick McCleary.

crete, brick, and other masonry being the most obvious solution. Masonry, however, exacted additional costs in labor and time, neither of which was available, so the efforts to increase wood supplies became ever more urgent. Smaller lumber mills were actively sought out and urged to expand their production, even as substandard lumber and other expedients were adopted for the short term. Nonetheless, the timber scarcity persisted throughout the war.[19]

One of the key ways in which wood supplies were stretched was in the manufacture of novel substitutes for wood panels and siding. For example, the Homasote Company of Trenton, New Jersey, promoted its Homosote board made of wood pulp and ground newspaper, bound with resin, by installing a miniature model home in an elegant Hartford department store, G. Fox and Company. For a full-scale model, eight-by-fourteen-foot premoistened panels were attached to a house frame for either walls or floors; and by allowing the panels to dry and shrink after being bonded, a very tight, economical construction resulted. Cemesto, created by Celotex, was another substitute material that came into common use for house building. It consisted of panels that

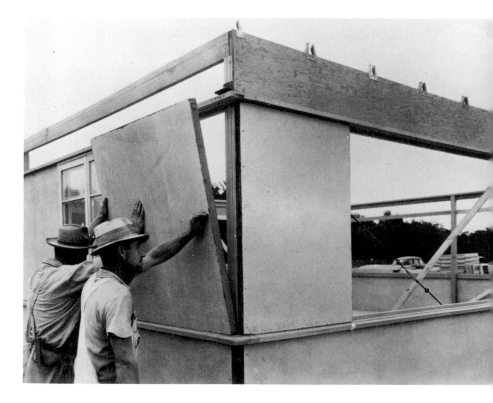

Workers fitting Cemesto wall panel into wood frame, ca. 1941. Courtesy National Archives. RG 208-EX-158-D-L-237.

were four feet wide, from four to twelve feet long, and made of one-eighth-inch-thick layers of asbestos-filled cement applied to a cane-fiber-composite core. These panels could be used in both exterior and interior walls, depending on the finish. Cemesto, easy to work with, was selected to speed up construction of large projects such as the one built at Oak Ridge, Tennessee, where from thirty to forty houses were erected in a single day. At Oak Ridge, the Cemesto houses were actually among the sturdiest and most attractive of the wartime constructions. Elsewhere they compared unfavorably with conventional wood-frame or brick structures.[20]

By all accounts, the most worrisome period of materials shortages was in mid-1942. Although the buildup of defense work had begun in the late 1930s and accelerated rapidly after the fall of France in June 1940, the move to total war after Pearl Harbor had sent shock waves through the economy. The control systems of the OPM, SPAB, and now the WPB were not very efficient instruments; and even if they had been, it is doubtful that a government and an economy so unaccustomed to working under such a radical new regime could have performed without considerable sputtering. And sputtering there was, and the list of "critical

Cemesto house, Middle River, Maryland, ca. 1941. Courtesy National Archives. RG 208-EX-D-L-240.

materials" continued to grow, until, as one Corps of Engineers officer put it, there was no problem of "critical materials, but rather
the conservation of *all materials*." For key metals such as aluminum, copper, and steel, the government embarked on an enormous program to increase production. In the case of aluminum,
for which the aircraft industry's needs were critical, the success
rate was spectacular—U.S. production rose from three hundred
twenty-seven million pounds in 1939 to a capacity of two and a
quarter billion pounds in 1943. Copper production was not so elas-
tic, but beyond increasing mine output, the WPB promoted ingenious substitutions, such as the allocation of the government's
silver reserves to the huge electrical bus bars required by the new
aluminum smelters and electrochemical plants. At Oak Ridge,
Tennessee, for example, fourteen thousand tons of silver (with a
value of about $.5 billion) were used in the gigantic uranium
diffusion plant. Steel sheet and plate continued to be a problem
throughout the war, and this was one area in which rationing and
conservation (including scrap recycling) continued to be the key
defense measures.[21]

Although rationing was the most notorious means for
controlling civilian consumption during the war, it was significant
only for a few items, such as gasoline, shoes, and certain food-
stuffs. The real curtailing of consumer goods came at the production end, where the system of materials allocations of the WPB,
bolstered by specific restrictions, quotas, and prohibitions, cut off
the supply of domestic needs from vacuum cleaners to tin cans. It
is important to remember that the enormous boost in military
and related production from 1939 to the end of the war was
largely due not to the diversion of resources from the civilian economy but to the extraordinary expansion of the entire economic engine. With the increase in output averaging fifteen percent per
year from 1940 to 1944 (the average from 1896 to 1939 was four
percent per annum), this period represented the greatest expansion of production in American history. Even those sectors of the

economy not directly devoted to war matériel expanded during these years (publishing and clothing were the lone significant exceptions), and overall consumer spending did not decline. Nonetheless, there was a perception of shortage and sacrifice. It was estimated that at the end of 1941 the liquid assets of individuals in the United States totaled $50 billion; by 1945 that figure had increased to $140 billion. In other words, the booming war economy put money in people's pockets, but they did not spend it.[22]

The perception of the need to sacrifice was encouraged by Madison Avenue, which provided an added incentive—the image of a bright future just over the horizon of war. The dilemma of the advertisers is worth remarking on, for it helped to shape visions of the postwar world and of the place of consumption in that world. The advertising industry prospered along with the economy, and agency budgets were at record levels before war's end. But at the war's outset it was clearly unpatriotic to promote consumption of most durable goods, and as allocations tightened, the goods were in fact in short supply. American corporations, nonetheless, were hooked on advertising and anxious to retain their name recognition. One solution, popular at the outset, was to associate the corporate name with the mobilization for war and with its aims. War bonds, conservation, and scrap drives were all drummed by soap, automobile, and radio advertisers. Magazine readers were told of each company's contributions to the war effort. Carrier was "turning out refrigeration and air conditioning equipment for hundreds of fighting ships and merchant vessels." Armco sheet steel was "doing valiant service" in tanks and battleships rather than refrigerators and pots and pans. Nash Kelvinator trumpeted "Ice Cubes for Japan," as its refrigerator lines were

Department store shoppers viewing quarter-scale model of Homasote house, *Architectural Forum,* June 1943.

converted to bomb production. Corporate America was not shy about telling the public of its contributions to victory.[23]

Wartime advertising, however, often went beyond simple reminders of a company's having done its patriotic duty. Most readers, after all, were well aware that the manufacturers had little choice but to do so. Advertisements began to appear that looked ahead to a brighter postwar world. "How to put the future on ice," read the headline in a Durez Plastics advertisement, which contained a drawing and description of a futuristic refrigerator (round in shape, it would have been an apt component of Buckminster Fuller's Dymaxion house or Wallace Neff's Bubble house). This product bore no seeming relation to the plastics for boat hulls, jettison fuel tanks, and helmet liners Durez was then supplying the military. An April 1942 issue of the *Saturday Evening Post,* for example, featured this promotion from Stromberg-Carlson, maker of radios: "With the new developments our labora-

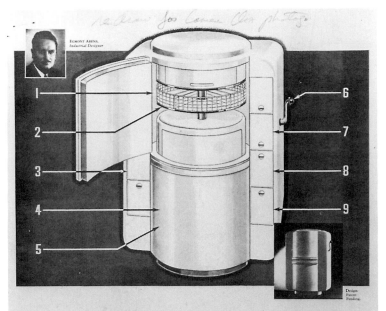

Advertisement, ca. 1943. Courtesy Occidental Chemical Corp. and Egmont Arens Collection/Department of Special Collections/George Arents Research Library/Syracuse University.

tories are now perfecting, the Stromberg-Carlson you buy when the war is won will be even finer than it is today." Diamond T Trucks promised, "Diamond T will build you even finer Super-Service Trucks than those which serve you today, when Victory brings Peace," and Servel Gas Refrigerators made this claim: "Looking beyond today, no one can say for sure what refrigerators are going to be like when peace returns. No one knows. But this *is* certain—that there *will* be refrigerators—that *we'll* be making them [and who knows what other modern appliances!]—and that they'll be *finer* than ever." Advertisements like these became common fare as the war went on and offered promises very like those found in this promotion from the makers of Sparton radios: "But don't you worry, peace will bring America's lost comforts back—and more. Home will be truly a House of Wonders in this after-Victory world. Science already knows how to make it comfortable beyond our dreams. Invention will fill it with conveniences we have never known. Methods developed by war will improve products and short-cut their manufacture. An abundance of materials, new and old, will make things plentiful." As John Morton Blum observed, "The house and all that went into it, 'the American home,' best symbolized of all things material a brave new world of worldly goods. The vision was in part a fantasy woven by advertising, in part a romanticizing of desires born of depression circumstances and wartime deprivations."[24]

Visions of the postwar world were not just Madison Avenue fantasies. From the beginning of American involvement in the conflict, industry and government called attention to the difficulties inherent in turning the economy back to peace. Motivated by memories of the problems arising at the end of World War I in 1918–19, and during the Great Depression in the 1930s, they were determined that they would not be caught unprepared again. Before the end of 1942, the National Association of Manufacturers had issued a report titled "Jobs—Freedom—Opportunity in the Postwar Years," which was the first in a series of annual recommendations for dealing with what came to be called "reconversion." By 1943, the debate over reconversion had become widespread, particularly as the tide in Europe turned decisively toward the Allies. Running throughout was a line of argument that the war mobilization had shown the flexibility and strength of the American economy, and now those characteristics must be mobilized to realize peacetime prosperity and abundance. Robert Nathan, a former WPB economist, asked,

If we can so speedily and effectively mobilize our resources for such an immense war production, can we not with equal effectiveness, from both the technical and organizational viewpoints, mobilize our economic resources for peacetime consumption? If we can build vast quantities of battleships, airplanes, guns, ammunition, tanks, and other weapons to kill our enemy, can we not devote the same resources after the war to building houses, automobiles, electrical devices, schools, hospitals, and other goods so much needed to raise the standard of living of all our people?

Nathan's answer was, of course, yes; moreover, the fruits of wartime research could be enjoyed in peacetime prosperity. Air travel and medical miracles would be commonplace in the new world, and synthetic materials, he said, will ensure against the depletion of resources.[25]

The materials suppliers themselves were among those most concerned about strategies for reconversion. The makers and fabricators of aluminum, artificial rubber, and many of the plastics were acutely aware that at war's end the gigantic demand created by the nation's war machine would recede. Having constructed huge new facilities, mainly at government expense, industrialists viewed with urgency the need to find civilian uses for their products, well before the guns fell silent. In 1943, the Kawneer Company commissioned architect William Lescaze to propose various aluminum storefront designs. A couple of the aircraft producers, Beech and Consolidated Vultee, attempted to

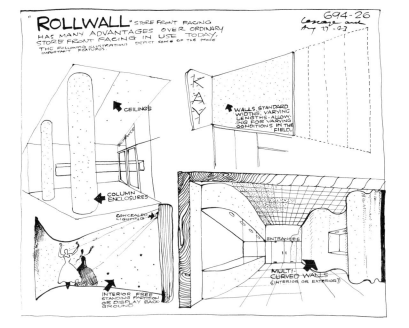

Advertisement, *Fortune*, n.d. Courtesy Reynolds Metals Co.

Sketch of proposed Kawneer aluminum storefronts, 1943. William Lescaze, architect. Courtesy William Lescaze Collection/Department of Special Collections/George Arents Research Library/Syracuse University.

translate directly the processes of making airframes into the manufacture of houses. Beech took up a new version of the radical Dymaxion house that Buckminster Fuller had designed early in his career, and Consolidated Vultee commissioned industrial designer Henry Dreyfuss and architect Edward Larrabee Barnes to design a house that relied on panels of aluminum-sandwiched paper for both walls and roof. The lightweight panels, it was thought, would allow factory production of house units, which could then be easily shipped and erected on site. ALCOA, the country's largest aluminum producer, underwrote a research team in the office of architect Wallace K. Harrison to come up with ways of promoting builders' use of the metal, with more success than the aircraft companies.[26] Some of the most important office buildings of the postwar era, such as the United Nations Secretariat in New York, used aluminum curtain walls, and in the early 1950s, ALCOA's own thirty-story headquarters in Pittsburgh by Harrison and Abramovitz (1951–53) showcased the light metal spectacularly.[27]

Builders looked ahead to the new postwar world as eagerly as anyone, both for the anticipated enormous demand for housing and other neglected construction and for the technical breakthroughs that the wartime experience had opened up. Soon after the invasion of Italy in the fall of 1943, when it looked to many as though the storming of Fortress Europe would be an unimpeded progress, Louis Kahn, the successor to Albert Kahn, wrote of his confidence that there would be a tremendous postwar demand to improve industrial buildings and take advantage of modern features, from higher levels of lighting to air conditioning. By the spring of 1944, with the Allies stalled in Italy, reconversion—and particularly housing—was a vital topic for many. The United Automobile Workers, for example, issued a hundred-twenty-page report to remind government and business leaders that the nation's housing needs were likely to be critical at war's end. The head of the National Housing Agency was quoted as saying that the country could support a program of building between a million and a million and a half houses for as long as two decades after the war. The WPB, sensing the pressure, proposed easing materials restrictions on building even before the end of 1943, but the military stepped in to stop this, and, in fact, lumber shortages remained a serious problem (more because of military crating requirements than building). And despite the glowing promises of technical marvels, the consensus among builders was that "the Buck Rogers adaptations of wartime discoveries—in light metals, plastics, and electronics"—would be less important than simply giving long-starved consumers simple luxuries, such as fancier bathrooms and built-in kitchen appliances.[28]

The question of how novel the postwar world would really be went to the heart of understanding the full effects of the war on the material dreams and aspirations of Americans. The prewar promises of the House of Tomorrow, combined with Madison Avenue's trumpeting of miracles to come, bolstered by the evident leading role played by science and technology in achieving victory, punctuated by the spectacle of the atomic bomb, all led to expectations of a postwar "Dreamworld." Early in 1947, about a year and a half after V-J Day, *Fortune* published a remarkable assessment of "What Happened to the Dreamworld?" "The American, in the postwar," *Fortune* wrote, "was going to live in a house built of glass, plastic, and maybe a slab or two of steel or aluminum, which was bought in a department store, delivered in a van, and erected in a few hours." The picture was further elaborated with fluorescent lighting, ultraviolet germ-proofing, "ultra-short-wave diathermic cooking controls" (microwave ovens?), and a host of other innovations in everything from cars to hosiery. In short, "the implication was that effort, pain, and death were to be eliminated from this earth—or at least from the U.S.A." Facetiousness aside, the article probed its central question carefully, concluding that "the unvarnished truth is that there is no consumer product of any kind on today's market . . . that can claim clear title to a postwar birthright." The only exception was, it claimed, the "ball-bearing [ball-point] pen." Meanwhile, "suspicion grows that the wonderful postwar world is not all that it was blown up to be back in the days when our troops stormed Anzio, and that, when it finally arrives, there'll be a lot less geewhiz and a good deal more hmmm." For all of the domains of the dream—transportation, communications, housing—the realities of a world in which new materials still cost much more than old, in which traditional wants and values dictated not only desires but fashions, in which the need to clothe, feed, and shelter a torn world took precedence over fantasies of the future, drove both producers and consumers to make a postwar world that looked remarkably, at least on the surface, like the old one.[29]

Of course, in the next decade or so the domestic world of Americans did change. Television took over the living room, just as tail fins and V-8 engines occupied the roads and garages. The material world changed as well. In the "Populuxe" era of the 1950s, chrome and glass found places in the home that would have been hard to imagine in the war years. In less than a decade after the war's end, kitchens and bathrooms were a repository for a bewildering variety of plastic goods, such as Formica countertops and vinyl floors, melamine dishes, and polyethylene storage containers sold through Earl Tupper's "Tupperware" parties. At the windows might be drapes of fiberglass (one of the war's most useful materials), touted not only for being fireproof but also for being carefree. Playrooms were littered with polystyrene toys, an odd choice in many ways, since this particular plastic was not very tough or sturdy—but it was cheap and colorful. Those cheap but easily breakable toys were no doubt a major contributor to the baby boomers' poor opinion of plastics in their mature years.[30] On the outside, the clapboard siding of the Levittown-style suburbs found new protection with alkyd resin (a form of polyester) and latex-based paints, or, increasingly, was replaced altogether by aluminum siding (which often, in those boom

Advertisement, 1950. Courtesy Dow Chemical Company.

Out of a Test Tube, Into Your Home
DRAPERY FABRICS
made of

GLASS

Can't Burn, Stretch or Shrink
Clean With a Whisk of a Damp Cloth

All the romance of Cinderella's slipper is woven into these lustrous glass drapery fabrics. For they're woven by Waverly of miraculous Fiberglas* Yarns . . . fibers finer than human hair, stronger than steel of equal size, yarns that will not burn, swell, stretch or shrink. These exciting materials of shimmering, indestructible beauty are ready now at your favorite store in new-as-tomorrow patterns for every window in your home.

Certified by Better Fabrics Testing Bureau, Inc.
Send for free booklet containing flame-test Fiberglas sample.

WAVERLY *Fiberglas* **FABRICS**
DIVISION OF F. SCHUMACHER & CO.
60 WEST 40th STREET, NEW YORK 18, N. Y.

*Trade-mark Reg.
U. S. Pat. Off. by
Owens Corning
Fiberglas Corp.,
Toledo 1, Ohio*

IN YOUR LIVING ROOM
*the graceful draping qualities
of this airy "Feather" pattern are
keyed to gracious living.*

IN YOUR BEDROOM
*blooms Fiberglas "Moss Rose."
As easily drapable, as permanently
dainty as any feminine heart
could wish.*

IN YOUR SUN ROOM
*"Horizontal Stripe" holds
sway. Can't help looking lovely
always because it's indestructible
Waverly Fiberglas.*

years, was not quite of the quality that its salesmen touted). The overall result, delayed for a few years while the domestic world caught its breath, was still not the Dreamworld of wartime visionaries, but it was a distinctive world, with a look and feel that differed—sometimes subtly and sometimes crassly—from the years before the war. The new world, not of dreams but of science and business, retained more of the past than the visionaries would have liked, but it was different. And in almost everyone's mind, the dividing line between the old material world and the new would be those years of wartime scarcity and promise.

Notes

1. Brian Horrigan, "The Home of Tomorrow, 1927–1945," in *Imagining Tomorrow,* ed. Joseph Corn (Cambridge, Mass.: The MIT Press, 1986), 145–153; Jeffrey L. Meikle, *Twentieth Century Limited: Industrial Design in America, 1925–1939* (Philadelphia: Temple University Press, 1979), chap. 9; Warren I. Susman, *Culture as History* (New York: Pantheon Books, 1984), 216; Frederick Simplich, "Chemists Make a New World," *National Geographic* (November 1939): 601–632; for a photograph of the "living symbol of the chemical age," see 609.

2. David A. Hounshell and John Kenly Smith, Jr., *Science and Corporate Strategy: Du Pont R&D, 1902–1980* (New York: Cambridge University Press, 1988), 270–271; *The New York Times,* (October 28, 1938); Simplich, "Chemists Make a New World," 603.

3. "U.S. Architecture, 1900–1950," *Progressive Architecture,* (January 1950): 78–83. On glass brick, see Henry J. Cowan, *Science and Building: Structural and Environmental Design in the Nineteenth and Twentieth Centuries* (New York: John Wiley & Sons, 1978), 279; Harry Parker, C. M. Gay, and J. W. McGuire, *Architectural Construction,* 3rd ed. (New York: John Wiley & Sons, 1958), 308–309. On metals, see Margot Gayle and David W. Lock, "A Historical Survey of Metals," in *Metals in America's Historic Buildings* (Washington, D.C.: U.S. Department of the Interior, National Park Service, 1992), 80–87. On plastics, see Horace G. Deming, *In the Realm of Carbon* (New York: John Wiley & Sons, 1930), 192–195; and Sheldon Hochheiser, *Rohm and Haas: History of a Chemical Company* (Philadelphia: University of Pennsylvania Press, 1986), 57–58.

Advertisement, *House Beautiful,* October 1945. Courtesy Waverly Fabrics.

4. Lee Kennett, *For the Duration* (New York: Charles Scribner's Sons, 1985), 19–21; Francis Walton, *Miracle of World War II* (New York: Macmillan Co., 1956), 116; Alan S. Milward, *War, Economy, and Society, 1939–1945* (Berkeley and Los Angeles: University of California Press, 1979), 64–65; John Morton Blum, *V Was for Victory: Politics and American Culture during World War II* (New York: Harcourt Brace Jovanovich, 1976), 118.

5. See, for example, Donald M. Nelson, *Arsenal of Democracy: The Story of American War Production* (New York: Harcourt, Brace and Co., 1946), especially chap. 5; Erling M. Hunt, *America Organizes to Win the War* (New York: Harcourt, Brace and Co., 1942), 167; Blum, *V Was for Victory,* 121; Walton, *Miracle of World War II,* 116–121; Milward, *War, Economy, and Society,* 103.

6. David Novick, Melvin Anshen, and W. C. Truppner, *Wartime Production Controls* (New York: Columbia University Press, 1949), 41–45; Kennett, *For the Duration,* 103.

7. Milward, *War, Economy, and Society,* 104; Kennett, *For the Duration,* 103–105; Nelson, *Arsenal of Democracy,* 124–128.

8. Kennett, *For the Duration,* 105–107; Nelson, *Arsenal of Democracy,* 283; Novick, Anshen, and Truppner, *Wartime Production Controls,* 46; "War Board's Building Conservation Order," *American Builder and Building Age* (May 1942): 39–41.

9. "Better Than the Headlines," *Business Week* (October 11, 1941): 13; "How Metals Stand," ibid., 17–18; "Plastics' Plight," ibid.; "Use of Copper Banned for Building Work," *Engineering News-Record* (October 23, 1941): 81; Robert B. Colburn, "How Priorities Work in Construction," ibid., 91–94; Herbert R. Simonds and Carleton Ellis, *Handbook of Plastics* (New York: Van Nostrand Co., 1943), 871–872.

10. Herbert L. Whittemore, "Materials Shortages: Redesign and Substitution," *Engineering News-Record* (January 15, 1942): 114–116.

11. "Housing for War," *Business Week,* (January 3, 1942): 18–19; Franklin D. Roosevelt to Abner H. Ferguson, Federal Housing Administrator, April

8, 1941; Walton, *Miracle of World War II,* 65–66; Blum, *V Was for Victory,* 102; "War Board's Building Conservation Order," 41; Nelson, *Arsenal of Democracy,* 283–285; "Total War and the Little Man," *Fortune* (January 1942): 78–84.

12. "War Buildings Are Different," *Engineering News-Record* (October 22, 1942): 99. Douglas Aircraft assembled the C-54, four-engine transport in the Chicago plant; according to Douglas, it saved twenty thousand tons of steel for the war effort by substituting wood for the columns, supporting trusses, window frames, and light reflectors of the six-bay structure.

13. Sylvia Katz, *Plastics: Designs and Materials* (London: Studio Vista, 1978), 70; Arthur Drexler, *Charles Eames: Furniture from the Design Collection of the Museum of Modern Art, New York* (New York: The Museum of Modern Art, 1973), 12–13, 24–25; the 1940 competition was titled "Organic Designs in Home Furnishings."

14. Cowan, *Science and Building,* 59–60, 150–151.

15. A. N. Carter, "Buildings of 1942 Were for War," *Engineering News-Record* (February 11, 1943): 102–105.

16. "Concrete and Laminated Wood Framing," *Engineering News-Record,* (October 22, 1942): 101–102; "Multi-Story Building Designed in Timber," ibid., 114–116; "Blimp Hangars Set New Timber Arch Record," ibid., 110–111; "Navy Develops All-Timber Blimp Hangar, part II," *Civil Engineering* (November 1943): 525.

17. Carter, "Buildings of 1942 Were for War," 104–105; Neff, Wallace Jr., *Wallace Neff: Architect of California's Golden Age* (Santa Barbara: Capra Press, 1986), 177–186; "Balloon Houses Designed for Defense Workers Bloom under Virginia Trees," *Life* (December 1, 1941): 34–35; "Bubble Houses for Defense," *Architect and Engineer* (January 1942): 20–21; "Inflated Balloon Provides Form," *Architect and Engineer* (January 1942): 22–23.

18. "Reducing Breakage in the Navy," *Modern Plastics* (November 1942): 80–81; H. E. Griffith, "Fabrication of Polystyrene," ibid., 79, 122; "Plastic Bottles?" *Modern Packaging* (November 1943): 65–67.

19. Carter, "Buildings of 1942 Were for War," 105; Lenore Fine, Jesse A. Remington, and Maurice Mattoff, eds. *The United States Army in World War II—The Corps of Engineers: Construction in the United States* (Washington, D.C.: Office of the Chief of Military History, United States Army, 1972), 545–553; "The Outlook," *Business Week* (February 19, 1944): 1.

20. "Army and Navy Try Out 'Demountable Houses,'" *American Builder and Building Age* (January 1941); "Six Houses a Day," *Business Week,* (September 13, 1941); "What to Expect in New Building Materials and Equipment," *Engineering News-Record* (October 18, 1945): 145–146; Charles W. Johnson and Charles O. Jackson, *City Behind a Fence: Oak Ridge, Tennessee, 1942–1946* (Knoxville: University of Tennessee Press, 1981), 21; "Historic and Architectural Resources of Oak Ridge, Tenn.," in U.S. Department of the Interior, National Park Service, National Register of Historic Places, Multiple Property Doc. Form, Oak Ridge, Tenn. [NPS 10-99-a], 16–17.

21. Quoting H. B. Zackrison, in Fine and Remington, *United States Army,* 554; Nelson, *Arsenal of Democracy,* 349–356; George O. Robinson, Jr., *The Oak Ridge Story* (Kingsport, Tenn.: Southern Publishers, 1950), 77.

22. Marquis W. Childs, *This Is Your War* (Boston: Little, Brown and Co., 1942), 19–25; Millward, *War, Economy, and Society,* 64–65; Blum, *V Was for Victory,* 100.

23. Blum, *V Was for Victory,* 100; "What Happened to the Dreamworld?" *Fortune* (February 1947): 91–93, 214–216; Carrier: *Saturday Evening Post* (April 18, 1942): 97; Armco: *Saturday Evening Post* (April 4, 1942): 85; Nash Kelvinator: *Life* (October 12, 1942): inside front cover.

24. *Saturday Evening Post* (April 4, 1942): 39, 60, and 73; Sparton: *Life* (October 5, 1942): 22–23; Blum, *V Was for Victory,* 102.

25. National Association of Manufacturers, Postwar Committee, *Report* (1942); National Association of Manufacturers, Postwar Committee, *Report* (1943); Robert R. Nathan, *Mobilizing for Abundance* (New York: Whittlesey House, McGraw-Hill Book Company, 1944), 10.

26. Conversation between Donald Albrecht and architect George Dudley, from the Harrison and Abramovitz office, July 8, 1993.

27. R. F. Seery, "Aluminum Curtain Wall Construction," in *Materials and Methods in Architecture,* ed. Burton H. Holmes (New York: Reinhold Publishing Corporation, 1954), 28–35; Burton H. Holmes, "Alcoa Building: Lightweight Construction," in ibid., 37–41.

28. George A. Bryant, Louis Kahn, and Morton C. Tuttle, "Construction after the War," *Engineering News-Record* (October 21, 1943): 106–109; "Building Waits for a Boom," *Business Week* (March 25, 1944): 17.

29. "What Happened to the Dreamworld?" 90–93, 214–216.

30. Thanks to Jeffrey Meikle for sharing this observation, as well as much else on plastics.

Margaret Crawford

Daily Life on the Home Front:
Women, Blacks, and the Struggle
for Public Housing

During 1943, Agnes Meyer and Selden Menefee toured America's war production centers. Meyer, a correspondent for the *Washington Post*, and Menefee, sent by Princeton's Office of Public Opinion Research, set out to examine the social impact of the war. Following separate itineraries, they arrived at similar conclusions, which were published in the *Post* in 1944. Both were deeply disturbed by what they found. With more than twenty-five million men, women, and children crowding into new centers of war industry, the fabric of American life had unraveled. Black and women war workers, new to the labor force, suffered the most. Both Meyer and Menefee judged the "plight of the Negro" to be the biggest social problem facing the nation. War work had given blacks hope, but they still faced segregation and discrimination. The war emergency strained a tenuous racial balance to the point of violence. The social turmoil produced by war also placed unprecedented pressures on family and home life. In the absence of social or governmental support, working mothers and their children bore a disproportionate burden. Meyer felt that these problems, uncovered by the war, challenged the basic premises of American democracy.[1]

Both Meyer and Menefee blamed much of the chaos on Washington. Although the government intervened in the lives of its citizens in unprecedented ways, its policies were rarely coherent or even consistently applied. New Federal agencies sprang into action to facilitate the war economy, but America never went as far as other countries, such as England, in taking control of essential labor, housing, and social services. Interagency rivalries generated bureaucratic red tape and made coordination almost impossible. At every level of government, political and ideological conflicts compromised and limited war measures. Liberals complained that President Roosevelt was selling out the New Deal by appointing businessmen to top government posts, while conservatives worried that civilian defense programs were socialism in disguise.[2] Local governments resisted wartime changes, particularly when Federal initiatives clashed with local priorities.

Defense housing programs embodied all of these contradictions. In 1940 the defense amendment to the U.S. Housing Act of 1937 channeled Federal slum clearance funds into housing programs for defense areas, converting more than half of the three hundred existing public housing projects into war housing. A radical piece of New Deal legislation, allocating Federal funds for low-income housing, the Housing Act had made it through Congress only by safeguarding local autonomy. This allowed cities to build and administer their own housing programs through municipal agencies "according to local customs." In contrast, the 1940 Lanham Act, which provided Federal aid for housing and services to communities affected by defense industries, imposed centralized control. Its conservative sponsor, Congressman Fritz Lanham of Texas, afraid of funding slum clearance or social programs, put the program under the jurisdiction of the Federal Works Agency, an engineering organization primarily concerned with construction. Competing programs still caused delays and bottlenecks, so in 1941, the government established the Division of Defense Housing to coordinate defense housing, then consolidated all housing activities into the National Housing Agency.

....."I helped cook 'em in my kitchen!"

"This is more of a woman's war than any war that has ever been fought!

"From the heroic nurses of Bataan . . . to the women at home faced with the problem of preparing nutritious wartime meals for their families . . . we're all playing a vital part in helping to win this war.

"But there's another way we can show our patriotism that many of us have probably never considered . . . and that is by avoiding wasteful use of Gas . . . in cooking and especially in house heating and water heating.

"Most people think of Gas only as a household fuel . . . the truth is, it's also used in making nearly every kind of fighting weapon that goes to our men . . . planes, ships, tanks, guns, bombs!

"Gas makes them faster . . . and that means lives saved! It's much more economical . . . and that affects all our pocketbooks. It's easier to control . . . and that means finer planes, better equipment for our husbands and sons!"

MEETING WARTIME NEEDS

1. For Gas fuel. Today the Gas industry is producing more Gas than at any time in history. Yet because of the difficulty in transporting fuel oil and coal to make manufactured Gas—and because of the shortage of materials with which to enlarge plants or build new natural gas pipe lines—there may be times in some sections when the demands of war production will reduce the amount of Gas normally available for household use. It is for these reasons you are urged to use Gas wisely—don't waste it!

2. For nutrition information. If you are one of the 85 million who depend on Gas for cooking, feel free to ask your Gas Company for the latest information on preparing nutritious wartime meals.

AMERICAN GAS ASSOCIATION

GAS

is vital to war production . . . use it wisely!

Buy War Bonds today—save for the Certified Performance Gas range of tomorrow.

15

ninety-three

Poster, n.d. Courtesy National Archives.

Women war workers at the Pacific Parachute Company, San Diego, California, 1945. Courtesy U.S. Office of War Information Collection/ Prints and Photographs Division/Library of Congress. LC-USW3-53881-E.

Women learning to build Boeing B-17 Flying Fortress bombers, n.d. Courtesy National Archives. RG 208-LU-38BB-3.

"I hope, Mary, you will never read this letter...

If you do, it will mean that you will have to go on from
here without me. You will have to face alone all these
things we started out so confidently to face together. • I have
wanted so much for you my darling. So many things I had hoped
to give you and to share with you. • Above all else,
I wanted you always to have
peace of mind, your dignity and
your independence. • Now it's too late for
me to have a part in that.
But perhaps I have been
able to help a little. For
sometimes, when things seem
clear to me, I feel that these are the things we over
here have been fighting for. • All my love, Mary.
We have had, at least, a little time together.*"

Tragedies like this—personal, individual tragedies—
are happening every day And they will continue
happening until the great tragedy of war is over—and our
victorious men start coming home. • America needs millions of
her women—needs *you personally*—to make
this day of victory come sooner. • *You*
can do a vital job in ending this
war *quicker. You* can save many and many an American
soldier from fighting needless extra days. • You are wanted
desperately in a war job—in the armed services—in essential
civilian work. Today, look in the classified section of your newspaper, or go to your nearest United States Employment Service office.
In most communities you will find the right job for you. If your choice
is the armed services, apply at your Army or Navy Recruiting Station.

The more women at war . . . the sooner we'll win

This advertisement sponsored by

HOFFMANN-LA ROCHE, INC.

Makers of Vitamins and Medicines of Rare Quality

Published in cooperation with the
Drug, Cosmetic and Allied Industries

Roche Park • Nutley, N. J.

Advertisement urging women to stay on the job, *Photoplay*, September 1943. Courtesy Kimberly-Clark Corp.

Opposite:
Advertisement, *Life*, February 1944.

Under these programs, the Federal government financed almost one hundred thousand units of defense housing across the nation. Five of these public projects demonstrate the conflicts, difficulties, and achievements of wartime housing in a particularly vivid way. Richmond, California, was torn apart by wartime changes. Reluctant to take actions that might permanently affect the community, Richmond's city government never solved wartime problems. In Detroit, the racial controversy ignited by the construction of the Sojourner Truth Homes uncovered the depth of the city's racial antagonism and the unwillingness of both Federal and local governments to address it. In Willow Run, Michigan, local resistance and Henry Ford's indifference to the needs of defense workers produced a disaster, described by Agnes Meyer as "a nightmare of substandard living conditions." Not all of the government projects were failures, however. Vanport, Oregon, and Marin City, California, were model communities, providing complete, if basic, living environments. At Vanport, Henry J. Kaiser created a community particularly addressed to the needs of women workers. In Marin City, a liberal housing authority took the notion of community seriously, making a positive effort to integrate housing and promote self-government.

"An Avalanche Hits Richmond"

The war turned Richmond, California, a small town of twenty-three thousand in 1941, into the quintessential boomtown. In 1943, Agnes Meyer found the area "in more of a turmoil" than any of the twenty-seven war centers she had already visited. Engulfed by war workers, the city government had lost control. Schools operated three and sometimes four shifts; police, fire, and sewer services broke down, and uncollected garbage piled up in the streets. Because government-operated industries and housing projects were tax-exempt, the city was broke. City Manager James McVitty wrote, pleading for Federal assistance, "Even normal social controls could not be maintained. The result was con-

Kaiser Shipyard, Richmond, California, ca. 1942. Courtesy Richmond Museum Collection.

Afternoon shift change at a Kaiser shipyard in Richmond, California, ca. 1942. Copyright Dorothea Lange Collection/Oakland Museum/ City of Oakland/gift of Paul S. Taylor.

Richmond, California, ca. 1942. Copyright
Dorothea Lange Collection/Oakland Museum/
City of Oakland/gift of Paul S. Taylor.

Oakland, California, ca. 1942. Copyright
Dorothea Lange Collection/Oakland Museum/
City of Oakland/gift of Paul S. Taylor.

gestion and utter confusion. Richmond was literally bursting at the seams."[3] Caught between the priorities of the war effort, the needs of Kaiser Shipyards, the demands of the Maritime Commission, and its own attempts to maintain control, the city government took actions that exacerbated rather than solved Richmond's problems. As a result, although Richmond housed the largest number of defense projects in the country, it never succeeded in providing decent living conditions for war workers.

Dominating Richmond's fifty-five other war industries, Kaiser Shipyards boosted industrial employment from four thousand five hundred in the summer of 1941 to nearly one hundred thousand by the end of 1943. The U.S. Maritime Commission invited Henry J. Kaiser to build Liberty ships at Richmond's deepwater port in 1941. Unlike Henry Ford, Kaiser had prospered by cooperating with the Federal government and the unions. Already famous for working miracles in the construction industry, Kaiser made his fortune by completing large-scale public works projects in record time. New to shipbuilding, the innovative Kaiser revolutionized the industry by introducing mass production techniques, based on assembly lines, and unskilled labor. Under pressure to meet the Maritime Commission's tight production schedules, the Richmond yards continually set new speed records, producing more ships than any other yard in the country. To meet his chronic labor shortages, Kaiser hired recruiters to scour the country. On peak days, more than one hundred men a day left for the West Coast yards. By the end of the war, Kaiser had brought nearly thirty-eight thousand workers to Richmond via paid train trips while another sixty thousand, referred by recruiters, came on their own.[4]

Like earlier migrants to California, many newcomers came from Texas, Oklahoma, Arkansas, and Louisiana, lured by the promise of work and a better life. For the first time, large numbers of blacks—such as Willie Stokes, a farm laborer from Desha County, Arkansas, his wife, and their two children—joined

"Okies" and "Arkies" on the road west. Arriving in Richmond, Willie Stokes quickly found work at Kaiser. Unlike other defense contractors, Bay Area shipyards opened their doors to black workers early in the war. In 1942, Kaiser recruited black workers in New York, transporting them west in special trains. Like the Stokes family, however, most blacks who moved to California came on their own.[5]

As shipyard employment surged, housing and transportation problems jeopardized Kaiser's production schedules. Absenteeism and turnover rates soared. In spite of extreme overcrowding, Richmond could house only twenty percent of shipyard workers. Hundreds of others poured into the city every day, from all over the Bay Area.[6] Because most workers commuted by automobile, this produced massive traffic jams. C. E. Miller, a Kaiser production engineer, claimed that "the principal cause for absenteeism is the transportation problem. We are losing about four

Shipyard workers' housing, 1944. Copyright Dorothea Lange Collection/Oakland Museum/ City of Oakland/gift of Paul S. Taylor.

thousand people a month who are quitting because they can't stand the strain." A Kaiser study revealed that length of commute was the most important factor determining turnover rates, comparing Richmond's one-percent rate with fifteen-point-three percent for East Bay residents and twenty percent for those who lived even further away.[7]

Kaiser found the pace of housing construction in Richmond inexplicably slow. Controlled by local real estate interests, the Richmond Housing Authority (RHA) moved carefully to ensure that public housing would not "hamper private building or rental." Reassured by the government's promise to destroy all temporary units within two years of the end of the war, the RHA agreed to set aside the swampy flatlands near the harbor for war housing.[8] Six thousand FHA units were under construction by the fall of 1942, followed by eight thousand Farm Security Administration (FSA) units. Even this boom in building did not meet Kai-

Richmond schoolchildren, ca. 1942. Every hand raised signifies a child not born in California. Copyright Dorothea Lange Collection/Oakland Museum/City of Oakland/gift of Paul S. Taylor.

ser's needs, so the Maritime Commission initiated its own housing program. Using Kaiser's shipyard engineers and construction expertise, the Commission built an additional ten thousand apartments and dormitories in record time, and even converted a Montgomery Ward warehouse into a dormitory for five hundred men.[9] To alleviate the worst conditions, the RHA opened its own trailer camp near the shipyards. The Federal government operated three camps just outside the city limits, including the El Portal camp, the largest trailer facility in the country. By the end of 1943, Richmond, with twenty-five thousand temporary units, had the largest public housing program in the nation. Almost overnight, enormous tracts of barrack-like housing covered Richmond's south side, providing shelter for seventy-two thousand people, more than half of the city's population.[10]

In the rush to build, government agencies sacrificed safety and comfort. Wartime shortages of materials and workers dictated cheap and quick construction. Federal specifications for temporary housing required seventy-eight percent less material than a permanent house. With characteristic efficiency, Kaiser broke records by completing the first Maritime Housing units only two weeks after the foundations were poured. Such flimsy materials and hasty construction made fire a constant danger. Numerous fires did occur, engulfing buildings in a matter of seconds. Health and hygiene were also problems. In 1943, influenza, polio, and tuberculosis spread through the projects. That same year, Harborgate residents complained that winter rains and poor drainage had produced a swamp of water and mud so large that their children could not get to school. That summer, health department investigators found little improvement. Water seeping up from the bay covered the ground. In desperation, tenants tried to soak up the water with floorboards and garbage, declaring that they preferred rats to mosquitoes.[11]

Expediency replaced aesthetic and social concerns. Harborgate was a complete community, furnished with playgrounds,

Shipyard workers' housing, ca. 1944. Copyright Dorothea Lange Collection/Oakland Museum/City of Oakland/gift of Paul S. Taylor.

schools, and landscaping, but most projects still provided only the basic necessities. Rows of drab two-story frame apartments lined up across the barren flats, unrelieved by trees or grass. In spite of tenants' demands, the RHA refused to furnish adequate services, forcing residents to make the long trip downtown for even the smallest purchase. In 1944, the RHA reluctantly built a supermarket only after Kaiser threatened to take over its own projects unless conditions improved. Tenants' unions sprang up, threatening rent strikes. Other disgruntled residents just left or refused to pay their rent. In July 1943, the RHA reported that over ten percent of all tenants were three or more months behind in their rent. Still, there was nowhere else to live, and for many southern and rural migrants the housing was the best they had ever had. In 1943, the RHA had a backlog of sixteen thousand applications.[12]

Constant turnover and class, religious, and ethnic differences prevented a feeling of community from developing. Race became a fundamental distinction; although no previous racial patterns existed in Richmond's industrial areas, the RHA introduced segregation as a basic principle of housing allocation.

Fore 'n' Aft

OCTOBER 15, 1943 • VOL. 3, No. 41

PISTOL PACKIN' MAMA
(See Page 3)

THE PERMANENTE METALS CORPORATION • KAISER COMPANY, INC. • KAISER CARGO, INC. • RICHMOND, CALIFORNIA

Margaret Crawford

one hundred six

Harry Barbour, the RHA manager, defended segregation as "a natural process, the result of the two different races naturally want-
ing to live with their own kind."[13] Afraid of violence, the FPHA
never challenged racial exclusion, adopting a cautious attitude in
order to maintain social harmony during the war emergency. Des-
ignating eight of the twenty projects and one of the dormitories
for blacks, the RHA rezoned Richmond's south side according to
race. Concentrating black residents on the west along the shore-
line, they inserted a buffer zone of all-white projects along its
northern edge, adjacent to commercial and residential areas.
Within the projects, the RHA grouped black workers and their
families in separate areas or in completely segregated buildings.
In the face of overwhelming black demand for housing, agency
quotas maintained the ratio of white to black at four to one.[14] Although selection procedures for the USMA units were officially
color-blind, preference for skilled workers acted as de facto segregation, resulting in housing that was more than ninety percent
white. In spite of protests by the United Negroes of America, the
NAACP, and other black organizations, the RHA refused to alter
its policies.[15]

The shipyard projects formed a wartime ghetto within
Richmond. Physically separated from the rest of the city, war
workers encountered natives only on crowded downtown streets.
Fortune magazine described the scene: "The sidewalks are
blocked by gaping strangers in cowboy boots, blue jeans and som-
breros. Women in slacks and leather jackets and shiny scalers'
helmets wait in long lines to buy food. Pale-haired children and
mangy hound dogs wander the treeless streets. Nobody knows
anybody."[16] Unpredecented social diversity provoked anxiety and
hostility. To reassert control, the city government imposed heavy
fines for trivial offenses. Police made four thousand arrests a
month, mostly of newcomers, who felt stigmatized and perse-
cuted.[17] Blacks from the South discovered that, although schools
and transportation were not segregated, discrimination still ex-

Fore 'n' Aft, October 15, 1943. Courtesy Richmond Museum Collection.

one hundred seven

isted. Immediately after stepping off the train from Texas, black migrant Cleophus Brown walked into a cafe and was refused service.[18] Because old-timers didn't know any migrants personally, stereotypes abounded. Black newcomers were either "Chicago Negroes"—slick, tough, urban criminal types—or "Southern Negroes"—ignorant, childlike yokels—while "Okies," "Arkies," and "hillbillies" were all lazy, illiterate, and unacquainted with modern ways. The *Richmond Independent* featured stories ridiculing project dwellers, reporting, for example, that many, failing to recognize modern plumbing, chopped holes in the floor to use as toilets.[19]

These deep social chasms astonished many observers. Sociologist Katherine Archibald's classic study *Wartime Shipyard* documents the depth of regional, class, and racial antagonisms among war workers. Employed at Moore Shipyards in Oakland, Archibald discovered a level of social disunity that made a mockery of patriotic calls for a united front. Her shipyard experience convinced her that such intense hatred went far beyond economic rivalry. Although they also suffered from prejudice, her white coworkers shared a basic hatred of blacks. An "Okie" responded to her pleas for tolerance with, "Well a nigger may be as good as you are, but he sure ain't as good as me." Statements such as this undermined liberals' assumptions that equalizing economic opportunities would eliminate prejudice.[20]

Detroit: Sojourner Truth and the Struggle for Black Housing

Just outside Detroit, another battle over war housing was taking shape. Most Detroit residents welcomed public housing, but as rapid wartime growth disrupted existing patterns of residence and social behavior, a confrontation erupted over the location of a housing project for black war workers. As automakers retooled for war, Detroit became the largest defense producer in the nation. Escalating demands for new workers drew migrants to the city. Actively recruiting in Kentucky and Tennessee, Ford spon-

Slum housing, Detroit, Michigan, 1942. Courtesy U.S. Office of War Information Collection/ Prints and Photographs Division/Library of Congress. LC-USW-3-16662-E.

Sojourner Truth housing project, Detroit, Michigan, 1942. Courtesy U.S. Office of War Information Collection/Prints and Photographs Division/Library of Congress. LC-USW3-16714-C.

sored mass meetings in rural areas, exhorting workers to do their
patriotic duty. Southerners responded in such large numbers that
a popular joke asked, "Why are there only forty-six states? Because Tennessee and Kentucky are now in Michigan!" Shut out of
training programs and defense jobs in the South, between 1940
and 1944 sixty-five thousand blacks arrived in Detroit. There,
white "hillbillies" and black migrants competed intensely with
natives and each other for jobs, housing, and services.[21]

Black demands for equal employment escalated, but Detroit's defense industries moved slowly in hiring black workers.
In 1941, A. Philip Randolph, of the Brotherhood of Sleeping Car
Porters, began organizing a massive march on Washington with
the slogan "We Loyal Negro American Citizens Demand the Right
to Work and Fight for Our Country." The threat of one hundred
thousand angry blacks descending on Washington convinced President Roosevelt to negotiate a settlement. Roosevelt would sign a
presidential order allowing blacks to work in defense plants if
Randolph would call off the march. Executive Order 8802 declared, "There shall be no discrimination in the employment of
workers in defense industries or government because of race,
creed, color or national origin."[22] The next year, the *Pittsburgh
Courier,* the largest black newspaper in the country, began the
"Double V" campaign, calling for "victory over our enemies at
home and victory over our enemies on the battlefields abroad." In
Detroit, the Negro Coordinating Committee for National Defense
complained to Roosevelt and pressured state officials, industrial
managers, and stockholders to hire black workers. Detroit's black
state senator Charles Diggs persuaded the Michigan senate to
adopt a resolution urging the state's defense producers "to employ
all qualified residents," regardless of race.[23]

Once employed, black migrants had to live in Detroit's
worst housing. In crowded ghettos, newcomers were forced to
double and triple up in substandard buildings. Rats infested the

ghetto, posing the threat of epidemic and occasionally biting sleeping children. As early as 1940, Charles Diggs and other black activists formed the Coordinating Committee on Housing, protesting exorbitant rents and unsanitary living conditions. In June 1941, aware of the desperate situation, the Federal Works Agency (FWA) and the Detroit Housing Commission (DHC) allocated two hundred FHA units to black war workers. The FWA began to plan a permanent housing project for black war workers in a mixed neighborhood in northeast Detroit, near the Polish community of Hamtramck, and dissension began immediately.

The plans for a black housing project crystallized black grievances and white fears. Middle-class blacks in the area, afraid of an influx of lower-class neighbors, initially expressed concern about the location of the project but withdrew their objections once the fight turned into a racial struggle. On one side, determined to prevent black occupancy, were white residents, led by local realtors. Both groups were convinced that property values would plummet. As opposition grew, agitators such as the National Workers League, a local fascist group, fanned the flames. Although initially a supporter of the project, local congressman Rudolph Tenerowicz switched sides and demanded that an alternative site be found or the project redesignated for whites. On the others side was the Sojourner Truth Citizens Committee, a coalition made up of black residents and war workers, the NAACP, white representatives from the CIO and UAW, and liberal Jewish and Protestant religious leaders. For blacks, as the NAACP's Roy Wilkins emphasized, the fight was more than a neighborhood brawl. Their basic interests were at stake: government housing and government protection. A local youth put it more bluntly: "If they take the Sojourner Truth Housing Project away from Negroes, they'll never draft me."[24]

The increasingly virulent campaign against the project uncovered the complexity of racial politics in Washington and Detroit during the war. While their political allies applied pressure, opponents inundated Washington with letters and set up daily picket lines outside City Hall. Federal and local authorities responded to insistent opposition with equivocation and indecision. When conservative southern legislators raised the issue in Congress, the Federal government wavered. Roosevelt saw wartime race relations "more as a problem of efficient industrial mobilization than as a fundamental moral problem."[25] Always mindful of his need for support by southern Democrats, Roosevelt made conflicting statements about racial issues.[26] In the space of a single year, the FHA reversed itself six times. The well-intentioned mayor, John Jeffries, hoping to satisfy both sides, also vacillated. The Detroit Housing Commission named the project after the celebrated ex-slave abolitionist and feminist poet, Sojourner Truth, then withdrew its support for the project. At this point the Citizens Committee mobilized its forces. Union members sent five thousand postcards to President Roosevelt, and the NAACP threw up its own picket line. Their efforts, supported by white liberals, finally shifted the political balance. The Detroit Housing Commission and the Common Council voted for black occupancy. Washington reversed its decision and ruled that blacks could move into Sojourner Truth.

Sign erected near Sojourner Truth housing project, 1942. Courtesy U.S. Office of War Information Collection/Prints and Photographs Division/Library of Congress. LC-USW3-16549-C.

Opposite:
A confrontation at the Sojourner Truth housing project in late February, 1942. Courtesy U.S. Office of War Information Collection/Prints and Photographs Division/Library of Congress.

Over the protests of angry whites, the Federal housing coordinator scheduled the first tenants to move in on February 28, 1942. The night before, a crowd of whites burned a cross outside the project. The next day, as a small group of black tenants arrived with moving vans, an angry mob attacked them, overturning the vans. As news of the incident spread, hundreds of blacks rushed to the scene to defend the tenants. Rioting started. The Detroit police refused to protect the tenants, instead arresting their black supporters. Of the more than one hundred arrests, only three were of whites; of thirty-eight people hospitalized, all but five were black. The violence ended, but the Sojourner Truth Homes remained empty. Demonstrations and picketing from both sides continued. Finally, two months later, the first tenants moved in with one thousand seven hundred fifty police and state militia standing guard. The first occupant, Walter Jackson, a war worker and father of five, declared, "I have got only one time to die, and I'd just as soon die here." The second family to move in, Mr. and Mrs. Joseph Battle, thanked the Citizens Committee, the NAACP, and the black press for their "courageous fight for democracy."[27]

The NAACP's role in the Sojourner Truth victory attracted new supporters, making the Detroit chapter the largest in the country. Meeting in Detroit that year, the national NAACP re-

affirmed its fighting stance: "We refuse to listen to the weak-kneed of both races who tell us not to raise controversies during the war. We believe, on the contrary, that we are doing a patriotic duty in raising them."[28]

The Sojourner Truth riot was, in fact, a portent. Increasing numbers of migrants, crowded housing conditions, and the influence of right-wing demagogues, such as Father Coughlin and Gerald L. K. Smith, heated racial tensions to the boiling point. Shortly after the Sojourner Truth incident, a government observer warned, "It now appears that only the direct intervention of the President can prevent not only a violent race riot in Detroit but a steadily widening fissure that will wreak havoc in the working force of every northern city."[29] *Life* magazine published a photo essay titled "Detroit Is Dynamite." On a sweltering night in June 1943, a full-scale race riot exploded. Violent street battles between black and white youths, migrants of both races, raged for two days. Thirty-four people died and six hundred seventy-five were injured before the army could stop the fighting. As Detroit returned to an uneasy racial truce, white officials saw the riot as further confirmation that any change in race relations would be dangerous. In spite of continuing pressure from the NAACP and the UAW, Detroit's housing projects remained segregated for the duration of the war. For Robert Weaver, one of Roosevelt's black advisers, the Detroit experience summed up the contradictions of wartime change: the color line in jobs weakened, but far stricter lines in housing emerged.[30]

The Battle of Willow Run

When Agnes Meyer arrived in 1943, Willow Run, Michigan, was already a national scandal. The Ford Motor Company had located an enormous bomber plant twenty miles outside of Detroit, anticipating that workers would commute from the city. Instead, gas and rubber shortages forced them to relocate closer to the plant. The initial influx of ten thousand workers overwhelmed local

Willow Village expansible trailers serving Willow Run bomber plant, 1943. Courtesy Collections of Henry Ford Museum and Greenfield Village. 94-845P833.788233.4.

Defense worker's family in a trailer home near Ypsilanti, Michigan, 1941. Courtesy U.S. Farm Security Administration Collection/Prints and Photographs Division/Library of Congress. LC-USF34-63706-D.

housing, services, and schools. By early 1942, not a single room to rent could be found within a fifteen-mile radius of Ypsilanti, the closest town. As workers continued to arrive, living conditions rapidly deteriorated. Newcomers occupied makeshift trailer camps, chicken coops, and abandoned garages. Visiting a frame house without water or indoor plumbing, Meyer found five men living in the basement, a family of five occupying the first floor, four men sleeping on the second floor, nine men in the garage, and four families parked in their trailers in the backyard. Willow Run, the stream that ran through the area, was filled with sewage from hastily erected privies. Dysentery was widespread. After studying the area, Meyer wrote, "it seems to me the Federal government will have to do something about the living conditions . . . or its orators will have to stop talking about the dignity of man."[31]

University of Michigan professors Lowell Carr and James Stermer painstakingly documented the wretched living conditions in the Willow Run area, even renting a trailer of their own. Always overcrowded, with insufficient toilets, showers, and laundry rooms, and blackouts and frozen pipes, the camps challenged even the most intrepid "trailerites." Mrs. John Castle, along with her husband, a bomber plant worker, and her seven-year-old son, Tommy, moved to Willow Run in 1942. A full-time schoolteacher, Mrs. Castle struggled with housekeeping. Faced with a limited supply of hot water, only two washing machines for sixty families, and no drying rooms, she found it nearly impossible to provide clean clothing for her family. Domestic chores were complicated by the constant presence of mud, and cooking proved equally difficult. Reluctant to pay the exorbitant prices charged by the only nearby store, Mrs. Castle attempted to bake cookies in her trailer's oven, only to find that, lacking a regulator, she had burned up her entire month's fuel ration. To keep the stove operating, she had to drive one hundred fifty miles in order to refill the tank.[32]

Mrs. Castle complained that a trailer camp was no place for a child. Crowded quarters and lack of services exacerbated normal problems of child rearing. Since the Castles' trailer camp had only one swing for thirty children, the rest amused themselves by playing in the mud. Keeping her son occupied inside their small trailer taxed Mrs. Castle's imagination and patience. In the evenings her son's model airplanes disturbed her husband, who was exhausted after a long day at the plant. John Dos Passos called women like Mrs. Castle, who could get no respite from their children or their cramped quarters, "trailer-wacky."[33] The Ford plant provided some child care facilities, but few workers knew about the service. When Mrs. Edsel Ford proposed showing women workers films publicizing the program, Henry Ford vetoed the suggestion. Like many employers, he was ambivalent about working mothers and preferred to ignore the issue altogether.[34] Most mothers working at Ford were reluctant to send their children to organized day care programs. Instead, they relied on family members or neighbors. Often, parents worked different shifts so one would always be home with the children. Such informal arrangements frequently broke down, however. Meyer, always concerned about children, recounted sensational stories of children locked all day in cars in factory parking lots or left alone in trailers.[35]

By early 1942, complaints from the UAW-CIO were mounting, adding to Willow Run's notoriety. Housing and transportation problems had produced an astonishing turnover rate of more than one hundred percent a month.[36] The plant was unable to maintain a stable work force. Production was lagging, averaging only one bomber a day instead of the anticipated five hundred planes a month. Taking stock of the situation, NHA administrators planned to construct a model community, which they named Bomber City. The massive project, covering fifteen square miles, would permanently house one hundred ten thousand workers and their families. Five sections, each with its own school, park, church, and shopping facility, would be surrounded by a mile-wide greenbelt with recreational facilities.[37]

The announcement produced a flood of opposition from local business, civic, and governmental groups. Denying that there was any need for public housing, the Washtenaw County Board of Supervisors sent the country prosecutor to Washington to protest this proposed "unnecessary social experiment." Anxious to maintain the status quo in the midst of overwhelming change, they regarded the war workers as unwanted "foreigners." From their point of view, the housing project would not only lower real estate values, it would inflict political damage by permanently relocating one hundred thousand UAW members in a Republican county.

Local pressure did not deter government planners, but Henry Ford's strenuous opposition did succeed in derailing Bomber City. Threatening to block the project "by every legal method," Ford sent company lawyers to testify against the project in Washington. Meeting with protesters, a Ford executive explained the company's position: "Ford Motor Company's business is to build the best bombers in the world, and how our workers live off the job is a community problem, not ours."[38] Scaling back the project by eliminating all permanent housing, the FPHA hastily constructed temporary projects. In the spring of 1943, Willow Lodge, which provided dormitory rooms for single men and women, opened, followed by Willow Village, with two thousand five hundred temporary family units. The government also opened a park furnished with a thousand Federally owned trailers. The entire complex supplied shelter for fifteen thousand people, but during the peak period of the plant's operation in June 1943 this amounted to only two-point-four percent of Willow Run's workers, rising to eight-point-eight percent in December.[39]

Living conditions in the temporary projects, although better than in the camps and shantytowns, were far from ideal. Until 1944, the closest store was three miles away. The lack of recreational facilities created a "drab social environment" that encouraged heavy drinking, wild parties, and extremely high rates of venereal disease. Professors Carr and Stermer abandoned academic language to express their outrage about the situation: "The first housing unit did not open till February 1943, one full year after the Japanese conquest of Malaya! One full year after the need for special housing at Willow Run had first become blatant. Nearly two full years after ordinary socially intelligent foresight could have foreseen the need!"[40] They attributed the Willow Run fiasco to an overall breakdown of social responsibility. Selden Menefee placed blame directly on Henry Ford's antilabor policies. Ford's opposition, Menefee argued, came from his determination to defend his power against assaults by unionized workers and the Federal government. Wherever the ultimate responsibility lay, Willow Run became a synonym for wartime disruption.

Vanport: A Total Community

In 1944, Kaiser's shipyard paper *Fore 'n' Aft* dramatized women's double duty in an article headlined "Women Must Do War Work, but a 17 Hour Day Is Too Long!" Telesis, a group of San Francisco Bay Area regional planners, described a day that began at dawn and ended at 10:30 or 11 at night. Before and after eight-hour shifts, working wives bought and cooked food, cleaned house, washed dishes, did laundry, took care of children, and ran errands using crowded public transportation. The lack of shopping, banking, and other services near the shipyards added at least an hour a day to their schedules. Banks, rationing boards, and medical services all closed early. Rationing and shortages made daily shopping for food a necessity, but the shelves were often empty long before closing, and few stores stayed open in the evening. Telesis urged Kaiser to lighten working women's burdens by providing services—from shopping to laundry, cleaning facilities, a catering kitchen, and child care centers—in each neighborhood clustered as close together as possible and supplemented by family health care and recreational facilities.[41]

In an interview in the *New York Times* the previous year, Kaiser agreed with this assessment. He argued that "factories should be equipped with child care centers, health clinics, shopping centers, food dispensers, banking facilities, dry cleaning shops, recreation centers, comfortable lockers and rest rooms." His statement had less to do with abstract concepts of community than with Kaiser's understanding of the link between daily life and productivity. Richmond had proved to be beyond Kaiser's control, but the company was determined to improve living conditions for workers in their three Portland shipyards. Michael Miller, a long-time Kaiser employee, explained: "From the outset we recognized the relationship of proper housing and adequate community facilities because we have had much experience on engineering jobs in remote places. The way people live and the way their families are cared for are bound to be reflected in production." [42] The Maritime Commission declared Portland a priority area and authorized Kaiser to begin building housing immediately. Costs would be reimbursed from subsequent Lanham Act

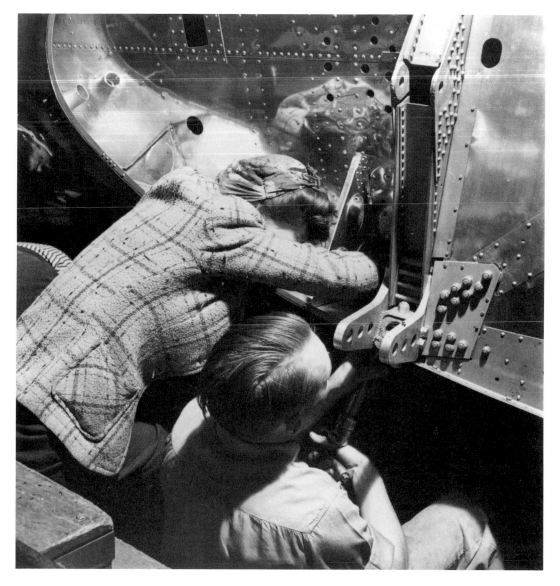

Exhausted woman worker at a Boeing aircraft
plant in Seattle, Washington, 1942. Courtesy
U.S. Office of War Information Collection/
Prints and Photographs Division/Library of
Congress. LC-USW3-41166-E.

Opposite:
Fore 'n' Aft, August 4, 1944. Courtesy Richmond Museum Collection.

appropriations. The company purchased six hundred fifty acres on the Oregon side of the Columbia River midway between the yards in Portland and Vancouver, Washington, and named the new community Vanport.[43]

Edgar Kaiser, Henry J.'s son and director of Oregon Shipyards, took charge of the project, over the objections of Portland's Housing Authority. Kaiser hired J. W. Moscowitz, a nationally known planner, as a consultant, and he chose the local architectural firm of Wolff and Phillips, designers of the Kaiser shipyards. In usual Kaiser fashion, construction of Vanport proceeded rapidly, reminding Agnes Meyer of a mirage, springing up like magic cities in the Arabian Nights. Kaiser had endless disputes with local and Federal housing authorities. Fighting for nursery schools, bus shelters, and landscaping, he was indignant when the FPHA called a halt on planting shrubbery, which they considered unnecessary in a temporary project. "How can anybody live there without some green trees?" he asked Meyer. After ten months' time, when housing, transportation, health, schools, and recreation programs took up more of Kaiser's time than shipbuilding, Vanport was a complete community, with seven hundred twenty-three apartment buildings, five schools, six nursery schools, five social buildings, a police station, four commercial shopping centers, a post office, sixteen playgrounds, three fire stations, an administration building, a library, a one-hundred-thirty-bed infirmary, and a theater.[44] Tenants could move into fully furnished apartments. If necessary, Kaiser would supply pillows and sheets. With a population of forty-two thousand, Vanport was the largest war housing project in the country and the second largest city in Oregon.

Kaiser had been a pioneer in hiring women workers, and by 1943 thirty-one percent of Oregonship workers were women.[45] Women's busy days translated into high absenteeism and turnover. In the Bay Area, a survey showed that, after illness and exhaustion, family duties were the most important reason for

Vanport, Oregon, ca. 1943. Courtesy Oregon Historical Society. OrHi 68762.

women's absences and high quit rates. In the Portland-Vancouver shipyards, the absentee rate among women was higher than the national average. An Oregonship survey revealed that women with children were losing more time than single women. This convinced Edgar Kaiser that providing top-quality child care was necessary to expedite production.[46]

Kaiser quickly discovered the deficiencies of Lanham Act nurseries, which provided minimal services and limited hours. Most closed at 6 P.M., rendering them useless to workers whose shifts let out at 6:30 P.M. Kaiser applied for Maritime Commission funds, arguing that adequate child care facilities were crucial to increasing working mothers' productivity. Impatient, Kaiser bypassed local day care committees and the Lanham Act's complicated procedures, appealing directly to Eleanor Roosevelt, who urged the Maritime Commission to give him the go-ahead. Kaiser spared no expense. Appalled at the low wages of nursery school teachers, he insisted on paying them shipyard wages. He turned the project over to experts Lois Meek Stolz and James Hymes, two well-known progressive educators,[47] who recruited a highly trained staff. Kaiser added the extra cost onto the price of his ships.

The result was unprecedented. Parents arriving at the center for the first time discovered a building specially designed for young children. Organized like the spokes of a wheel, fifteen playrooms surrounded an outdoor play area with a wading pool.

Vanport apartment interior, 1942. Courtesy Oregon Historical Society. OrHi 90397.

Each playroom had a covered area so children could play outside on Portland's numerous rainy days. The architects planned the entire building from a child's point of view, lowering the windows of the playrooms to fit a small child's sight-lines, designing child-sized furniture for each age group, and even redesigning bathroom fixtures to meet the needs of young children. Bathtubs were high enough so teachers could bathe children without bending and deep enough for children to have fun splashing. Scaled-down toilet seats were placed twelve inches from the ground. The children ate from special flat-sided plates with miniature forks and spoons. The rooms were painted cheerful hues of blue, apricot, or lemon. The staff developed innovative play equipment, designed to foster adventure and inquiry. To build the centers, Kaiser expediters, cajoling suppliers across the country, requisitioned hard-to-find materials and ordered custom-made goods, accomplishing a wartime miracle.[48]

Government policies toward mothers were contradictory, and child care was a controversial issue. Although the War Manpower Commission directed employers not to discriminate against mothers, it also urged that women with children should not be encouraged to work until all other labor was exhausted. Until 1943, official policy discouraged women with children under fourteen from working. The Children's Bureau, echoing the position of most child care experts, believed that mothers should care for young children at home. As more women entered the labor force,

Swan Island Child Service Center, ca. 1944.
Courtesy Oregon Historical Society.
OrHi 78700.

this position was no longer tenable. After much debate, Congress reluctantly extended the Lanham Act, providing matching funds to local programs to ensure that at least some child care arrangements were available.

The Kaiser centers responded wholeheartedly to the needs of working families. By March 1943, almost half of the fourteen thousand women in the Kaiser yards were mothers, and about one-third of them had children between the ages of one and six.[49] To save parents extra trips, Kaiser located identical centers at the entrances to the Oregonship and Swan Island shipyards. Open to children aged eighteen months to six years, the centers ran on a twenty-four-hour-a-day schedule, seven days a week. At 6:15 A.M. parents on the day shift brought their children in their pajamas. Teachers dressed them and gave them a hot breakfast. At 2 A.M. swing-shift parents wrapped up sleeping children in blankets and carried them home, still asleep. Nurses cared for sick children and monitored children's health with preventive care and immunizations. The staff saw the centers as a resource for parents and children; they took in children when parents needed to attend a union meeting or go shopping, and allowed older children to join their siblings on sleeping shifts. They also

Child Service Center, Portland, Oregon, ca. 1944. Courtesy National Archives. RG 208-EX-244-197.

provided a mending service for children's torn clothing, offered
help for any family problem, and, most revolutionary, provided
hot meals for parents to take home when they picked their children up.[50]

Despite these extraordinary efforts, few children showed
up on opening day. This low attendance was a national trend.
Only five percent of working mothers used child care centers, forcing many Lanham Act centers to close because of underenroll-
ment. Child care was still a novelty, and New Deal programs,
operated by the WPA, had unwelcome associations with poverty
and relief. Many parents distrusted institutions, preferring traditional forms of individual care. Augusta Clawson, a Swan Island
welder, reported that her co-workers were initially suspicious of
the center. "I don't want my kid playing with just anybody's kid,"
said one. "My Dickie's fussy about eating. I have to watch his
food," protested another. Assured that it was "not a charity
thing," their interest picked up.[51] Kaiser's enthusiastic publicity
attracted others; by 1944 more than one thousand children were
enrolled in the centers. Although this was still slightly under capacity, the Kaiser centers were among the most successful in the
country.[52]

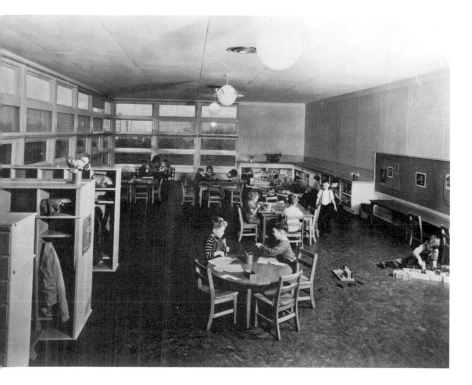

Child Service Center, ca. 1944. Courtesy
National Archives. RG 208-EX-244-196.

Tolerance and Diversity in Marin City

Marin City, California, known for its progressive policies, was a
rare instance of local planning and support for war housing. Although Marin County, an area of expensive residential communities, was almost completely without industry, its newly
constituted Housing Authority was not composed of the usual
real estate and commercial interests. The chairman, Ernest
White, was president of the Marin Central Labor Council, and
Guy A. Ciocca, a local lawyer and judge without previous housing
experience, became executive director. The authority began working with Marinship and the Maritime Commission to coordinate
transportation and housing before the shipyard was completed.[53]
Marin City, housing one thousand five hundred families and more
than one thousand single workers, opened along with the ship-

yards. Like Vanport, it was a complete community, providing all the necessities: a supermarket, shops, cafeteria, post office, clinic, school, and social buildings.[54]

Unlike most defense projects, Marin City followed a policy of nondiscrimination and nonsegregation, along with New York, Seattle, and Los Angeles. Marin City began in August 1942, without debate or discussion, to assign dormitory housing to black employees. By September, whites in the dorm were complaining about their neighbors. The project manager, Milen Dempster, was a community organizer who had managed a migrant labor camp during the New Deal and had run for governor of California on the Socialist ticket. Like other "right thinking people," New Deal liberals, and leftists, Dempster saw war housing as an opportunity to create a sense of community among disparate Americans. Dempster, after consulting with Ciocca, responded by stating that Marin City would house all shipyard workers without regard to "religion, race, color, or position in the shipyards." When whites protested, Dempster appealed to their patriotism, saying, "These men are Americans. They are needed just as you are—to build ships." Although he encouraged nonwhites to participate fully in all of the project's services and programs, Dempster's housing allocation policies were color-blind. Marin City continued to follow this policy throughout the war, and by 1945, blacks lived in all sections of the project and composed over one-third of its total population.[55]

Dempster also encouraged self-government in Marin City. Although the project was part of Marin County, he organized an elected city council as a vehicle for residents' concerns. Council politics attracted the project's most socially concerned residents, who elected female and black members. One of the new council's first acts was to publish a weekly newspaper, the *Marin Citizen*. A source of community information and a house organ for progressive values, the *Citizen* mixed social notes and complaints about local merchants with editorials denouncing racial preju-

Foreman Kay Daws and welding crew at Marinship near San Francisco, California, n.d. Courtesy Marinship 1942–1945/Bay Model Visitor Center.

勝
利

VICTORY

CHINES

Cheerful W. S. Fa
a cook for 18 yea
naturally, be bec
burner in Sub-Ass

A. W. Toy is the only Chinese certified welder at Marinship. He is 35, youngest of 8 children, and former headwaiter. (Below left) Y. P. Wong is engineering graduate of Brown University, was a builder for Chinese government. Mother is still in China.

THERE'S one thing you'll notice about Marinship Chinese workers. They're always working.

This probably goes back to a tradition of hard work which they and their ancestors have observed for millenniums in China. It is also due to the serious view they take of a war which for over five years has torn their homeland and now almost threatens its existence.

There are about 350 Chinese workers at Marinship, and the largest proportion of them are on the swing shift. Virtually all live in the famous Chinatown in San Francisco, where their life is a strange blend of Oriental tradition and Occidental education. Their home language is Cantonese; elsewhere they speak English.

Their spirit is amazing. Scarcely a department of Marinship is not profiting by their

(Below) Roger Quan operates a burning machine in Sub-assembly. Father of two children, he was formerly a truckdriver.

(Above) Lonnie Young is very shy. Only 22, she is a flanger. She was born in Salinas, formerly worked in a cannery there.

These colorfully dressed Chinese girls are holding a model of the Liberty ship YAT SEN. They are Lai Chuck (left) and Gladys Low, first Chinese girl to be ployed here. Behind them is a recruitment poster sent by clipper from Chun

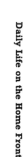

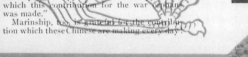

er Ying W. Lee looks ive on the job. She a laborer, and be- that a seamstress.

Albert Yee, former Chi- nese typesetter, began as a scaler and studied to be marine electrician.

Attractive Margaret Leung is supervisor of distribution for the im- portant bills of material.

Andrew Tseng saw friends blown to bits by Jap bombs in China in 1938. An engineer, he is a graduate of Columbia. (Below left) This is the deckhouse for the S.S. SUN YAT SEN, launched on March 25. The characters read, "Victory for the United Nations!" This was inscribed by George Kwock (below right), shipfitter, with daughter, Arlene, 8.

The Mariner's Journey

ORKERS AT MARINSHIP

endeavor. Some of the Chinese are among the best educated persons in the yard. They include many fine engineers. Others are old Chinese women and men with almost no education. But all see clearly the job they are here to do.

Typical of their spirit is a recent incident. The Liberty ship SUN YAT SEN was launched in honor of Mme. Chiang Kai-shek. Spontaneously the Chinese volunteered to pledge a day's pay to the relief of Chinese war orphans. In only a few days a check for $2,002.94 was on its way to China's first lady. Recently came back the reply:

"Madame Chiang desires me to convey to all of you her appreciation of the spirit with which this contribution for the war orphans was made."

Marinship, too, is grateful for the contribu- tion which these Chinese are making every day!

. Chan and B. T. Chang are hull engineers. Both are graduates in eering of American universities. Chan was formerly in aeronau- engineering. He publishes a youth magazine. Chang is from Hawaii.

Lovely Frances Jung makes all Marinship travel reserva- tions. At Stanford she grad- uated in Physical Education.

Marin-er, the Marinship newsletter, June 26, 1943. Courtesy Marinship 1942–1945/Bay Model Visitor Center.

dice. In spite of these efforts, the *Citizen*'s constant reproaches about the lack of participation suggests that most of Marin City's residents had little interest in community activities. Residents did not necessarily share the *Citizen*'s progressive attitudes. A survey of Vanport's residents listed the presence of black workers in housing and schools as one of their main complaints about the community.[56] A housing authority official admitted that if the white majority at Marin City were given the power to eject blacks from the project, "they would probably do so."[57] Still, the Housing Authority, the City Council, and the *Citizen,* by taking a strong stand for integration and equality, created an atmosphere of tolerance that was rare in war housing projects.

Postwar Promise and Peril

As the end to the war approached, defense production was already winding down. Within hours of the Japanese surrender, the government began canceling armament contracts.[58] The shipyards, always intended to be expendable, wrapped up their operations within a year after the end of the war. The war boomtowns collapsed, but many migrant and defense workers remained, hoping to find new jobs and houses in the peacetime economy. Reconversion and demobilization drastically reduced the shipbuilding and aircraft jobs that had employed women and blacks. As returning veterans and laid-off defense workers sought new jobs, employment patterns changed dramatically. Competition for jobs increased. Women and blacks, hired late and reluctantly, were the first to be fired. They had been recruited during a crisis and were now expected to give up their jobs to returning veterans. In spite of intense propaganda encouraging women to return to traditional domestic roles, however, many women stayed in the labor force. By 1950, the percentage of employed women had risen higher than the wartime peak. With high-paying wartime manufacturing work now closed to them, women moved back into traditionally female jobs in sales, clerical, and service occupations.[59]

Advertisement, *Fortune,* November 1944. Courtesy Smith-Corona.

When it becomes a souvenir...

What then? Stay home...do nothing? You *know* you won't! Like our fighting men, you've earned the right to choose work you enjoy. And the time to prepare is ... now!

A surprising number of war workers are going to learn to type ... a skill easy for them to acquire.

For women who want careers, typing is the opening wedge to the world's most fascinating professions. For women who plan marriage, typing brings contacts with the world outside ... keeps distant friends in touch, leads to club, business, and social activities that less accomplished women miss.

So *do* think about learning to type. Even today, some Smith-Corona typewriters, under certain conditions, are available for civilian use—or you can "beg, borrow, or rent" for practise purposes. It's a wise move for post-war planners. L C Smith & Corona Typewriters Inc Syracuse 1 New York.

SMITH-CORONA
Typewriters
Groton   Plant

MORE L C SMITHS FOR CIVILIANS!

Note to Industry: W. P. B. has increased our fourth quarter allotment of new typewriters to be made for *necessary* civilian use. If you can qualify under "W. P. B.—1319," we may be able to supply you; in any event, talk with our local branch office or L C Smith dealer.

Black workers, male and female, fared even worse. In 1945, the number of black persons employed declined twice as fast as all employment.[60] In order to maintain the economic gains achieved during the war, blacks would have to continue fighting for equal employment.

Wartime social services disappeared quickly. At the end of the war more than one hundred thousand children were attending federally funded child care centers. The WSA planned to terminate all Lanham Act child care centers in 1945, but a national campaign kept them open for another year. The Kaiser centers' director had hoped that the centers would serve as a model for a "vast postwar development," but in late 1945, once Maritime Commission funds dried up, Kaiser closed the centers as the last ship left the yard. By 1948, even though one in every four working women were mothers, none of the wartime centers was still in operation.[61] Temporary war housing, in contrast, turned out to be more permanent than anyone had anticipated. In 1945, the Federal government postponed the demolition of temporary housing indefinitely, and Title V of the Lanham Act opened the remaining war housing to returning veterans. In the midst of a national housing shortage, veterans and their families, many studying under the G.I. Bill, flocked into the defense projects. Willow Run housed so many students that it became known as the "second campus" of the University of Michigan. In 1954, Ypsilanti Township bought the project from the Federal government to operate as public housing.[62] Vanport, home to many veterans, disappeared forever in a sudden and dramatic flood on May 30, 1948, when high water from the Columbia River surged over its dikes and wrenched houses off their temporary foundations.[63]

Other projects had more significant fates. The Sojourner Truth Homes, built as permanent housing, became an important symbol of black pride in Detroit. The struggle over their occupancy forged a tradition of tenant activism. Over the decades, residents organized to fight for local improvements, picketed City

View of Vanport flood, May 30, 1948. Courtesy Oregon Historical Society. OrHi 24149.

Hall for a bus line, and fought school officials for a PTA. Tenants cooperated in taking responsibility for the projects and looking after each other. The fight for Sojourner Truth Homes became a legend, passed on to each new wave of residents. Even though many of the original buildings were replaced with townhouses, former residents still gather and celebrate with an annual picnic. For its residents, Sojourner Truth remains one of Detroit's most desirable public housing projects.[64] The struggle over the project crystallized the issues that would generate the civil rights movement a decade later and brought together the black and union coalition that would continue fighting for jobs and fair housing.

Richmond and Marin City were more typical examples of the racial polarization that marked the postwar era. In 1950 just over fifty percent of Richmond's population, including seventy-eight percent of the city's blacks, still lived in the defense projects. Willie Stokes was a typical resident: by 1947 he was unemployed, occasionally finding work as a laborer while his wife worked as a domestic. Hoping for better times, he was determined to stay in California. During the 1950s, the south side projects became a battleground as the city's business leaders embarked upon a redevelopment plan intended to attract industry and middle-class white residents to the city. Words like "slum" and "blight" took on clear racial connotations as the city targeted the war housing for eradication. By razing war housing without building public housing, the city hoped to rid itself of war migrants. Although they were shut out of most private housing in the area, however, black migrants remained. "What I can't understand," asked a black tenant in the Canal projects, "is where can we go if we can't stay here?"[65] As whites gradually moved out of private housing in the area surrounding the wartime projects, blacks moved in. By the end of the decade, the south side formed a new black ghetto, still socially and spatially separate from the rest of the city. Marin City suffered a similar fate. As white war workers gradually moved out, finding new jobs and homes

Reverend Mother Julia Span at the Canal housing project in Richmond, California, 1949. Courtesy Richmond Museum Collection.

nearby, the project became primarily black. By the 1960s multistory concrete buildings had replaced the temporary wooden structures, and Marin City was an island of black poverty in the midst of an otherwise affluent white county. Once a model community, it became a typical housing project, beset by the same problems as the inner city.[66]

Richmond's redevelopment plans failed to prevent whites from following the national pattern of moving out to the suburbs. Blacks rarely had this option. In Marin City, black residents who could afford to move discovered that no one in Marin Couty would sell or rent to them, forcing them to relocate to black neighborhoods in San Francisco and Oakland. If restrictive covenants, approved by the FHA, did not exclude blacks, their neighbors made it clear they were not welcome. In 1952, Wilbur Gary, a black veteran and ex-shipyard worker, finding his Harborgate apartment too cramped for his seven children, bought a house in Rollingwood, a wartime subdivision built expressly for shipyard workers. Moving in, the Garys found a cross on their lawn and a mob jeering and throwing rocks. After Gary appealed to the local NAACP to protect his family, they mounted an around-the-clock guard on their house. Although the violence eventually subsided, the Garys remained the only black family in Rollingwood.[67]

The worst aspects of public wartime housing shaped the postwar American city. The withdrawal of the government's interest in child care and other social services left working women to fend for themselves. Inevitably, in both suburb and slum, family and home life suffered. Segregated defense housing coupled with all-white FHA suburbs set the postwar pattern of black inner cities and white suburbs, creating segregation where it had never existed before. Federal indifference and local hostility to racial integration continued to affect government housing and employment policies. As a result, the wartime issues of equal employment and fair housing remained the focus of struggles by the NAACP and other civil rights groups during the 1950s. Although their wartime cooperation with unions and progressives had laid the groundwork for interracial coalitions, McCarthyism silenced many of their white allies. By the 1960s, these groups' wartime expectations were still unsatisfied. Renewed demands for equality and a rebirth of resentment ultimately exploded in the riots that rocked Richmond and many other American cities. As Agnes Meyer and Selden Menefee warned in 1944, racial conflict would remain an enduring aspect of American life.

Notes

I would like to thank Andrew Liu, Marc Tedesco, and Greg Hise for their invaluable assistance; Kathleen Rupley of the Richmond Museum of History for her very helpful introduction to Richmond; Heather Burnham for her research skills and interests; Georgette Hasiotis for her sensitive editing; and especially Donald Albrecht for his knowledge, enthusiasm, and patience.

1. Agnes Meyer, *Journey through Chaos* (New York: Harcourt, Brace and Co., 1944); Selden Menefee, *Assignment: U.S.A.* (New York: Reynal and Hitchcock, 1944).

2. Alan Clive, *State of War: Michigan in World War II* (Ann Arbor: University of Michigan Press, 1979), 99.

3. James McVittie, "An Avalanche Hits Richmond," City Manager's Office, Richmond, California, July 1944, 10.

4. Alyce Mano Kramer, "The Story of the Richmond Shipyards," Carton 288, Kaiser Papers, Bancroft Library, University of California, Berkeley, n.p.

5. Cy W. Record, "Willie Stokes at the Golden Gate," *The Crisis* (June 1949): 175; Marilynn S. Johnson, "The Western Front: World War II and the Transformation of the West Coast Urban Life" (Ph.D. diss., New York University, 1990), 78.

6. "Transportation and Housing Problems' Effect on Labor Turnover," Carton 288, Kaiser Papers, Bancroft Library, University of California, Berkeley, n.p.

7. Ibid., n.p.; Gerald Nash, *The American West Transformed: The Impact of the Second World War* (Bloomington: Indiana University Press, 1985), 7.

8. Hubert Owen Brown, "The Impact of War Worker Migration on the Public School System of Richmond, California" (Ed.D. diss., Stanford University, 1978), 28; Joseph C. Witnah, *A History of Richmond, California* (Richmond: Chamber of Congress, 1944), 128–124.

9. Frederick C. Lane, *Ships for Victory: A History of Shipbuilding under the U.S. Maritime Commission in World War II* (reprint, New York: Harcourt, Brace and Jovanovich, 1976), 482–483.

10. Witnah, *Richmond,* 126.

11. Brown, "Impact of War Workers," 184.

12. Johnson, "Western Front," 169; Brown, "Impact of War Workers," 134–136.

13. Moore, *The Black Community in Richmond, California* (Richmond, Calif.: Richmond Public Library, 1987), 20.

14. Roy Hamachi, "Postwar Housing in Richmond, California" (master's thesis, University of California, Berkeley, n.d.), 31.

15. Minutes, Richmond Housing Authority, vol. 4; Moore, *Black Community,* 21.

16. "Richmond Took a Beating," *Fortune* 31, no. 2 (February 1945): 262–264.

17. Ibid., 267.

18. Moore, *Black Community,* 27.

19. Brown, "Impact of War Workers," 188, 308; interview with Donald Hardison, Richmond, California, January 23, 1994.

20. Katherine Archibald, *Wartime Shipyard* (Berkeley: University of California Press, 1947), 64–65.

21. Clive, *State of War,* 130–169, 170–185.

22. John Morton Blum, *V Was for Victory: Politics and American Culture during World War II* (New York: Harcourt Brace Jovanovich, 1976), 185–188.

23. Dominic Capeci, *Race Relations in Wartime Detroit: The Sojourner Truth Housing Controversy of 1942* (Philadelphia: Temple University Press, 1984), 120.

24. Ibid., 128.

25. Frank Freidel, *Franklin D. Roosevelt: The Triumph* (Boston: Little, Brown and Co., 1956), 43.

26. Ibid., 132.

27. Ibid., 136–137.

28. Clive, *State of War,* 161.

29. Clive, *State of War,* 156.

30. Robert Weaver, *Negro Ghetto* (New York: Harcourt, Brace and Co., 1948), 94.

31. Meyer, *Journey through Chaos,* 33.

32. Lowell J. Carr and James E. Stermer, *Willow Run: A Study of Industrialization and Cultural Inadequacy* (New York: Harper and Brothers, 1952), 87–115.

33. John Dos Passos, *State of the Nation* (Westport, Conn.: Greenwood Publishing Group, Inc., 1944; reprint, 1973), 48.

34. Carr and Stermer, *Willow Run,* 254.

35. Meyer, *Journey through Chaos,* 206–208.

36. Menafee, *Assignment,* 109.

37. "What Housing for Willow Run?" *Architectural Record* 92, no. 3 (September 1942): 52–53.

38. Carr and Stermer, *Willow Run,* 11.

39. Ibid., 62.

40. Ibid., 10–11.

41. "Women Must Do War Work," *Fore 'n' Aft* (August 4, 1944): 12–13.

42. Meyer, *Journey through Chaos,* 169.

43. Lane, *Ships for Victory,* 432–433; Manley Maben, *Vanport* (Portland: Oregon Historical Society Press, 1987), 44–49.

44. Meyer, *Journey through Chaos,* 168.

45. Gerald D. Nash, *World War II and the West: Reshaping the Economy* (Lincoln: University of Nebraska Press, 1990), 58.

46. Sheila Tropp Lichtman, "Women at Work, 1941–1945: Wartime Employment in the San Francisco Bay Area," (Ph.D. diss., University of California, Davis, 1981), 172, 286.

47. Amy Kesselman, *Fleeting Opportunities: Women Shipyard Workers in Portland and Vancouver during World War II and Reconversion* (Albany: State University of New York Press, 1990), 76–78.

48. "Designed for 24 Hour Child Care," *Architectural Record* (March 1944): 84–89.

49. Kesselman, *Fleeting Opportunities,* 67; Susan M. Hartmann, *The Home Front and Beyond: American Women in the 1940s* (Boston: Twayne Publishers, 1982), 58.

50. James L. Hymes, "The Kaiser Answer: Child Service Centers," *Progressive Education* 21, no. 5 (May 1944), 223–226; Interviews #4 and #24, Karen Beck Skold Interviews, Oregon Historical Society, Portland, Oregon.

51. Augusta H. Clawson, *Shipyard Diary of a Woman Welder* (New York: Penguin Books, 1944), 165.

52. Kesselman, *Fleeting Opportunities,* 84–87.

53. Richard Finnie, *Marinship: The History of a Wartime Shipyard* (San Francisco: Marinship, 1947), 65–68.

54. "Marin City, California," *Architectural Forum* (December 1943): 67–68.

55. "Review of City's Non-Segregation Policy Appears in National Publication," *Marin Citizen,* February 23, 1945, 2.

56. Charlotte Kilbourn and Margaret Lantis, "Elements of Tenant Instability in a War Housing Project," *American Sociological Review* 11, no. 1 (February 1946), 59.

57. Charles Wollenburg, *Marinship at War: Shipbuilding and Social Change in Wartime Sausilito* (Berkeley: Western Heritage Press, 1990), 91.

58. Clive, *State of War,* 225.

59. Karen Anderson, *Wartime Women: Sex Roles, Family Relations and the Status of Women during World War II* (Westport, Conn.: Greenwood Press, 1981), 182–186.

60. Richard Polenberg, *War and Society: The United States, 1941–1945* (New York: J. P. Lippincott Co., 1972), 103.

61. Kesselman, *Fleeting Opportunities,* 89, 122–123.

62. Marion F. Wilson, *The Story of Willow Run* (Ann Arbor: University of Michigan Press, 1956), 127–134.

63. Maben, *Vanport,* 104–120.

64. Zachare Ball, "Sojourner Development Puts Other City Projects to Shame," *Detroit Free Press,* February 21, 1992, 1B.

65. Richard Reinhardt, "Richmond: The Boom That Didn't Bust," *San Francisco Chronicle,* August 16, 1954.

66. Wollenberg, *Marinship,* 96.

67. Johnson, "Western Front," 856–858; Moore, *Black Community,* 29.

Greg Hise

The Airplane and the Garden City: Regional Transformations during World War II

In 1945, noted urban theorist Lewis Mumford articulated his vision for the postwar era, a time when the airplane would be "as much a part of our daily lives as the motor car."[1] He wrote, "At the beginning of the twentieth century, two great inventions took form before our eyes: the airplane and the Garden City, both harbingers of a new age." Mumford believed this new transportation technology would transform urban regions into Garden Cities, with wide belts of open land. Contrary to Mumford's assessment, however, the coupling of the airplane and the Garden City was already in place, although not in a form the doyen of rational urbanism would endorse.

World War II transformed the American city. Three factors—modern community planning, industrial location, and migration—informed these changes. During the war, Federal policies designed to meet defense production quotas intersected with the objectives of regional planners and social reformers. The War Production Board, for example, encouraged defense contractors to disperse manufacturing. Design professionals promoted the garden suburb, a complete community composed of housing, neighborhood services, schools, and retail centers, all in close proximity to employment. Private-sector builders capitalized on these initiatives. In fact, the war accelerated the emergence of community builders, who consolidated land sub division, sion, construction, and sales into a single organization. Although the implications of this new spatial and social order were national in scope, western cities—Los Angeles in particular—prefigured future trends. In short, defense-related manufacturing was the necessary foundation for home builders to experiment in constructing communities for "balanced living."[2] These large-scale developments were in many cases virtually new towns, and they ultimately helped shape America's contemporary urban landscape.

Modern community planning was a two-part package. The first component was a low-cost, efficient dwelling that met minimum requirements for space, light, and air. This basic house had its roots in the workingman's bungalow and mail-order housing from the 1910s and 1920s. During the 1920s and 1930s, social and environmental reformers, industrial engineers, and advocates for building prefabrication, ranging from the American Public Health Association to the National Forest Products Laboratory, worked independently and in concert to identify and codify a standard dwelling unit. Following passage of the 1934 Housing Act, the Federal Housing Administration adopted a popular plan variant—a square, four-room plus bath, basement-less unit they designated the minimal house.[3]

This effort to transform home building into a modern industry extended beyond the house type to encompass quantity production and site planning. Reformers conceived the minimal house as a basic module for self-contained, satellite communities, the second component of the package.[4] Mumford, an outspoken proponent for modern community planning, drew explicit links between an individual dwelling and the community: "A good house can not exist in a city by itself; it can only come as part of a community plan, and until we learn to design our communities and our houses cooperatively, treating each separate unit as part of the whole, we shall not succeed much better than the jerry-builder does today."[5]

Illustration from "Private Enterprise in Defense Housing," *Insured Mortgage Portfolio*, fourth quarter, 1940. Courtesy U.S. Department of Housing and Urban Development.

Chart, *Homes for Defense: A Statement of Functions*, 1941. Courtesy U.S. Department of Housing and Urban Development.

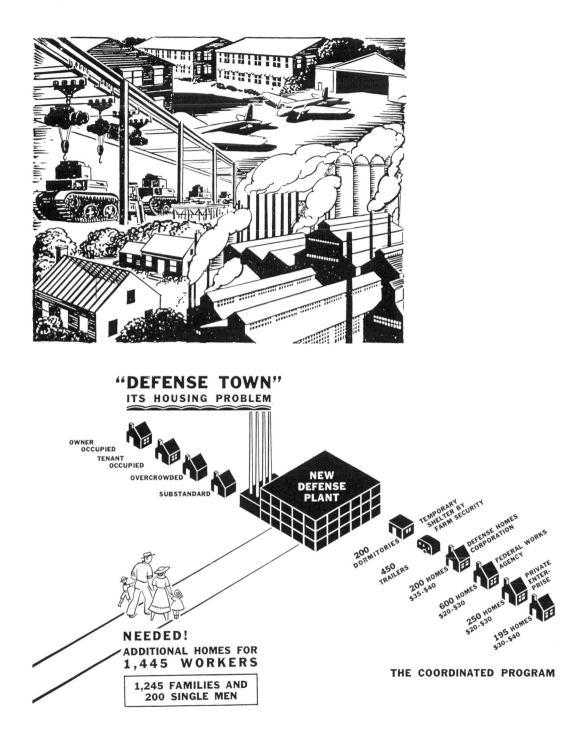

Clarence Perry offered the most comprehensive and influential articulation of these principles in his 1920s design for a neighborhood unit. Formally the concept employed superblock planning and a hierarchical, functionally segregated street system. Major arterials, built to encourage and accommodate through traffic, would bound each neighborhood. Internal streets were designed for circulation and access only. Retail shops were placed at specific intersections; the implication, in plan, was that contiguous, interlocking units would form a commercial district.

Socially the neighborhood unit was a product of the Progressive-Era settlement house movement. Each community-scaled project would house the families required to fully enroll a primary school; each child would live within a half-mile of the facility. In Perry's diagram, community institutions cluster around a central green or common; small parks, planned to meet neighborhood needs, are sprinkled throughout the site. Physical and social planning intertwined in an emphasis on neighborhood consciousness and a sense of belonging. In other words, the neighborhood unit represented a tightly planned and replicable module that, Perry argued, would be applicable throughout the country.[6]

Although the neighborhood unit and, more broadly, modern community planning presented a highly coordinated landscape, design professionals and theorists remained silent concerning implementation. In their polemic "New Homes for a New Deal," Mumford and Henry Wright articulated the need for scale economies in planning and production, including comprehensive plot and building design, centralized material purchasing, and rationalized site operations. Implementation, however, required an unintended convergence of defense-related government policy with the objectives of community builders.[7]

The 1931 President's Conference on Home Building and Home Ownership and subsequent New Deal agencies provided an institutional framework for the combination of these constituencies.[8] The Federal Housing Administration (FHA) played a critical role in this process. The FHA's mortgage insurance incentive assured that their technical bulletin series became a blueprint for community design. Seward Mott, a landscape architect, directed the agency's Land Planning Division. When developers submitted their projects for approval, FHA staff applied a standard template to evaluate everything from room layout to land use patterns. The FHA derived standards from progressive subdivision planning practices first advanced by land developers and then adopted by municipalities, counties, and state government.[9] For example, in bulletin 5, "Planning Neighborhoods for Small Houses," the agency reproduced comparative site plans illustrating developments they had rejected and endorsed. Approved site plans featured differentiated street patterns to restrict traffic hazards and avoid visual monotony. The FHA promoted a Radburn-

THE NEIGHBORHOOD UNIT FORMULA

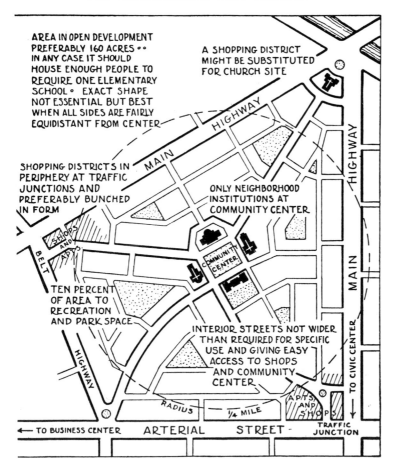

Clarence Perry's Neighborhood Unit Formula, *Regional Plan of New York and its Environs*, 1929. Courtesy *Housing for the Machine Age*, published by Russell Sage Foundation, 1939.

type plan based on superblock principles with a minimal area devoted to circulation and more emphasis on recreation.[10]

During the war, private builders followed FHA guidelines to secure guaranteed mortgages and construction financing. They produced over one million housing units, which represented eighty percent of the total built, and home ownership climbed significantly. In their 1946 report on the effect of wartime housing shortages on home ownership, the Bureau of Labor Statistics documented a fifteen-percent increase between April 1940 and October 1945. The authors compared this gain with similar intervals and found the wartime increase outpaced any comparable time span on record.[11]

Defense workers secured home ownership through the Administration's loan insurance program, which revolutionized the conditions for purchasing a dwelling. FHA guarantees encouraged lenders to loan a greater percentage of the mortgage face value, thereby reducing down payments. Lenders, backed by FHA guarantees, jettisoned their customary three- and five-year repayment periods and adopted fifteen- and eventually twenty- and

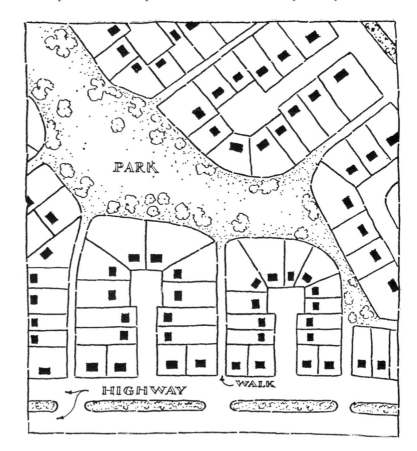

FHA interpretation of Radburn planning principles, "Planning Neighborhoods for Small Houses" (FHA Technical Bulletin 5), 1936. Courtesy U.S. Department of Housing and Urban Development.

twenty-five-year plans. The FHA also standardized loan procedures, eliminated second mortgages, and lowered interest rates.
All these features were in marked contrast to the prevailing system for financing the purchase of a house.[12]

In February 1940, the FHA launched a concerted campaign to promote home ownership among families with $2,500 an-
nual earnings, sufficient to own a home on a budget of $25 a
month.[13] FHA promotions included displays, booklets, and newspaper and radio advertisements whose copy enticed renters with
slogans such as "Now you can own a modern home—comfortable
to live in, attractive to look at, convenient to pay for." Mortgage
institutions, builders, real estate firms, building material manufacturers, and dealers actively supported this program.

Local conditions informed the nature and timing of defense housing, which varied within and across regions. In the San
Francisco Bay Area, for example, the Federal Works Agency oversaw a program of temporary housing, trailers, and demountable
dormitory units. The urgent need for community-scale projects
was underscored by a local civil defense official who, in March
1941, noted that "whole new towns are springing up, a thousand
houses at a clip, where yesterday were empty fields and where today there are no provisions for sewers, playgrounds, fire and police protection, hospital facilities, and all other local services."[14]

In Los Angeles housing was available, albeit not always
in close proximity to employment. Immediately preceding the
war, the pace of residential construction there compared favorably to the 1920s boom; in 1941, there were over sixty thousand
units for sale or rent. In San Diego, by contrast, home building
was stagnant; there were only five-and-a-half thousand dwellings
available, and the city was experiencing an immediate and severe
housing shortage.[15]

Eugene Weston, the National Housing Agency (NHA) rep-
resentative for California (Region IX) addressed the problem of regional disparities in his testimony before the Subcommittee on

Naval Affairs, noting that "during peacetime there was more FHA Title II housing built in [Los Angeles] than any other place in the United States. There is money and land and contractors willing and able to go ahead with private housing. In many other areas . . . we have been unable to produce any private housing, and practically all the [NHA's production] has been public."[16] Acknowledging the marked disparities between regions and among cities within a region does not reduce a discussion of wartime production, housing, and jobs to mere particularism. On the contrary, modern community planning and industrial location informed defense housing projects throughout the country.

In April 1941, Mr. and Mrs. Darrell Ratzlaff moved into a new two-bedroom house at 8406 Vicksburg in Westchester, ten miles southeast of Los Angeles's City Hall. According to Gertrude Ratzlaff, "In 1940, Darrell and I were looking for a place to build. . . . We drove [past] La Tijera often, and noticed when a sign was posted stating '400 Homes to be Built—FHA 10% Down.' The address was in Bell, [w]e immediately checked into it and found a beautiful tract of homes by Silas Nowell . . . we picked out our lot on a map and started to build in January 1941." At the time, the area was known for a hog farm and the surrounding bean fields; however, Gertrude Ratzlaff added, "the FHA assured us the hogs would be gone before anyone moved in."[17]

Airesearch Manufacturing Company, Los Angeles, California, 1947. The plant was constructed in 1941. Courtesy Wittington Collection/Department of Special Collections/University of Southern California Library.

Darrell Ratzlaff was a buyer for Airesearch Manufacturing Company, a Glendale-based firm, which produced aircraft heat transfer equipment, air coolers, and cabin pressure control valves. In January 1941, Airesearch purchased a twenty-acre site in Westchester, adjacent to Mines Field (now Los Angeles International Airport). The company had an eighty-thousand-square-foot plant under construction on this site when the Ratzlaffs moved into their new dwelling.[18]

Airesearch supplied equipment to prime airframe contractors. In March 1941, the firm moved into its new facility, located equidistant from the Ratzlaffs' house and nearby North American Aviation and Douglas plants. North American had chosen their site following a nationwide search. In 1934 J. H. "Dutch" Kindelberger, a Douglas vice-president, assumed control of North American's predecessor firm in Baltimore, Maryland. After securing a contract for an Army Air Corps basic trainer, the NA-16, Kindelberger leased a twenty-acre site in Inglewood, California, at the southeast corner of Mines Field. In November 1935, seventy-five employees relocated into temporary quarters; three months later, two hundred fifty workers entered the new roughly one-hundred-and-fifty-eight-thousand-square-foot assembly plant. The first production NA-16 came off the line in February. Aircraft orders, output, and employment steadily increased for two years; then, between September 1939 and December 1941, the company's growth accelerated. North American increased monthly output from seventy units to three hundred twenty-five, added fourteen thousand employees to its work force, and expanded floor space to over one million square feet. In addition, by 1940 North American had over one thousand firms under subcontract and had begun construction of branch plants in Dallas and Kansas City.[19]

Home builders anticipated an influx of defense workers drawn by these employment centers, and they selected sites in close proximity for community projects. Westchester is a premier example. In just three years, four sets of developers converted a five-square-mile parcel owned and master-planned by Security Bank into a complete community for ten thousand residents housed in three thousand two hundred thirty units.[20] In addition to Silas Nowell, developer of Westport Heights, the participants included Bert Farrar (Farrar Manor), Frank Ayers and Sons (Kentwood), and Fred W. Marlow and Fritz B. Burns, who marketed their tract as "Homes at Wholesale." Marlow-Burns brought to this development their recent experience at Westside Village, a seven-hundred-eighty-eight-unit project two miles from Clover Field, Douglas Aircraft's parent facility in Santa Monica; and Toluca Wood, a four-hundred-unit development three miles from Vega and Lockheed's Burbank plants; both showcased elements central for a community-scale project such as Westchester.[21]

At Westside Village, Marlow-Burns made the transition from developing raw land and selling lots to community building. And it was there that they first applied the principles of mass building, organizing the site into a continuous production process. At Westchester, suppliers delivered materials to a staging area

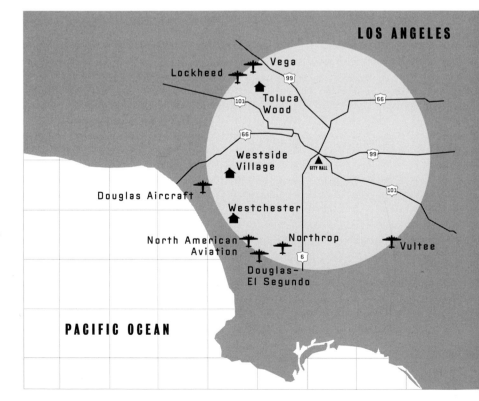

Location of the Big Six airframe contractors and community projects developed by Marlow-Burns, all within a ten-mile radius of City Hall, Los Angeles, California, ca. 1941. Courtesy Greg Hise and Lisa Padilla.

where workers precut and preassembled individual framing or plumbing components into subassemblies for eventual trucking throughout the site. Specialized teams of laborers and tradespeople moved sequentially through the project, grading and grubbing, preparing and pouring foundations, framing and sheathing building envelopes, and applying finish materials. Thus, a full decade before Levittown, we find factory practices applied to the on-site production of housing.[22] Using these techniques, the Marlow-Burns organization built over one thousand houses in Westchester during the war years.

"Homes at Wholesale" formed Westchester's southeastern quadrant. Here the Board of Education constructed a primary school on property Marlow-Burns deeded to the city.[23] Real estate advertisements highlighted the proximity to Los Angeles Municipal Airport and the cluster of ancillary industry extending along Century Boulevard at the northern boundary of the airfield. A map in the *Los Angeles Evening Herald and Express* noted substantial business enterprises employing many thousands of workers, and they identified twelve important plants and allied projects.[24] The *Los Angeles Daily News* touted Westchester as "the

Westchester district, 1941. Courtesy Aerial Photo Archives/University of California at Los Angeles Department of Geography.

Westchester under construction, 1941. Courtesy Wittington Collection/Department of Special Collections/University of Southern
California Library.

Westchester, 1942. Courtesy Huntington
Library.

Westchester, ca. 1945. Courtesy Bancroft
Library/University of California at Berkeley.

model residential community of the decade" in May 1942, citing
unidentified city planners from all over the country who visited
the "expertly planned community." In August, the *Los Angeles
Downtown Shopping News* extolled the project, encouraging readers to visit Westchester and see the advantage of modern community planning over old-fashioned guesswork.[25]

The demand for housing and services encouraged modern community planning in mid-size and smaller cities as well.
For example, in 1942 the Maritime Commission selected Vancouver, Washington, as the site for a new Liberty ship and airplane
carrier yard, a decision based primarily on access to a deep-water
port and cheap energy from the recently completed Bonneville
Dam. The Henry J. Kaiser Company, whose Aluminum Company
of America (ALCOA) division had established a regional plant in
the area, agreed to build the shipyards for the government. Kaiser officials estimated forty-five thousand additional employees
would be needed for this operation.[26]

Within two years, in-migrating workers and their families tripled Vancouver's population. In response, the city established a local housing authority, which worked with the Federal
Public Housing Authority (FPHA) to implement a short- and
long-term program. The agency authorized a small number of dormitories and temporary units to serve immediate needs, but the
preferred solution was a large-scale development, designed to provide postwar Vancouver with a complete-community infrastructure. The Federal government acquired an eleven-hundred-acre
site cobbled from dairy and garlic farms north of the shipyards,
two miles from the town center. Here the local housing authority,
the FPHA, six design firms, and local contractors planned and
constructed McLoughlin Heights. The FPHA installed sewer and
water systems, electrical distribution, and streets and sidewalks.
By the war's end, McLoughlin Heights contained six thousand
dwelling units, four schools, recreation and day care centers, a
branch library, medical clinic, and two retail centers. The latter

Greg Hise

McLaughlin Heights, ca. 1942. Courtesy Vancouver Housing Authority.

McLaughlin Heights shopping center, ca. 1942. Pietro Belluschi, architect. Courtesy National Archives. RG 208-EX158-C-161.

included the Boulevard Shopping Center, a fifty-thousand-square-foot complex with thirty-three merchants and the region's largest food store. The site plan, attributed to Pietro Belluschi of A. E. Doyle and Associates, drew all the shops into a permeable block surrounding an internal pedestrian green. To maximize the separation of automobiles and pedestrians, the designers oriented the complex away from the main boulevard, providing access off a side street. The project, profiled in *Architectural Record,* was an early realization of a ubiquitous postwar retail building type.[27]

Following the war, the Federal government transferred public buildings in McLoughlin Heights to the city, which annexed and sold the permanent housing to residents. Over the next decade, developers completed a series of new neighborhoods around the existing infrastructure. In Vancouver, this conversion of a wartime public housing project provided a framework for the postwar expansion of a small metropolitan region.[28]

These planning principles and design strategies were not exclusive to the FHA and private builders. In the journal *Civil Engineering,* Leon Zach, Chief Site Planner for the Military Construction Branch, noted that "housing at military installations has to be planned as an integral part of the whole base just as residential areas of a city must take their proper place in the total plan. Housing areas . . . are 'zoned' for officers, troops, and WAC's. The [city's] industrial area becomes . . . the 'warehouse-utility area.' The division's 'civic center' includes its town hall (Administration Building), bank, post office, shops (Exchange), and theater."[29]

Zach identified three land-planning variables: siting community housing in relation to industry, designing an efficient circulation system, and developing standard plans for varied settings—the same criteria the FHA site planners and community builders had singled out. More important, the Military Construction Branch's preferred solutions aligned precisely with guidelines the FHA had established and large-scale builders had adopted.

Like his FHA counterparts, Zach included alternative site plans illustrating good and bad planning features. Each diagram included a neighborhood center, school, and recreation area serving a community project with mixed housing types. The first scheme, which Zach designated rectangular and regimented, covered sixty-eight acres and required sixteen thousand linear feet of roadway. An irregular layout with the same number of units and equivalent community amenities required eleven fewer acres and twenty percent less grading, while offering a thirty-one percent reduction in streets. In addition, the latter avoided visual monotony, and this benefit could be enhanced by mixing dwelling types, siting two-story units as cul-de-sac termini, and using a variety of building materials. In effect, the military implemented all the formal principles the FHA promoted through its technical bulletins. Zach concluded his précis on planning efficiencies with a brief concerning the relationship between civilian war community housing and the place of work.

In Chicago, the Planning Commission's Master Plan Division capitalized on the war's profound effect on industrial patterns to draft a set of postwar subdivision design standards. The showpiece of their document *Building New Neighborhoods* was a one-point-eight-square-mile parcel adjacent to the Dodge plant on the city's south side. The planners diagramed alternative configurations contrasting current development patterns with the advantages offered by modern community planning. According to Executive Director T. T. McCrosky, "People have shown conclusively that they want to live in comfortable homes located in . . . neighborhoods . . . [that] offer more than buildings on narrow lots, facing long straight streets. They want . . . good schools and

"Neighborhood Standards," Chicago Plan Commission, *Building New Neighborhoods*, 1943.

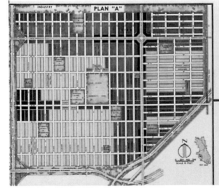
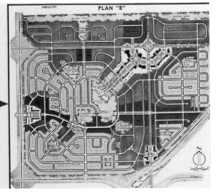

adequate playgrounds within walking distance of home . . . [and] marketing in conveniently located shopping centers."[30]

Defense-related community development was not restricted to prime contract sites such as Los Angeles, Vancouver, and Chicago. As the war progressed, new materials, security concerns, and the need to reduce transit time and costs encouraged the War Production Board and the Plant Site Board to develop satellite facilities. Planner Clarence Stein argued that the threat of air strikes demanded a national policy for dispersing industry beyond existing population and manufacturing centers, where residential areas could be separated from factories and other communities by open greenbelts: "Modern industry can be run more effectively and more economically in less congested centers. The cost of building new communities is less than that of rebuilding old and obsolete cities. The total cost of carrying on industry and business in the United States would be greatly decreased by a more scientific distribution . . . of goods and people."[31]

By early 1942, the War Production Board had engaged prime contractors to construct and manage decentralized modification centers and feeder plants. These projects took two forms. The first were isolated company towns designed to bring the labor force to a strategic site. Douglas Aircraft, for example, created Daggett, a town thirteen miles from Barstow in the Mojave Desert. More important in terms of modern community planning and the postwar landscape were projects along the urban periphery such as Midwest City, Oklahoma. Nine miles southeast of Oklahoma City, an enterprising community builder secured a three-hundred-thirty-acre tract opposite a new Douglas cargo plane plant. Working with the Army Air Service Command, the state FHA office, Douglas officials, and sixteen Oklahoma builders, W. P. Atkinson created an "air industry city" promoted in *Insured Mortgage Portfolio* as the "first FHA city." In 1944 the Urban Land Institute (ULI) featured an aerial view of Midwest City on the cover of *Urban Land* under the heading "Model Community."[32]

Planners and public officials equivocated when predicting whether the end of the war would alter or stem migration. Homer Hoyt, a location theorist and FHA consultant, predicted a vast, floating postwar population:

At the close of the war nine to thirteen million men in the armed forces and twenty million workers in war factories will form a great mobile population that will be ready to move to any city promising jobs. A great number of industries will, of course, remain tied to old locations and will resume their prewar types of manufactures. However, many new, well-located war factories suitable for conversion into peacetime production will draw industries away from obsolete plants. A vast reshuffling of plant locations will in turn cause great shifts in sites for new housing.[33]

Hoyt questioned whether postwar urban development would follow old patterns or if a new structure might usher in a new type of city. In response, planners, industrialists, business leaders, and developers from regional centers such as Vancouver and urban regions such as Los Angeles began to explore ways to capitalize on wartime industry in the postwar era.

The Los Angeles Regional Planning Commission (RPC) spoke directly to this intersection of modern community planning and industrial dispersion. Their vision of a coordinated metropolitan region composed of discrete, satellite communities was consistent with a fifty-year discourse concerning the creation of a new kind of city. In "Congestion de Luxe—Do We Want It?" (1926), Clarence Dykstra argued that, contrary to the "centralization complex" manifest in the East, "the city of the future ought to be a harmoniously developed community of local centers." In Los Angeles he foresaw "a great city population which for the most part lives near its work, has its individual [homes] and gardens, finds its market and commercialized recreational facilities right around the corner, and which because of these things, can develop a neighborhood with all that it means."[34]

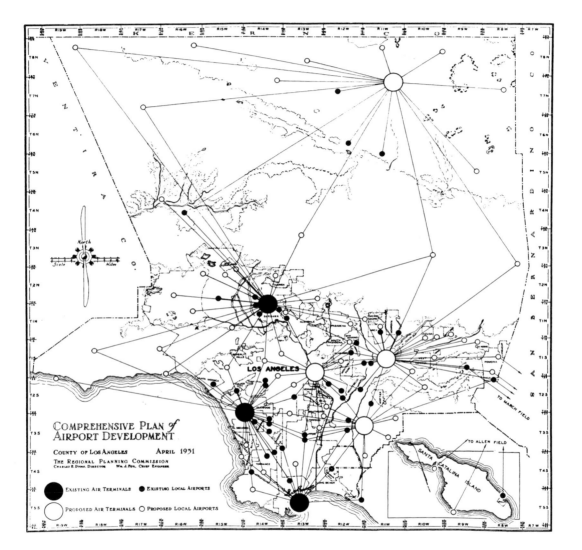

Master Plan for Airports, Los Angeles Regional
Planning Commission, *Regional Plan of Highways*, 1931.

LOS ANGELES AIRPORT
Lloyd Aldrich City Engineer
John C. Austin E. ... Sutton Arc.

Postwar air terminal proposal for Los Angeles.
Office of the City Engineer, 1943. Courtesy
Whittington Collection/Department of Special
Collections/University of Southern California
Library.

From their vantage point, the RPC commissioners noted a tendency in recent subdivisions toward the development of complete communities. Private-sector builders shared this view. Testifying before Congress, Seward Mott, former FHA director for land planning and current director of the Urban Land Institute (ULI), noted that in the past these projects were exclusively for "high-class homes." During the war, according to Mott, the FHA had stimulated communities of low-cost housing. In 1945 ULI President Hugh Potter wrote, "Nobody should undertake to develop less than a neighborhood."[35] The Institute, in turn, promoted these objectives through publications, forums, and exhibitions devoted to subdivision planning and community building.

One of the industries the RPC focused on was aircraft manufacturing. During the defense emergency, airframe assembly and ancillary industries became one of the region's most significant manufacturing sectors in terms of jobs, payroll, and multipliers. Postwar conversion posed a vexing problem; the peacetime market could not guarantee output comparable to what the war had generated. For example, on V-J Day, North American Aviation held orders for eight thousand aircraft. Within a few months, that number plummeted to twenty-four. Employment followed suit, dropping from a peak of ninety-one thousand to five thousand, and the firm shuttered its Dallas and Kansas City feeder plants.[36]

Along with the Los Angeles Board of Public Works and Bureau of Engineering, the RPC undertook or revised a series of land use surveys as projections for postwar public works.[37] The objective was to construct an infrastructure attractive to additional defense contracts.[38] *The Master Plan of Airports* (1940, revised 1945) was a critical component with direct ties to military and defense. The plan identified fifty airstrips judiciously located across the region. It was a crystalline diagram, simultaneously a reflection, reinforcement, and projection of the region's spatial pattern.[39]

Business and civic leaders, planners, and organized labor in San Francisco, Oakland, and San Diego, to cite only examples in California, also campaigned and secured funding for new or expanded airport facilities.[40] The Chicago Planning Commission published a diagram that, not surprisingly, placed their city at the epicenter of a branched and ever-expanding network, stretching in a series of concentric circles to Bangkok, Sydney, Santiago, and Nairobi. Closer to home, a special committee, representing the Commission, the Chicago Association of Commerce, and the Regional Planning Association, issued a report in 1941 forecasting the city and region's postwar needs. After stating that no city planner could afford to overlook the necessity of providing for the future accommodation of air transportation as a part of their city's long-range program, the committee released a set of proposals calling for three major air terminals within three to ten miles of the Loop, a second set of four major inner-belt airports, and an outer ring of five fields, forty to sixty miles from the city center, all publicly owned and managed. In addition, they cited the need for thirty private airports clustered around secondary fields. The composite plan revealed a fifteen-county urban region stretching from Racine, Wisconsin, to LaPorte, Indiana.[41]

Thus, the transformation Mumford predicted was already underway. The airplane and Garden City ideals had transformed Los Angeles and Southern California, and planners, business leaders, and civic elites in other metropolitan areas were grappling with the spatial implications of industrial and residential dispersion in the postwar era. Urban expansion was proceeding, however, in a manner contrary to what Mumford and the regionalists envisioned. For Mumford, Los Angeles and other sprawling regional cities were the Garden City's antithesis. In a *New Yorker* column, Mumford denounced the physical planning of the 1939 New York World's Fair "Town of Tomorrow," calling it a "Coney Island out of Los Angeles." The exhibition's streets accounted for "traffic circulation . . . as ample as Wilshire Boulevard" requiring everyone to "spend the greater part of the day circulating needless distances," a condition he ascribed to the modern metropolis.[42]

Others viewed postwar prospects in a more positive light. Addressing the legacy of the defense effort for large-scale planning and community design, *New Pencil Points* editor Kenneth Reid argued that the "needs of war housing brought problems of greater magnitude, involving whole communities of hundreds and even thousands of houses. These projects had to have shops and stores, schools, community centers, and other facilities to serve [residents]."[43] The design team responsible for Fort Drive Gardens in Washington, D.C., was more bold: "The war has taught us to think big about housing; to evaluate entire communities in terms of accommodations and social resources, and to build complete new towns."[44] According to planner Tracy

Auger, this was precisely why American servicemen went to war. "The American home that we are fighting for is not just a well-built building, not even a building equipped with gleaming bathtubs and refrigerators. It is a dwelling place composed of house, neighborhood, and community rolled into one."[45] The Bureau of Labor Statistics's home-building forecast was equally sanguine. Their reports cataloged the industry's wartime coming-of-age.[46]

A Los Angeles example illustrates the type of development Reid and Auger envisioned. Following the war, the Regional Planning Commission fixed the "area of greatest growth at . . . a radius fifteen miles from the Civic Center."[47] Within the fifteen-mile circle, sections such as the two-hundred-twelve-square-mile San Fernando Valley were still predominantly agricultural. A 1943 "Los Angeles Master Plan" document stated that the "Valley should be planned as a self-contained unit . . . industry and commerce should be introduced to supplement the agricultural economy and supply employment for present and future residents."[48] According to director of planning Charles Bennett, the plan would result in a "regional city . . . a number of well-planned and moderately sized communities separated by agricultural areas."[49]

To encourage their objectives, the Planning Commission published a series of special studies; one featured a planned community at the Panorama Ranch. In 1946, when builder Fritz B. Burns was negotiating the purchase of this property, General Motors had begun construction of its new assembly plant at the southwest corner of the site. Developed and built by Kaiser Community Homes, a joint venture of Burns and Henry J. Kaiser, Panorama City included a site north of Roscoe Boulevard for a recreation center and primary school. One block south was the public high school. Burns developed a linear commercial district with department stores, supermarkets, and a theater on Van Nuys Boulevard, a north-south arterial for the Valley. In the bend of Woodman Boulevard, Kaiser constructed a Permanente Medical Center.[50]

Greg Hise

As constructed, Panorama City epitomized the convergence of a planning ideal, the decentralized regional city, with the production emphasis and community-building expertise of a corporation such as Kaiser Community Homes. Panorama City underscores the point that the complete community, including the requisite proximity to employment, continued to be a highly touted objective, one that planners, builders, and home buyers actively pursued. Analyzing postwar development patterns in California, Edward Eichler and Marshall Kaplan wrote, "If suburbia means large groups of housing developments with little or no major shopping facilities or employment centers, most of the development in California in the last fifteen years should be given another name."[51]

Historians routinely single out Levitt and Sons and their Levittowns in Long Island and Pennsylvania as the paradigm of postwar community building. Often presented as revolutionary, Levitt's postwar developments were in fact part of an ongoing evolution. The FHA's *Technical Bulletins* were a paean to rationalization and modern industrial organization. *American Builder* and other trade journals alerted readers to the advantages these innovations could secure. For his wartime housing projects in Norfolk, Virginia, Levitt adopted many of the time- and cost-saving methods that reformers advocated and that Los Angeles community builders had already put into practice.

While Levitt was building in Virginia, the United Associates Corporation, a Jamaica, Long Island, concern, completed a series of projects for defense workers in Bellmore, a thriving little town near the aviation firms that had located in the Farmingdale area. Six years later, Levitt and Sons acquired a four-thousand-acre parcel in nearby Hempstead. Here the Levitts capitalized on the employment offered by Grumann Aviation, Republic Aviation, and other aircraft, and later aerospace, firms. The later Pennsylvania project was sited in close proximity to United States Steel's Fairless Works, and the Levitts dedicated industrial tracts in their site plan for Landia, an unrealized 1951 community proposed for Jericho, Long Island.[52]

Surveying our contemporary metropolitan landscape, the home-front legacy seems obscured by fifty years of city building. Recent accounts of postwar urbanism refer to the outer city, postsuburb, and technoburb as scattered satellites in a galactic metropolis.[53] In his well-known "edge city" thesis, Joel Garreau asserts that during the past thirty years Americans have launched the most sweeping change in one hundred years in how they live, work, and play. According to Garreau, edge cities are the third wave in a causal ocean that has inundated the postwar landscape. The first wave was residential, followed in turn by retail and services and, more recently, business and jobs. Business and jobs, he argues, followed people "weary of returning downtown for the necessities of life."[54]

In his uncritical examination of our contemporary metropolitan landscape, Garreau reiterates the traditional suburban thesis. But edge cities are not, as Garreau states, exclusively postwar phenomena. We can trace their conceptual roots back to Ebenezer Howard's Garden City and the planned dispersion of the nineteenth-century industrial city. America's World War II defense programs accelerated this urban morphology when epochal migration coupled with rapid industrial expansion and a dispersed spatial pattern for aircraft and other industry. Garreau is incorrect as well when he claims that housing led and continues to lead urban expansion. Rather, wartime satellite developments were dynamic centers with a mix of land uses. Industry provided an economic base, jobs, and people, the foundation necessary for large-scale builders' experiments in modern community planning.

Levittown, New York, ca. 1950. Courtesy the National Building Museum/gift of Richard Wurts.

Notes

Heather Burnham, Curatorial Assistant at the National Building Museum, and Patrick Wirtz at the University of Southern California provided invaluable research assistance; Richard Longstreth of George Washington University offered sage advice regarding wartime commercial development. Colleagues in the History, Theory, and Design Seminar at USC critiqued an earlier version of this essay, as did the editor, Donald Albrecht. The *Journal of Urban History* granted permission to reprint sections of the Los Angeles case studies. In a forthcoming study (Johns Hopkins University Press), I examine these themes in detail.

1. Lewis Mumford, "An American Introduction to Sir Ebenezer Howard's 'Garden Cities of Tomorrow,'" *New Pencil Points* 24 (March 1945): 73.

2. The term *community* was applied imprecisely in contemporary sources. Few authors limited the term qualitatively or quantitatively, which may account for its wide usage. Depending on the author and reference, *community* connoted the areal boundaries of the project under discussion; the physical plant of infrastructure, business, commerce, and residences; or the social institutions and social life of inhabitants. I use the term *complete community* to denote the sum of the project area, physical plant, and social institutions, a usage that parallels the most inclusive contemporary sources. *Balanced living* appeared in the writings of planners and reformers during the 1930s. The members of Southern California Telesis offered the most concise definition in the exhibition catalog . . .*and Now We Plan* (n.d.), published by the Los Angeles Museum of Natural History.

3. Greg Hise, "The Roots of the Postwar Urban Region: Mass-Housing and Community Planning in California, 1920–1950" (Ph.D. diss., University of California, Berkeley, 1992), chap. 2.

4. American regionalists planned to harness industrial dispersion and emergent technology to craft a network of managed population centers connected by transit and surrounded by greenbelts. Greg Hise, "Building the World of Tomorrow: Regional Visions, Modern Community Housing, and America's Postwar Urban Expansion," *Center: A Journal for Architecture in America* 8 (1993): 52–61.

5. Lewis Mumford, "American Architecture," *American Federationist* 34 (December 1927): 1484.

6. Clarence Arthur Perry, "The Neighborhood Unit, Monograph I," in *Neighborhood and Community Planning,* vol. 7 of *Regional Survey of New York and Its Environs* (New York: Russell Sage Foundation, 1929). See Perry, *Housing for the Machine Age* (New York: Committee on the Regional Plan of New York and Its Environs, 1939) and Howard Gillette, Jr., "The Evolution of Neighborhood Planning: From the Progressive Era to the 1949 Housing Act," *Journal of Urban History* 9 (August 1983) for Perry's formulation of the neighborhood unit concept.

7. Harold Mayer, Lewis Mumford, and Henry Wright, "New Homes for a New Deal," *The New Republic,* ca. 1934. Reprinted as a pamphlet in the Special Collections of the College of Environmental Design, UC Berkeley.

8. John M. Gries and James Ford, eds., *The Final Reports of the President's Conference on Home Building and Home Ownership* (Washington, D.C.: The President's Conference on Home Building and Home Ownership, 1932–33).

9. Marc A. Weiss, *The Rise of the Community Builders: The American Real Estate Industry and Urban Land Planning* (New York: Columbia University Press, 1987). See for example San Mateo County Planning Commission, *The Subdivision of Land in San Mateo County California* (San Mateo: San Mateo County Planning Commission, 1932).

10. United States Federal Housing Administration, "Planning Neighborhoods for Small Houses," *Technical Bulletin No. 5* (Washington, D.C., July 1, 1936).

11. U.S. Bureau of Labor Statistics, *Monthly Labor Review* (Washington, D.C., April 1946), 560–561. The majority of publicly financed housing for war workers was completed before Pearl Harbor. On February 24, 1942, President Roosevelt consolidated all Federal housing agencies into the National Housing Agency (NHA). Charles F. Palmer, Defense Housing Coordinator, was a real estate developer and past president of the National Association of Real Estate Boards who responded favorably to private builders. John Carmody Papers (Box 103, FWA Defense Housing,

1940–41 Folder), Franklin Delano Roosevelt Library, Hyde Park, New York.

12. Gertrude S. Fish, "Housing Policy during the Great Depression," in *The Story of Housing,* ed. Gertrude S. Fish (New York: MacMillan, 1979) and Nathaniel S. Keith, *Politics and the Housing Crisis since 1930* (New York: Universe Books, 1973).

13. United States Federal Housing Administration, "A New Small-Home Ownership Program" in *Insured Mortgage Portfolio* (Washington, D.C., February 1940).

14. California State Planning Board, *Hearing on the Establishment of a San Francisco Bay Regional Planning District, March 28, 1941* 35, quoted in Roger Lotchin, "World War II and Urban California: City Planning and the Transformation Hypothesis," *Pacific Historical Review* 62, no. 2 (May 1993): 147.

15. For Los Angeles, see the Security First National Bank report "Number of Dwelling Units Compared with Population: Los Angeles County," August 17, 1958 in Fletcher Bowron Papers (Box 59, Population Folder); Eugene Weston's testimony before the Subcommittee of the Committee on Naval Affairs, *Investigation of Congested Production Areas, Part 8: Los Angeles-Long Beach, California, November 10–13, 1943* (Washington, D.C.: U.S. Government Printing Office, 1944). For San Diego, California, Eugene Weston, testimony before the Subcommittee of the Committee on Naval Affairs, *Investigation of Congested Production Areas, Part 2: San Diego, California, April 6–10, 1943* (Washington, D.C.: U.S. Government Printing Office, 1943).

16. Weston, *Investigation of Congested Areas* (November 13, 1943).

17. Mrs. Darrell Ratzlaff, handwritten statement dated 1981, in the Westchester Historical Society Collections, Loyola Marymount University. Los Angeles Chamber of Commerce, *Southern California Business: New Series* 1 (January 1941).

18. Ibid.

19. For unit output and employment see Civil Aeronautics Administration, *United States Military Aircraft Acceptances, 1940–1945: Aircraft, Engine, and Propeller Production* (Washington, D.C.: U.S. Government Printing Office, 1946). Floor space is noted in North American Aviation, *A Brief History of Operations Immediately Prior to and during WWII* (Los Angeles: North American Aviation, 1945). Contrary to the accounts of industry leaders and an earlier generation of business historians who cited topography and California's temperate climate as critical factors, airframe production concentrated in Los Angeles because of the innovations developed by engineers such as Douglas, the presence of a skilled, nonunion labor force, and institutional support, including the California Institute of Technology. See Roger Lotchin, *Fortress California, 1910–1961: From Warfare to Welfare* (New York: Oxford University Press, 1992), especially chap. 5.

20. Regional Planning Commission, "Statistical Areas and Jurisdictions: Dwelling Units and Population," *Regional Planning Commission, County of Los Angeles* 16 (July 1945).

21. Greg Hise, "Home Building and Industrial Decentralization in Los Angeles: The Roots of the Postwar Urban Region," *Journal of Urban History* 19, no. 2 (February 1993), 95–125.

22. Author interview with William Hannon, sales manager for Marlow-Burns, July 29, 1991. See Hise, "The Roots of the Postwar Urban Region," for a detailed discussion of this revolution in building practice.

23. Marlow-Burns site-planned schools and religious institutions for their developments; dedications and purchases were noted on property maps. See Trefethen Papers (Carton 11, Folder 9, Kaiser Community Homes Property Maps, Tract 13711) in the Henry J. Kaiser Papers, Bancroft Library, University of California, Berkeley.

24. The University of California, Los Angeles, Department of Geography's Spence and Fairchild Aerial Photo Collections contain low-altitude oblique images of Westchester. For "Homes at Wholesale," see the *Los Angeles Evening Herald and Express* March 28 and April 25, 1942 and January 2, 1943; *Los Angeles Daily News* December 25, 1942; and *Los Angeles Examiner* April 12, 1942.

25. *Los Angeles Downtown Shopping News* August 15, 1942, 12.

26. City Planning Commission, *Columbia Rivers Port City for Homes and Industries: A Report to the Citizens and City Commissioner* (Vancouver, Wash.: The City Planning Commission, 1945), 80.

27. Vancouver's 1940 population was eighteen thousand seven hundred eighty-eight; in 1943, it stood at eighty-six thousand. See Walter Gordon, "Cities While You Wait: Housing in Washington and Oregon," *New Pencil Points* 24 (April 1943) and Housing Authority of the City of Vancouver, *Housing in War and Peace: The Story of Public Housing in Vancouver, Washington* (Vancouver: The Housing Authority, 1972). *Architectural Record Building Types Study No. 70* (October 1942): 63–78.

28. Vancouver Housing Authority, *Vancouver's Plan . . . for the Utilization of War Housing Projects Located at Vancouver, Washington* (Vancouver: The Housing Authority, 1945); "How Vancouver Plans for Disposition of War Housing Properties," *Western City* 21, no. 5 (May 1945): 17–19; and Vancouver Housing Authority, *Housing in War and Peace* (Vancouver: The Housing Authority, 1972).

29. Leon Zach, "Site Planning of Cantonment and Community Housing," *Civil Engineering* 15, no. 8 (August 1945): 363–366.

30. The Chicago Plan Commission, *Building New Neighborhoods: Subdivision Design and Standards* (Chicago: The Chicago Plan Commission, July 1943), 6.

31. Memo dated June 20, 1940, in the John Carmody Papers (Box 103, FWA Defense Housing Reports 1940–41 Folder), Franklin Delano Roosevelt Library, Hyde Park, New York. See also Benton MacKaye's "Defense Time Conservation" (July 25, 1940) in the Catherine Bauer Wurster Papers (Carton 10, Defense Housing Folder), Bancroft Library, University of California, Berkeley, which advocates the "scatterization" of industry to "draw to such new uncrowded plants and towns the workers and families now overconcentrated in metropolitan seaports."

32. Chet Miller, "Douglas Town on the Mojave," *Douglas Airview* (March 1943): 10–12; editorial "It's no Mirage," *Douglas Airview* (September 1943). *Insured Mortgage Portfolio* (Fourth Quarter 1943): 21–22, 40–41; *Urban Land* 3, no. 5 (1943): 1, 3.

33. Homer Hoyt, "The Structure of American Cities in the Post-War Era," *The American Journal of Sociology* 48 (January 1943): 475–481. For accounts of the uncertainty posed by conversion, see the testimony of Los Angeles mayor Fletcher Bowron and Paulson Viesel of the Alhambra Chamber of Commerce, U.S. Senate, *Hearings before a Subcommittee of the Special Committee on Post-War Economic Policy and Planning, September 11–18, 1943* (Washington, D.C.: U.S. Government Printing Office, 1943).

34. *1944–1945 Annual Report* (Los Angeles: The Regional Planning Commission, 1946); Clarence Dykstra, "Congestion de Luxe—Do We Want It?" *National Municipal Review* 6 (July 1926): 394–398. See also William E. Smythe, "Significance of Southern California," *Out West* 32, no. 4 (April 1910): 287–302; Sherley Hunter, *Why Los Angeles Will Be the World's Greatest City* (Los Angeles: H. J. Mallen Company, Inc., ca. 1923).

35. U.S. Senate, *Hearings before the Subcommittee on Housing and Urban Redevelopment of the Special Committee on Post-War Economic Policy and Planning: Part 9* (Washington, D.C.: U.S. Government Printing Office, 1945), 1599. *Urban Land* 5, no. 1 (January 1945).

36. "Aviation History Made on a Street Corner," *Rockwell News* 6, no. 20 (October 9, 1978), 3.

37. Los Angeles Board of Public Works, *Aliso Viaduct and Ramona Parkway, City of Los Angeles, August 14, 1944* (Los Angeles: The Board of Public Works, 1944); Los Angeles Bureau of Engineering, *A Proposed Six Year Program of Postwar Construction for the City of Los Angeles* (Los Angeles: The Bureau of Engineering, 1944).

38. Lotchin, *Fortress California;* Allen J. Scott, *Technopolis: High Technology Industry and Regional Development in Southern California* (Los Angeles and Berkeley: University of California Press, 1993).

39. *A Comprehensive Report on the Master Plan of Airports for the Los Angeles County Regional Planning District* (Los Angeles: The Regional Planning Commission, 1940). The region benefited materially, for example, when the military deeded Van Nuys and Palmdale airports to the city and county respectively. The subsequent *Master Plan of Heliports,* a

scheme the county Department of Aviation promoted as the first plan "officially adopted anywhere in the world," underscored the spatial bias of the airport plan. It showed a network of one hundred fifteen landing sites clustered around air terminals at Long Beach, Los Angeles Municipal Airport, Burbank, Palmdale, and a proposed terminal at Puente in the San Gabriel Valley. *Annual Report: 1951–52* (Los Angeles: The Regional Planning Commission, 1952), 49–50.

40. Lotchin, *Fortress California,* 250–255.

41. "Chicago Plans," *New Pencil Points* 24 (March 1943): 34–63.

42. Lewis Mumford, "The Skyline in Flushing: West Is East," *The New Yorker,* 15 (June 17, 1939): 37–41.

43. Kenneth Reed, "The Invisible Client," *Architectural Forum* 24 (March 1943).

44. Vernon DeMars, Carl Koch, Mary Goldwater, John Johansen, and Paul Stone, "Mixed Rental Neighborhood, Washington, D.C.," *Architectural Forum* (October 1943): 79.

45. Tracy Auger, "Defense Housing—Now and Afterward," *Proceedings of the National Conference on Planning, May 12–14, 1941* (Chicago: American Society of Planning Officials, 1941), 137–141.

46. U.S. Bureau of Labor Statistics, *Bulletin No. 825, Probable Volume of Postwar Construction* (Washington, D.C.: U.S. Government Printing Office, May 14, 1945), 7–8. Postwar commentators noted this explicitly. Kathryn Murphy's "New Housing and Its Materials, 1940–1956" in the U.S. Bureau of Labor Statistics *Monthly Labor Review* (Washington, D.C.: U.S. Government Printing Office, 1958) placed changes in the "pattern and pace of homebuilding" squarely in the war period when shortages "forced the abandonment of many customary practices and encouraged the application of large-scale production methods and experimentation with new designs and layouts in housing for military personnel and civilian war workers." See also Howard P. Vermilya, "Potential Technical Development of Post-War Houses," *Insured Mortgage Portfolio* (Third Quarter 1943): 24–25, 37.

47. Regional Planning Commission, *Statistical Areas and Jurisdiction* 46 (1954).

48. Los Angeles City Planning Commission, *Accomplishments 1944* (Los Angeles: The City Planning Commission, 1945).

49. Charles Bennett and Milton Brievogel, "The Plan for the San Fernando Valley," *New Pencil Points* (June 1945).

50. Hise, "Home Building and Industrial Decentralization."

51. Edward Eichler and Marshall Kaplan, *The Community Builders* (Los Angeles and Berkeley: University of California Press, 1967).

52. "Builders Rush Small Defense Homes with Aid of Priorities" *American Builder* 63 (November 1941): 46–49; Alfred S. Levitt, "A Community Builder Looks at Planning," *Journal of the American Institute of Planning* 17 (Spring 1951): 80–88.

53. Jack Rosenthal, "The Outer City: U.S. in Suburban Turmoil," *The New York Times,* May 30, 1971; Rob Kling, Spencer Olin, and Mark Poster, eds., *Postsuburban California: The Transformation of Orange County since World War II* (Los Angeles and Berkeley: University of California Press, 1991); Robert Fishman, *Bourgeois Utopias: The Rise and Fall of Suburbia* (New York: Basic Books, 1987); Pierce Lewis, "The Galactic Metropolis," in *Beyond the Urban Fringe: Land Use Issues of Nonmetropolitan America,* ed. Rutherford Platt and George Macinko (Minneapolis: University of Minnesota Press, 1983).

54. Joel Garreau, *Edge City: Life on the New Frontier* (New York: Doubleday, 1991).

Joel Davidson

Building for War, Preparing for Peace: World War II and the Military-Industrial Complex

At the conclusion of World War II, weapons were scrapped and soldiers returned to civilian pursuits, but a massive defense infrastructure endured, providing a ready framework for the permanent militarization of American society during the cold war. Although a significant symbiotic relationship between the military and industry had existed as far back as the Civil War, no previous conflict had required mobilization on the scale that took place from 1940 through 1945. The very existence of these massive facilities, from aircraft plants to cities devoted to nuclear research, provided its own argument for continued defense production. This defense infrastructure supported an interwoven community of military officers, bureaucrats, corporate executives, scientists, and politicians; a powerful constituency whose well-being depended on military spending. These rising political and economic forces and the escalating U.S.-Soviet arms race ensured that the wartime military-industrial base would remain an active element on the national and world scene.

Joel Davidson

By focusing on three areas—the aerospace industry, the government-owned arms industry, and the defense-academic cooperative—I will explore how construction of specialized factories and research facilities contributed to winning the war but also helped perpetuate a wartime economy through the fragile peace that became known as the cold war. On September 1, 1939, when German forces marched into Poland and war broke out in Europe, the United States was psychologically and physically ill-prepared to play a major military role. The U.S. Army could field just over a quarter of a million men, a far cry from the eight-million-man force that eventually helped spread American power from Okinawa to the Elbe. The Navy, though large, had yet to acknowledge that aircraft carriers had eclipsed big-gun surface ships in military significance, and the Army Air Corps was just beginning to emerge as an independent branch of the armed forces.[1] Perhaps most alarming, however, was the near total absence of a modern arms industry. During World War I, the United States had relied on its allies for much of the Army's planes, weapons, and ammunition. During the 1920s and 1930s, the Army maintained just six arsenals dedicated to weapons manufacture—capable of producing less than a tenth of the armaments required for a major war.[2]

The German blitz across France in May and June of 1940 shattered the assumption that the war could be confined to Europe. With France defeated and Britain in jeopardy, the United States began a crash program to arm itself. Unimpeded by blockade, bombing, or invasion, American war industries expanded with amazing rapidity. In many cases, existing factories, some of which had been idle during the Depression, could be converted to war production with the proper machine tools. The automotive industry, the country's largest, included over a thousand plants. After Pearl Harbor the government banned private automobile production, and almost all of these plants converted to war work. The industry eventually accounted for more than half the na-

one hundred eighty-six

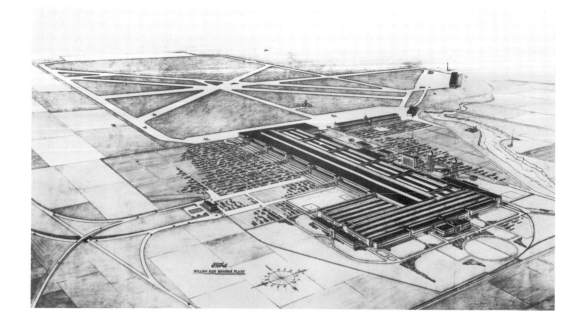

Willow Run bomber plant, Ypsilanti, Michigan, built by Ford Motor Company to manufacture B-24 bombers. The main building turned ninety degrees to avoid crossing a county line. Albert Kahn Associated Architects and Engineers, designers. Courtesy Collections of Henry Ford Museum and Greenfield Village. P.833.80489.1.

Advertisement, n.d. Courtesy Chevrolet Motor Car Division/General Motors Corp.

Fuselage sections of B-29 Superfortress bombers awaiting final assembly, n.d. Courtesy National Archives. RG 208-PRA-8-1.

tional output of tanks and aircraft engines, in addition to millions of military trucks.[3]

However widespread and successful, conversion of plants from civilian to war production could not meet American defense needs, and the Federal government undertook to create a wide range of new industrial facilities. In 1940, Congress approved funding techniques that involved government to an unprecedented degree in industrial finance. Before 1940 Federal funding provided less than five percent of the nation's capital investment; from 1940 to 1943 this contribution jumped to sixty-seven percent.[4] The government agency largely responsible for industrial construction was the Defense Plant Corporation (DPC). By 1945, the DPC had funded over a thousand industrial facilities worth almost $7 billion, mostly aircraft factories and shipyards.[5] Major corporations, motivated by patriotism, increased wartime profits, and new tax laws, invested a nearly equal amount. With a "certificate of necessity" issued by the armed forces, factory owners could deduct the entire cost of new construction over five years rather than the usual twenty.[6]

Marietta, Georgia, known as Bomber City, with the Bell B-29 bomber plant in the background. Courtesy National Archives. RG 208-PRA-17-1.

The third major funding source for industrial expansion was the military. With annual appropriations reaching billions of dollars, the Army and Navy built their own manufacturing base for arms, explosives, and other specialized defense items. Many new plants were operated by the armed services, employing the military for the first time in mass industrial production and plant management. Most, however, were run under special management contracts by major corporations such as E. I. Du Pont De Nemours and Remington Arms. Plants operated under contract were known as GOCO—government-owned, contractor-operated—factories. In both cases, the new facilities gave the armed forces direct control over a large and modern weapons industry.

As the armed forces expanded their administrative payrolls to handle the burgeoning military and industrial infrastructure, they rapidly outgrew prewar offices scattered around Washington, D.C. In 1941, the War Department proposed a new headquarters building for forty thousand workers. As no single Washington site could accommodate such a structure, a parcel of land across the Potomac in Virginia was selected.[7] Critics opposed

Army M-3 tanks on the assembly line at the Detroit Tank Arsenal, Detroit, Michigan, 1941, Albert Kahn Associated Architects and Engineers and Chrysler Corporation, designers and builders. Hedrich-Blessing photograph/courtesy Chicago Historical Society. HB-06539-B.

Oakland Naval Supply Depot under construction, Oakland, California, January 1942. Courtesy NAVFAC Historical Program/Port Hueneme, California.

Oakland Naval Supply Depot, September 1943. Courtesy NAVFAC Historical Program/Port Hueneme, California.

spending $35 million on a four-million-square-foot building that would destroy the picturesque quality of nearby Arlington Cemetery and have no postwar use.[8] President Roosevelt placated these critics by predicting that the building would become a storage records facility, and the project went ahead.

Construction of the five-story Pentagon began in September 1941, and within sixteen months crews had completed the largest office building in the world. The reinforced-concrete structure sits on a two-hundred-eighty-acre site and contains over seventeen miles of corridor and a five-acre landscaped central courtyard. A system of highways—and today a subway—connect the building to downtown Washington. Built to house the bureaucracy that managed World War II, the Pentagon remains the major nexus of American military, corporate, and political power.

Aircraft Facilities

Without a doubt the most spectacular and far-reaching wartime industrial growth occurred in the field of aircraft production. The aircraft industry received a major boost following the fall of France. President Roosevelt made a nationally broadcast speech calling for manufacturers to increase production from thirteen thousand to fifty thousand planes a year, which the government estimated would require tripling existing factory space.[9] Once the United States entered the war, production targets rose even higher; in early 1942 Roosevelt demanded that plane makers build sixty thousand aircraft in 1942 and one hundred twenty-five thousand in 1943.[10]

In response to these demands, the government and industry launched a major building program. A prime example was Douglas Aircraft Company's Long Beach, California, assembly plant, located across town from Douglas's existing facilities at El Segundo and Santa Monica. Built with Federal money in 1940–41, the one-point-four-million-square-foot factory was one of the most advanced aircraft plants in the world. Forty-three thousand

Temporary office buildings for Federal workers line the reflecting pool below the Lincoln Memorial in this wartime view from the Washington Monument. Courtesy National Archives. RG 80-G-46524.

The Pentagon under construction, Arlington, Virginia, January 1942. Courtesy Pentagon Office of History/Department of Defense.

Douglas Aircraft plant, Long Beach, California, with roofs painted to resemble nearby streets and houses. Courtesy Douglas Aircraft Company/McDonnell Douglas Corporation.

Workers place metal siding over a layer of fireproof thermal insulating board at the Douglas Aircraft plant in Long Beach, California, 1941. Edward and Ellis Taylor, architects, Walker Construction Company, builders. Courtesy Douglas Aircraft Company/McDonnell Douglas Corporation.

Joel Davidson

Camouflage village atop Douglas Aircraft
plant, Santa Monica, California, ca. 1943.
Courtesy Douglas Aircraft Company/McDon-
nell Douglas Corporation.

Douglas Aircraft plant, Santa Monica, California, ca. 1943. Courtesy Douglas Aircraft Company/McDonnell Douglas Corporation.

Joel Davidson

Exterior of U.S. Army bomber plant, Tulsa, Oklahoma, 1942. Courtesy Office of History/Army
Corps of Engineers.

Main assembly building of U.S. Army bomber
plant with B-24 Liberator bomber in fore-
ground, Tulsa, Oklahoma, ca. 1943. Courtesy
Douglas Aircraft Company/McDonnell Douglas
Corporation.

Joel Davidson

Basic Magnesium plant under construction near Las Vegas, Nevada, 1942. Courtesy U.S. Office of War Information Collection/Prints and Photographs Division/Library of Congress. LC-USW3-3881-E.

Movable wooden forms used to build concrete arch hangars at the Naval Air Station, Patuxent River, Maryland, 1943. Courtesy National Archives. RG 71-CB-98-V-1.

Opposite:
Open hearth furnaces and stacks under construction at the Columbia Steel mill, Geneva, Utah. Courtesy U.S. Farm Security Administration Collection/Prints and Photographs Division/Library of Congress. LC-USW3-43151-C.

thereby freeing western shipbuilders from dependence on eastern steel sources. In a speech dedicating the new government-funded steel mill in Fontana, California, master industrialist Henry Kaiser observed, "For the first time on this side of the Rockies we begin the manufacture of iron, the fundamental element in modern industry, from ore mined in our own mountains. . . . The westward movement which began so long ago has not come to an end on the Pacific Slope. It is poised now for the next great thrust. The day of the West is at hand."[23]

While increased industrial muscle helped integrate the Far West into the American economy, additions to the nation's air transportation system ensured that political and cultural integration would soon follow. With planes pouring off the assembly lines, the growing U.S. air forces required thousands of new airfields to train pilots. In 1939, the Army and Navy together had only twenty-eight air stations. During the war, the Army built more than one thousand air bases, while the Navy built over sixty major air stations, including a flight-testing facility at Patuxent, Maryland. Begun in 1942, this air station featured six twin-arch reinforced-concrete hangars.[24] Patuxent continued to serve as the Navy's principal flight-testing station throughout the following decades.

Patuxent and hundreds of new flying fields like it confirmed the ascendancy of military aviation in the postwar world, but the true revolution occurred in the nation's civilian air transportation system. Many existing civilian airports such as Denver, Colorado's, Municipal Airport were expanded and upgraded by the military, and areas that had never been near commercial air transportation routes suddenly became homes to busy modern airports. After the war, over five hundred surplus military airfields were transferred to municipal authorities, making possible a truly national system of air travel.[25] One example is Windsor Locks Army Air Base in Connecticut, built in early 1941 as a fighter station to defend southern New England. State authori-

Workers building aircraft hangar in 1941 at municipal airport, Denver, Colorado, one of thousands of new facilities built to accommodate the nation's growing air forces. Courtesy National Archives. RG 69-N-21197.

ties took over the base in 1946 and began laying the groundwork for Bradley International Airport, the region's principal air transportation facility.

Airfield technology also improved as wartime advances in navigation and electronics soon made their way into civilian planes and control towers. A crash wartime research program improved runway pavements to handle seventy-ton B-29 Superfortress bombers; advances in runway design allowed large civilian aircraft to use even small municipal airports.

Continual improvements and refinements of military aircraft designs prompted the industry to fund sophisticated structures for research and testing. Wartime profits allowed aircraft companies to finance installations that would previously have been beyond their reach. In 1942, four large California aircraft producers—Douglas, Consolidated Vultee, Lockheed, and North American—agreed to cooperatively finance construction of the nation's most technologically advanced wind tunnel. The Southern California Cooperative Wind Tunnel was built in Pasadena, California, and operated by the California Institute of Technology. Clark B. Milliken of Caltech, who became director of the project, had actively lobbied for the wind tunnel, seeking first government and then corporate funding. The thirty-one-foot-diameter tunnel, which was completed in early 1945, required two and one-half million pounds of welded steel plate nearly an inch thick to withstand the tremendous pressures generated during tests.[26] A nearly identical tunnel was built in Buffalo, New York, by the Curtiss-Wright Company. Updated and improved, the Southern California Cooperative Wind Tunnel continued to serve the aerospace industry for a decade and a half after the war, linking the academic community and the military by performing vital testing on major military and civilian aircraft designs.

The wartime building boom in aircraft plants and related facilities created a large, integrated industry out of what had been a collection of small specialized producers. The war not only enhanced the status of airframe and engine companies, the latter now including giant General Electric for jet turbines; it also fostered the growth of specialized interests that relied on continued aircraft production for their survival. Plants that made parts and instruments, high-octane gasoline and jet fuel, or specialized lightweight forgings had as much at stake in the aircraft industry's survival as the aircraft producers themselves. In some areas, entire communities depended on the aircraft industry for their economic well-being. In Los Angeles, for example, local governments tried to sustain the industry's postwar health by encouraging airport construction and civilian air travel. Corporate and civic interests allied with bureaucratic forces in the government attempted to influence policy decisions that would help maintain a large and modern Air Force.

Munitions Plants

The German victories of 1940 spurred the hurried construction of ordnance plants of all kinds. By early 1941, the Army had thirty-four new munitions factories under construction, and by 1944 U.S. factories led the world in armaments production. Typical of the new munitions facilities was the Radford Ordnance Works, a four-thousand-acre explosive-powder plant begun in rural Virginia in 1940. The first of the new armaments factories to enter service, Radford could turn out three hundred thousand pounds of explosive powder a day.[27] Pursuant to a typical GOCO plant agreement, Radford was designed, built, and operated by the Hercules Powder Company under a cost-plus-fee contract. From 1941 through 1944, the plant produced over three hundred million pounds of smokeless powder for the Army.

To minimize the danger from highly volatile propellant charges, production at Radford was dispersed over three hundred fifty separate buildings. Like many ordnance factories, buildings were erected with concrete partitions between bays and with special "blow-out" exterior walls of corrugated steel or cement-

Cut-away of Southern California Cooperative
Wind Tunnel, Pasadena, California, 1945, California Institute of Technology, designer. Courtesy National Archives. RG 208-LU-11-HH-2.

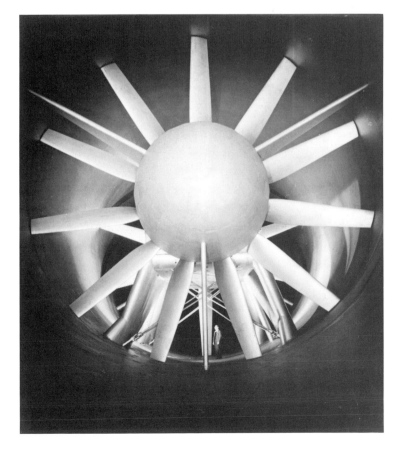

Wind vanes in Southern California Cooperative Wind Tunnel. Courtesy National Archives. RG 208-LU-11-HH-5.

Tandem twelve-foot fans in Southern California Cooperative Wind Tunnel, capable of producing winds over seven hundred miles per hour. Courtesy National Archives. RG 208-LU-11-HH-1.

two hundred eleven

Barrel-vaulted ammunition storage bunkers at the Hoosier Ordnance Works, Charlestown, Indiana, 1941. Courtesy U.S. Army Center for Military History.

asbestos siding, thereby directing explosions outward and limiting damage in the event of an accident.[28]

The wartime ordnance plants were conceived and created as part of an integrated munitions industry. The Radford factory, for example, was served by an ammunition-loading facility at the nearby New River plant. Explosive powder produced at Radford was loaded into live ammunition and stored for shipment at New River.[29] Explosives and ammunition required special storage facilities as well. The Army adopted a standard design for a barrel-vaulted ammunition storage bunker made of steel-reinforced concrete, and tens of thousands of these simple bunkers were built at ordnance factories, ammunition depots, and training bases around the country.[30] In addition to powder and shell plants, the Army built factories for tanks, cannons, and machine guns, as well as proving grounds and storage depots. By the war's end, the military owned over $5.5 billion worth of munitions plants and supporting facilities, most of which were operated by private contractors.[31] These plants represented a quantum leap in munitions production capacity, and gave the armed services a degree of independence and control that military leaders would be loathe to relinquish.

Research and Testing Facilities

World War II was the first war for which basic scientific research was harnessed to produce war-winning weapons. By far the most advanced and far-reaching research project was the massive, secret, and science-intensive industry devoted to developing a nuclear weapon. The Manhattan Project helped turn scientific investigation into a national security endeavor that blurred the lines between industry, universities, and the armed forces. At its peak, the Manhattan Project employed over two hundred thousand workers at thirty-seven installations in the United States and Canada.[32] Some of these installations contained specialized structures never before built or even imagined. At Oak Ridge, Tennessee, for example, scientists and architects designed a gaseous diffusion plant that would collect U-235 by pumping uranium-enriched gas through a series of microscopic filters. The main diffusion building, built by J. A. Jones Construction Company, measured nearly half a mile long; its series of precisely engineered and aligned pumps, filters, and instruments made it the most technologically sophisticated factory of its time.[33]

The atomic bomb was only the most impressive of many scientific-military ventures launched during the war. Advances in radar and electronics revolutionized warfare, and the military financed laboratories at leading universities to continually refine this new technology. Government contracts financed new construction at the Massachusetts Institute of Technology, where the secret Radiation Laboratory perfected military radar and guid-

K-25 gaseous diffusion plant, Oak Ridge, Tennessee, which captured U-235 bomb material by forcing uranium-enriched gas through a series of filters. J. A. Jones Construction Company, builder. Courtesy J. A. Jones Construction Company.

Atomic pile area, part of the plutonium production facility at Hanford, Washington, 1945. Courtesy National Archives. RG 111-SC-209932-S.

Los Alamos, New Mexico, the key research
and design center for nuclear weapons
throughout World War II and the cold war,
1946. Courtesy Los Alamos Historical Museum
Archives.

Joel Davidson

Radar aerials from the secret Radiation Laboratory line the roof of Building 20 at the Massachusetts Institute of Technology, Cambridge, Massachusetts, 1945. Courtesy MIT Museum.

Interior of the main testing tank at the David Taylor Model Basin, with carriage used to tow ship models to simulate the movement of actual ships at sea, Carderock, Maryland, 1946. Courtesy David Taylor Model Basin.

ance systems.[34] At Harvard, the Radio Research Laboratory
searched for ways to confuse enemy radars.

Not all government research work could be farmed out to
universities and private industry. Federal dollars were also used
to create or expand sophisticated government testing facilities
that would supplement academic and corporate resources. The
David Taylor Model Basin, for example, built in 1938–39 just outside Washington, D.C., tested warship designs by running scale
models through an artificial ocean created in a large tank. So precise were the measurements required that the tank's foundations
followed the curvature of the earth.[35] The original main testing
tank was twelve hundred feet long, but in 1945 an emergency
project to expand the facility more than doubled the length of the
tank and added new apparatus to work with high-speed torpedoes and flying boats. The basin continues to serve as the nation's
premier nautical test facility.

To test faster and larger ships and torpedoes,
the Navy more than doubled the length of the
main testing tank at the David Taylor Model
Basin, 1945. Courtesy David Taylor Model
Basin.

Postwar Conversion

In September 1945, the termination of hostilities brought significant dislocation to these aerospace, ordnance, and defense research facilities. In each case, however, initial cutbacks were followed by a period of continued government intervention. Government interest in creating a permanent defense-production establishment was reflected in the measures taken to maintain the industrial base created during the war. While many war plants were retained by the military, other government-financed defense plants not directly under military control continued to be used for national security purposes. Although certain plants were sold outright after the war, Congress designated over two hundred surplus plants as vital to national security in the event of a future conflict. These factories could be sold to private firms, but only on the condition that they be available for military production in an emergency. Approximately one hundred plants that did not find buyers were retained as a national industrial reserve.[36] These and other government-controlled plants formed the physical basis for the military-industrial cooperative that thrived during the cold war.

Growing markets in the postwar world allowed many corporations that produced consumer goods to reconvert and utilize their expanded wartime plants. Where government-owned facilities were intermingled with private facilities, as in the steel and auto industries, private companies were in a very strong bargaining position. Many government-funded facilities consisted of additions to existing factories. With no rival bidders for these "scrambled" plants, original owners could usually purchase them at a fraction of the original cost. Experienced in mass-production techniques, automobile manufacturers were able to quickly reconvert aircraft engine or tank factories into auto plants. The net effect of the government building program was to help established firms expand their facilities without large capital outlays.

In some instances, wartime facilities were of little use to anyone. For example, the massive shipbuilding industry created

Advertisement, 1947.

KAISER
SPECIAL

PRODUCT OF KAISER-FRAZER

TRAIL BLAZERS

IN

POSTWAR STYLING!

BUILT AT WILLOW RUN

ONLY ONCE in a decade comes a distinctly new trend in motor
car styling—a trend so clearly in accord with public preference that
it is only a matter of time until all manufacturers fall into line. The
KAISER SPECIAL and the FRAZER, America's first 1947 motor cars,
have set a trend in body styling, passenger comfort and driver
convenience that will be reflected in other automobiles in the years
to come. You can see *these* cars at your dealer's showroom now.

FRAZER
PRODUCT OF
GRAHAM-PAIGE

for the war had literally produced itself out of existence. A post-war glut of durable cargo vessels dictated that all but a few war-time shipbuilders would leave the business. The government considered certain industries so strategically important, however, that it created an artificial demand to ensure the continued operation of wartime plants. For example, to keep synthetic rubber factories running, Congress legislated a market for the product by requiring the use of synthetics in tires and other rubber products.

The enormous expansion of the aircraft industry created perhaps the most difficult postwar disposal problem. Aircraft assembly plants were generally vast single-story structures with open bays; their sheer size and high utility costs made them uneconomical to operate. By the end of 1945 only sixteen of sixty-six airframe plants were in use, and only five of twenty-three engine factories. As aircraft orders were canceled, most major manufacturers abandoned their branch plants and concentrated production in their prewar facilities, reversing the industry's wartime geographic spread. By the end of 1949, only one of the twenty large wartime plants built in the heartland was still in operation.

Where desirable plants existed, their wartime operators were often able to buy them from the government at fire-sale prices. For example, in 1946 Douglas Aircraft bought the Long Beach plant for $3.6 million, less than a third of its original cost.[37] Douglas hoped to cash in on what was expected to be a burgeoning market for civilian transports and personal planes. Nonmilitary orders never materialized on the scale predicted, however, and Douglas rented out parts of the Long Beach plant for the production of auto parts.

Some of the abandoned aircraft plants were taken over by other industries. For example, Henry Kaiser occupied the huge Willow Run bomber assembly plant to build his unsuccessful line of Kaiser Frazer autos. In attempts to keep their trained workers employed, the Consolidated Vultee plant near Los Angeles and the Beech Aircraft plant in Wichita turned to the production of aluminum houses that ultimately proved to be unmarketable. In Columbus, Ohio, the Lustron corporation leased a massive DPC-financed aircraft plant to build its unique enamel-coated steel homes.

For most wartime aircraft plants, however, the end of the war brought a period of enforced idleness. A few factories operated at partial capacity as the industry work force shrank to less than seven percent of peak wartime levels.[38] Like many wartime plants, the Tulsa bomber plant remained in government control, serving as a repair facility and warehouse.

The advent of global competition with the Soviet Union in the late 1940s and 1950s revitalized the partnership between the Pentagon and aerospace firms. Increased aircraft production during the Korean War was the catalyst that brought many defunct plants back into service.[39] To expand production, the industry relied heavily on government-owned standby plants, which accounted for over a quarter of total factory space in 1950.[40] The Korean conflict proved a boon to the giant aerospace firms, which quickly reoccupied some of their old World War II facilities. For example, the Tulsa bomber plant reopened, and Douglas Aircraft returned to build and modify a new generation of cargo planes and jet bombers.[41] Henry Kaiser gave up on autos and reconverted Willow Run to build Air Force transport planes, while jet fighters replaced the failed Lustron houses at North American Aviation's plant in Columbus, Ohio. As old branch plants sprang to life, aircraft factory space grew from sixty-three million square feet in 1950 to one hundred twenty-six million in 1953.[42] Thus, World War II–era structures continued to serve as a vital link between the government and the burgeoning aerospace industry.

The large and highly specialized ordnance industry presented an even greater challenge for postwar conversion. Many arsenals had been built at a particular location for purely strategic reasons, with little thought given to their postwar viability.[43] Not surprisingly, the armed forces retained many of these plants, en-

Model of proposed neighborhood of Dymaxion Wichita houses. © 1994 Allegra Fuller Snyder. Courtesy Buckminster Fuller Institute, Santa Barbara.

suring a significant postwar capacity for weapons production. For example, in 1956 the Army had over one hundred industrial facilities, including forty-six active GOCO factories and thirty-seven standby plants.[44] The wartime ordnance works were larger and more modern than the prewar arsenals, and they represented a new capability for sustained munitions production completely under military control. During the ensuing decades these factories cycled through various levels of production as American involvement in international conflicts flared up and died down. The Radford Arsenal, for example, made propellant charges for every rocket fired by U.S. forces in Korea and Vietnam.[45]

Though aircraft and munitions production facilities were cut back after the war, government-sponsored research programs

... the house America has been waiting for

expanded. Eager to perfect and exploit scientific breakthroughs that had helped win the war, the government retained exclusive jurisdiction over the scientific-industrial base created to develop the atomic bomb. The advent of nuclear weapons laid the groundwork for an ongoing program of directed scientific research to improve the bomb and to anticipate any nuclear breakthroughs by potential rivals. Government-owned laboratories at Los Alamos and other locations were managed by civilian contractors, further linking the scientific and academic communities.[46] Scientific endeavors at America's leading research universities often depended on military funding, ensuring government access to almost all high-technology research.

Advertisement, *Life*, April 19, 1948.

Joel Davidson

Permanent Preparedness

The World War II construction program was the most significant
and enduring legacy of America's home-front war effort, for the
buildings remain long after playing their role in history's most de-
structive conflict. Their existence helped ensure that the United
States would maintain a state of permanent postwar military
readiness. As international tensions rose and fell, these facilities
provided an ongoing impetus to defense spending and had a dramatic effect on the nation's physical and political landscape.

War construction transformed many of America's predominantly rural areas, especially in the Midwest and Southwest. Factories and the trained work forces they attracted shifted the
nation's political and economic balance away from traditional
eastern power centers. To the nation, these advanced facilities
and trained technicians represented a significant investment in
defense production capability, one that could not be re-created easily if allowed to deteriorate. As Federally sponsored labs devised
ever more sophisticated military technologies, the desire to replace outmoded defense items provided the rationale for continued production and employment. In turn, profits from defense
work allowed corporations to finance research and development,
producing concrete results that encouraged continued government investment. Federal ownership of a large part of this infrastructure gave the military increased independence from the
vagaries of national funding priorities, and at the same time facilitated military-corporate partnerships in weapons development
and production.

As the arms race continued and defense production stabi-
lized, the wartime infrastructure became the source of middle-
class prosperity for thousands of Americans. Permanent suburban developments grew where emergency war workers' camps
once stood; in Long Beach, for example, developers created the
planned community of Lakewood to provide housing for workers
from the revitalized Douglas plant. A small city of office buildings

grew up around the Pentagon as corporations established outposts for easier access to the officers who controlled military purse strings. Universities continued to upgrade their laboratories and hired top faculty in hopes of obtaining more government contracts, skewing an entire generation of high-technology research toward military applications.

In his farewell speech in 1960, Dwight Eisenhower, the war hero who went on to become the country's first postwar president, warned of the "conjunction of an immense military establishment and a large arms industry . . . new to the American experience. The total influence—economic, political, and even spiritual—is felt in every city, every state house, every office of the Federal Government." By the time Eisenhower left office, the aircraft, munitions, and scientific facilities built for the war were so embedded in the national economy that a disengagement from permanent war production was all but impossible. Even a President was powerless to undo this mutually supporting cartel, carrying as it did the patriotic stamp of approval. A permanent state of readiness was the price the nation paid for its survival and ascendancy to global preeminence, a price symbolized by buildings that were built for war alone.

Notes

1. In 1941 the Air Corps achieved quasi-independent status and was renamed the Army Air Forces, but it did not attain the status of an independent Air Force until after the war.

2. R. Elberton Smith, *The Army and Economic Mobilization,* United States Army in World War II (Washington, D.C.: Office of the Chief of Military History, United States Army, 1959), 498.

3. Donald M. Nelson, *Arsenal of Democracy: The Story of American War Production* (New York: Harcourt, Brace and Company, 1946), 213–217.

4. Gregory Hooks, *Forging the Military-Industrial Complex: World War II's Battle of the Potomac* (Urbana: University of Illinois Press, 1991), 127.

5. Gerald T. White, *Billions for Defense: Government Financing by the Defense Plant Corporation during World War II* (University, Ala.: University of Alabama Press, 1980), 10.

6. Smith, *The Army and Economic Mobilization,* 458–459. The tax breaks for new construction proved especially lucrative because they helped offset high wartime taxes during a period of increased productivity and profits.

7. The original design team included Lt. Col. Hugh J. Casey, Col. Leslie R. Groves, Col. Edmund H. Leavey, and George Bergstrom. Architect David Witmer directed the detailed design.

8. Alfred Goldberg, *The Pentagon: The First Fifty Years* (Washington, D.C.: Office of the Secretary of Defense, 1992), 22.

9. Irving B. Holley, *United States Army in World War II, Buying Aircraft: Material Procurement for the Army Air Forces* (Washington, D.C.: Office of the Chief of Military History, United States Army, 1964), 293.

10. Alfred Goldberg, "Equipment and Services," *Men and Planes,* vol. 6 of *The Army Air Forces in World War II,* ed. Wesley Craven and James L. Cate (Chicago: The University of Chicago Press, 1955), 278.

11. "McDonnell Douglas 50 Years in Long Beach," *Long Beach Business Journal* (1990): 28.

12. Donald Douglas, quoted in "Building Begins at Long Beach," *Douglas Airview* (November 1940): 7.

13. William G. Cunningham, *The Aircraft Industry: A Study in Industrial Location* (Los Angeles: Lorrin L. Morrison, 1951), 57. When the war began, Los Angeles and San Diego alone accounted for almost half of the nation's airframe production capacity.

14. Irving B. Holley, *United States Army in World War II*, 324.

15. Cunningham, *The Aircraft Industry,* 141.

Joel Davidson

16. "Assembly Plant for Four-Motor Bombers," *Architectural Forum* (February 1942): 98.

17. Lou R. Crandall, *The George A. Fuller Company: War and Peace, 1940–1947* (New York: George A. Fuller Company, 1947), 169–170.

18. Wesley W. Stout, *Great Engines and Great Planes* (Detroit: Chrysler Corporation, 1947), 45.

19. Nelson, *Arsenal of Democracy,* 237.

20. John B. Rae, *Climb to Greatness: The American Aircraft Industry, 1920–1960* (Cambridge: MIT Press, 1968), 153. This number increased from approximately thirteen thousand in 1940. The actual increase in output is even greater than the number of planes would suggest, because aircraft produced in 1944 were on the average much larger than those produced in 1940.

21. J. R. Charles and Sherman Mason, "Basic Magnesium—the Desert Giant," *Civil Engineering* (January 1945): 21.

22. White, *Billions for Defense,* 74.

23. Henry Kaiser, quoted in Albert P. Heiner, *Henry J. Kaiser: Western Colossus* (San Francisco: Halo Books, 1991), 175.

24. Bureau of Yards and Docks (compiled from their records), *Building the Navy's Bases in World War II: History of the Bureau of Yards and Docks and the Civil Engineer Corps, 1940–1946,* vol. 1 (Washington, D.C.: U.S. Government Printing Office, 1947), 248–249.

25. *Quarterly Reports to Congress, 1946–1949* (Washington, D.C.: War Assets Administration, 4th Quarter 1948), 13.

26. "The Southern California Cooperative Wind Tunnel," *Engineering and Science Monthly* (July 1945): 4–8. The tunnel featured a two-element electric motor that generated twelve thousand horsepower, driving tandem twelve-foot fans to create wind speeds of over seven hundred miles per hour.

Cadillac

Craftsmanship is still our stock in trade

The rhythmic roar of the P-38 tells more eloquently than words of the superb fighting qualities built into its two perfectly synchronized engines. Foremost of the American designed and built liquid-cooled aircraft engines is the Allison, which powers several of our top fighter craft and for which we at Cadillac produce vital precision assemblies.

It was natural that Cadillac should be entrusted with this war production assignment,

because for forty years Cadillac has exemplified the ultimate in craftsmanship and precision. The long-remembered Cadillac motto, "Craftsmanship a Creed—Accuracy a Law," is far from being an empty, meaningless phrase. It is, in fact, the very credo by which we live because it calls for the fullest exercise of our highest traditional skill.

Another assignment is the production of M-5 light tanks, for which the Cadillac automotive-

type V-8 engines were adapted. This se to keep the same Cadillac craftsmen o same production line on which they we in time of peace.

Thus, while serving the nation at war full-time basis, we are also maintaining efficient peak everything that the Ca name and crest represent in time of pe the peace which must ultimately be our

Michael Sorkin

War Is Swell

WHERE *Pride* IS A DIVIDEND!

It has been said, in song and in verse, that the best things in life are free.

And we must say that we side with this romantic conjecture in at least one small regard. For we know that the finest reward of Cadillac ownership costs you nothing.

We have reference, quite naturally, to that wonderful feeling of pride that comes inevitably to new owners of new Cadillacs. It is, in the truest sense of the word, a dividend for your wisdom in choosing the "car of cars."

Of course, when a motorist takes title to his Cadillac, he *expects* to find great pride in his new possession. But we doubt if ever he is fully prepared for the heart-lifting moments which await him behind the wheel.

There is, for instance, the unforgettable memory of his first journey home . . . and of the joyous welcome of family and friends.

There is his unending pride and joy in the car's great beauty and performance and mechanical perfection.

There is his deep-felt satisfaction at seeing his family surrounded with Cadillac's great comfort and safety and luxury.

And there is his keen awareness of membership in the world's most distinguished fraternity of new car owners.

Won't you come in soon and let us give you a demonstration "preview" of these remarkable "Cadillac dividends"?

We know you would find it the most enlightening experience of your motoring life— and, for our own part, it would be a pleasure to introduce you to the Standard of the World.

YOUR CADILLAC DEALER

Michael Sorkin

I was born after the war, a boomer. "My" war was Vietnam, which I experienced as a resistor. For me, World War II is history, pure mediation, and my primary visual source an engineer father who worked virtually all of his professional life at the Defense Department. I recall visits to his office on the Mall where I was entranced by the display of remarkably accurate model ships, a sight that still inspires my work. I remember the blue-bound copies of *Jane's All the World's Aircraft* and *Jane's Fighting Ships* that my father brought home every year with their mesmerizing photos, performance data, and elegant line drawings. And I remember childhood war games and fantasies, enacted either outdoors in roaming bands or indoors at the side of a paralyzed friend where the action consisted in narration, the dying of heroic deaths, he lying in his dystrophied bed, me in a chair alongside. I remember sitting at the back of my grade school class, drawing aircraft in my notebook, their bomb loads dropping to the bottom of the page.

The image of the war was ubiquitous then, and I approached it with both fascination and embarrassment. Because I was forbidden war toys by a liberal-minded mother, my consumption of the war took a covert turn, part of a larger family drama. War games were fought with the toy guns of neighbor children, my reading done in bookshops and libraries, *Sands of Iwo Jima* switched off at the sound of parental footfalls. Thus enjoined, the war and its images assumed the fascinations of the forbidden, an erotogenic turn. And not just the puerile phallomorphism of bombers and subs but florid irresistible death. Images of bodies dismembered and still were the unspoken object of the war research that absorbed so much of my childhood—of the childhoods of so many boys, turning the pages of old *Life* magazines for photographs of Marines mangled on Tarawa beach, of Chinese civilians with bodies blown naked by Japanese bombs at Nanking, of the corpses stacked at Birkenau.

Preceding pages:
Advertisement, *Fortune*, October 1943. Courtesy Cadillac Motor Car Division/General Motors Corp.

Advertisement, *Life*, August 23, 1954. Courtesy Cadillac Motor Car Division/General Motors Corp.

This furtive, varnished pleasure stimulated broad inquiry, and I amassed an astonishing breadth of knowledge. Even now, I can identify hundreds of aircraft, ships, tanks, guns, uniforms. I know the battles and the strategies, still experience the anxiety of a series of might-have-beens—had the cloud cover held above the Ardennes, had the bomb killed Hitler, had the radar signals been correctly interpreted at Pearl Harbor, had the U-boat buildup begun a year or two earlier, had the rail lines to the camps been bombed. The war was my first big body of knowledge, with its vast classifications of things, masses of narrative, and its endless style. Every schoolboy of my generation had a complex lexicon of favorite war machines based on a careful connoisseurship. For many of us, the war provided the grist for our first real systems of objects. However, unlike those other great taxonomic reveries of American boyhood, motorcars and athletes, the hobbying of war objects begged an ethics, some engagement with the question of why. Indeed, it is in the space defined by this gap between the consumability of these images and the lassitude of the constraints on their enjoyment that a characteristic American consciousness is constructed.

Simply put, the message America received in the forties and fifties was that the war had been beneficial, a war unlike other wars, the "good" war. For us, it had been so in many ways. Between 1939 and 1945, the GNP increased from $88 billion to $135 billion. Real compensation of industrial workers rose twenty-two percent. Net farm income doubled. Corporate profits had an after-tax growth of fifty-seven percent in 1943 alone. Average plant utilization went from forty hours a week to ninety hours. The number of skilled black workers doubled. The percentage of women in the work force grew dramatically. By the end of the war the United States was responsible for over fifty percent of the world's industrial production, including forty percent of its production of arms. The war rescued America from its economic and psychic depression, thrust us to the forefront of global power, established us as the dominant national culture of the twentieth century.

In *Wars I Have Seen,* Gertrude Stein describes the Second World War as a cultural equivalent of the "dark and dreadful days of adolescence," marking a moment of transition from the childhood of the nineteenth century to the adulthood of the twentieth. For Stein, the war represents modernity, a modernity that is situated in a condition of uncertainty, of strangeness. She sees the war as a kind of epistemological break, a juncture after which the certainties bred of positivistic, nineteenth-century science were ruptured, destabilized, throwing the idea of progress, with its secure relations of means and ends, into radical doubt. For Stein, too, the war marked the end of the possibilities for the realist text, its supersession by the more disjunctive relations of modernism. Bring on the hounds of hyperreality.

Indeed, can there be any doubt that those hydra-horrors, the Holocaust and the A-bomb, yielded a level and character of anxiety that was entirely fresh? Here the Clausewitzean means are attenuated beyond comprehension. Yet postwar America—birthplace of the Strangelovean theory of Mutually Assured Destruction—bankrupted itself precisely to enable this straining disjuncture between means and ends (freedom guaranteed by global Holocaust) to be resisted. Of course realism had to die. The language we were forced to use was so unreliable, so fundamentally mendacious, that such a literature was impossible.

My own adolescence was also marked by that ripest of postwar graphics, the encircled black on yellow trigram of the fallout shelter/radiation logo. It's a symbol that cuts two ways, a certification of its own impossibility, trying to mean opposites (radiation and safety from radiation) at once. The most readily available summer design jobs during my college days—a brilliant piece of co-opting make-work—were assisting in a nationwide fallout shelter survey, an invitation to read every building in America with the eyes of a paranoid.

Not that the feeling was strange to me; I'd been brought up on it. I remember—during the late-fifties mania—going to the familial backyard and beginning to dig. I was afraid, of course, horrified by the flood of images the media were whipping up in those days, but also angry, disappointed that my parents showed no interest in this latest consumer (it was hoped) durable, not keeping up with the Joneses, another sign that my parents were simply inattentive to the needs of the (post)nuclear family.

The fallout shelter was a malignant inversion of the historic modernist housing fantasy, the notion of a guaranteed *Existenzminimum* for every worker, a fantasy played out on the bright side of planning for the war in those sunny and cooperative communities that so aptly merge sensibility and purpose. Indeed, if one were to parse the descent of the interwar urban ideal, one stream leads from the planned communities of the war down to the enfeebled New Towns (such as Reston and Columbia) of the sixties and seventies. Another crests at Levittown, the egalitarian automobile suburb. And a third—the ultimate revenge of the windowless monad—leads to the shelter craze, the ultimate one-family home with its global hearth. The shift was very rapid. If the image of sheltering during the war was collective, of civilians huddled together in the London subways (as depicted, for example, in those remarkable Henry Moore sketches), the standard-issue equipment for the A-bomb shelter always included a rifle, to keep everyone else out.

Reporting on the trial of Adolf Eichmann in Jerusalem, Hannah Arendt remarked—indelible phrase—on the "banality of evil." In postwar America, our embrace of the evils of war as a national project resulted in a discourse that was not so much banal as bizarre. The happy techno-talk, the cults of euphemism, the very insistence on describing nuclear war in the antique terms of military tactics and strategy was not simply an instance of "generals always preparing to fight the last war" but of postmodernity itself. The postmodern environment is one in which old notions of

combination and sequence have broken down. Indeed, the fetishi-
zation of the implements of the Second World War is surely a nos-
talgia for the "conventional" in both senses, for preapocalyptic
means and for the immemorial master narratives of conflict.

The notion that the war was something to be looked back
on sanctified its artifacts. Such reverence for raw instrumentality
is very American. We romance handguns as "equalizers," confer-
ring a democratic aura on a thing, converting it to a right. The
six-gun, symbol of the frontier, allegedly enshrined in constitution-
ality, serves simultaneously as instrument of romance, self-
individuation, and citizen-power and of the manifest destiny of
the American imperium. In World War II, we had myriad good
and undeniable reasons for taking up the gun. But can the satis-
fied pursuit of national violence, however just, fail to expand the
envelope of individual propensity?

I've never before written expressly about the war, and—
not being a historian—I write about its effects on the territory of
my own interests, on architecture, urbanism, and design, on the
transformation of their contexts of possibility. I agree with Gertrude Stein that the war was a high-water mark of modernism,
one that enshrined its dominant construct—functionalism—as a
virtual national aesthetic. Functionalism, enamored of the "objec-
tivity" of industrial objects, argued for a theory of absolute ac-
countability, for the singular legibility of every aspect of the
artifacts under its view. Although functionalism was a theory of
pure purposiveness, its investment was always in means rather
than ends. This led to its characteristic myopia, its focus only on
the efficient elegance of the bomber's design, celebrating its capacity for maneuver and flight, ignoring its lethality, or rather,
translating it into pure allure.

Functionalism is an aesthetic of adolescence, sustainable
only because of the narrowness of its preoccupations, its immatu-
rity vis-à-vis any larger notion of consequences, whether in use or
in expression. In the postnuclear, postmodern, postwar climate,

this functional reading of objects—no longer undergirded by a national consensus about their meaning and purpose—unraveled. Forms were easily wrested from their original contexts and endlessly recombined, destabilizing original meanings with profuse substitutions and modifications. Emptied, the objects of war became mere insignia. For consumer culture, the result was an avalanche of metonomy, of things that looked like things. In the art world, functionalist efficiency devolved into minimalism, a last-gasp run on the proprietorship of meaning, an attempt to keep the faith with the idea of pure, unassailable expressiveness, by a deliberate evisceration of all scope for nuance, the optimism of pessimism.

But let's get down to cases.

P-38

One of the preferred aircraft in my adolescent war fantasies was the Lockheed P-38. Legendarily a "hot" fighter, it still commands the enthusiasm of buffs and collectors. In part, this is because of its functional pedigree: the P-38 was a fast, agile, technologically advanced aircraft, appreciated by its pilots. It was also extremely distinctive visually with twin engines and twin fuselages, its cockpit suspended between the two fuselage booms. P-38 was the aircraft that Frank Sinatra flew (and crashed) in *Von Ryan's Express,* an apt technical haberdashery for Old Blue Eyes, an American plane, big, throbbing, powerful.

As symbolic postwar object, though, the P-38 reentered the culture in transmuted form. The aircraft was the favorite of Harley Earl, the legendary General Motors styling chief and father of the automotive tail fin. The P-38 first crossed over in the 1948 Cadillac whose pubescent fin-buds were direct emulations of the rounded twin-tails of the P-38. That appropriation was already nostalgic—jets were flying by then—but Detroit quickly caught up with the jet age and then the rocket age via the styling medium, converting tragedy into farce in a familiar process.

For aircraft, form does follow function: visual differences enjoy a direct translation into differences in capability, performance, or mode of control. The automotive system—and the entire system of consumer machinery for which it sits at the apex—flattens the legibility of such readings by surrounding them with a set of signifiers that sit at greater and greater distance from their practical points of origin. The tail fins of the Caddy—growing yearly topsy-like larger—may have originated in the memory of the control surfaces of one of the machines that contributed to the winning of the war, but in their descent into the rococo stylings of the early sixties their meaning became ever more purely engaged with the signification of mere, sheer excess. We simply believed that the cycle of prosperity would never cease.

Eisenhower

It is no coincidence that the election of Dwight Eisenhower to the American presidency coincided with the germination of the tail fin. The human and material instrumentalities of victory in a war regarded with great positive feeling by Americans were thus doubly celebrated. The reassuring Eisenhower, architect of victory and by imputation of the great prosperity it engendered, was a logical choice to continue and expand those very values.

In his way, Eisenhower was also an avatar of fashion. As general, he was known for the short "Eisenhower jacket" that was his preferred uniform. This outfit signified a senior staff officer dressed with an attitude both sufficiently casual to evoke a disdain for rigid hierarchy and sufficiently practical to take the field (all those photos of Ike getting out of the jeep driven by Kay Summersby, another unspoken subtext). In studied contrast to the buffoonery of the uniforms of Goering and the Germans, the anachronistic cutaways and toppers of the Japanese government, or the jackboots and swords of its generalship, Eisenhower, Patton—even the aviator-shaded MacArthur—conveyed the image of men at work, differing in appearance only in degree from workers on the factory floor—or ordinary soldiers.

In his postwar, presidential incarnation, Eisenhower continued to set the tone. Here, a double image prevails. The first is the Brooks Brothers, narrow-lapelled haberdashery of the organization man. The simple suits of the "conformist" society of the fifties offer up a mufti analogue to the G.I. drag, drab and regimented but with an acute slippage of purpose. Madison Avenue, after all, was the emblematic locus of fifties employment. For the consumer leviathan, advertising was the extension of war by other means. The sacrifice of war rotated around the axis of prosperity to become the leisure of peace.

Which brings us to the second classic postwar Eisenhowerian image: the golfer. Like some invert Cincinnatus, Ike forsook carbine for niblick, launching his spheroid missiles toward the halcyon green of American happiness. This image of Eisenhower offered copious sanction for a new sort of national enterprise, the conversion of the ethics of work and struggle into the project of recreation and leisure time. Ike, after all, was carpingly accused of being a president whose mind was too much on his golf game. Yet in this he displayed a remarkable prescience about the real nature of postwar America, about the true quality of private time in an era of abundance. What, after all, were we to do with our prosperity, with the fruits of our victory, if not enjoy them?

But Ike was no mindless duffer. He recognized not simply the product of war but the means of its achievement. In what was possibly the most important cultural observation to be made by an American President, Eisenhower left office with a warning. The "conjunction of an immense military establishment and a large arms industry is new to the American experience," Ike cautioned. And he continued, "We must not fail to comprehend its grave implications. . . . In the councils of government, we must guard against the acquisition of unwarranted influence, whether sought or unsought, by the military-industrial complex. The potential for the disastrous rise of misplaced power exists and will persist." No clearer statement of the dangerous basis of our war-won prosperity was ever uttered.

The Interstates

If there is a single physical legacy of the Eisenhower era, it is the enormous national highway system initiated during his presidency, forty-one thousand miles at completion, joining every joinable state. Indeed, the largest "thing" bequeathed to the nation by the war was the interstate system, easily the biggest single artifact ever built, ever imagined. The Hitlerian antecedent (". . . but he did build the autobahn") is not irrelevant. The Nazi road system responded to two imperatives: the stitching together of the nation and the creation of a transport infrastructure for the movement of armies. Our system—enabled by legislation calling for a National System of Interstate and Defense Highways—did the same. The war had begged the question of the purposive coordination of the entire nation, and it was in the physical movement of people and goods that this integration found its highest expression.

The interstates, however, were built after the fact of the war. They expedited not the movement of war material but the dissemination of a single form of national prosperity. The interstates were the venous system that infused a vast network of cultural homogeneity, the consumer version of the univalent apparatus of war. At every interchange rose an identical McDonald's, Roy Rogers, Holiday Inn, Mobil station, Seven-Eleven. Down the exit ramp were the FHA-stimulated suburbs, the shopping centers, and the boomer schools. On the roadway itself, tens of millions of new cars tooled across the nation, finned like fighters. As Charles Wilson, Ike's Secretary of Defense, famously remarked, "What was good for General Motors was good for the country." The interstates brought the happy ethos—victory and prosperity through the mass production of mobile machines—of the war back home.

In many ways, the interstate system and its effects represent the high-water mark of American federalism. Funded at ninety percent, they were lusted at by the states, eager not simply for the almost free money but for inclusion in the new American system of prosperity. Their construction also coincided with that other great war-stimulated effort at integration: the extension of civil rights of black Americans. It was Eisenhower who called out the troops to defend the desegregation of the schools of Little Rock. Ike was clearly fixed on a vision of the spreading good.

Of course, there was a down side. What was good for General Motors was not uniformly good for the country, and the concrete ties that bound could also destroy. The interstates foundered precisely where they encountered the complexities of the urban, where form and the deployments of class were not the sparse and regular monotone of rural and suburban America. Spilling the clot of cars into spaces that could not accommodate them, bulldozing neighborhoods for efficient passage through them, the highway program became a kind of carpet bombing, warring on hapless civilians who simply happened to find themselves in the way of some higher aspiration to order and efficiency.

Opened Cities

In many American cities today buildings have their addresses painted in enormous numerals on their roofs. This is intended to increase the efficiency of aerial surveillance by the police, to make the order of the city more visible. The war recast the very idea of the landscape. Rendered surveillable by the universal possibility of overflight, the city was suddenly exposed, vulnerable not simply to attack but to new modes of comprehension. Cities were reunderstood from the point of view of the bomber. World War II, after all, was the first great "war of the cities." Even the insane carnage of the First World War had been largely a phenomenon of the battlefield. Total war—directed against civilian populations with the same vigor as against armies—was the strategic contribution of the Second World War.

An immediate effect of this visibility was the proliferation of strategies of camouflage. On the vast roofs of western aircraft factories mock landscapes were constructed, complete with roads, houses, and foliage. To frustrate the bombers, urban installations were made to disappear, suburbanized. Although the United States was never under serious threat of aerial attack, the fear remained and gave the efforts at camouflage their compelling logic. The logic of camouflage also extended to a logic of dispersal. Great wartime facilities were often located outside of cities—at Oak Ridge, Hanford, Los Alamos in the case of the atomic program—both to protect them from attack and to bring the entire American landscape within the orderly regimen of the war effort.

The scopic mentality of the bomber system became that of the planner as well. No need to rehearse the tribulations of urban renewal, the careful wantonness with which "dangerous" parts of towns were measured and destroyed, made safe for another vision, for the modernist rationalities of cars and commerce. The perishability of the metropolis was reseen in light of the experience of war, both physically and conceptually. The blazing cities of Europe and Asia and the dissipated motor archipelago of America both gave the project of postwar urbanism a kind of confidence.

The war made the world safe for Disneyland. For the first time in history, a global vision of cities had truly emerged. Habituated to single comprehension of the world by the speed and scope of the war, to the possibility for truly enormous cycles of destruction and reconstruction, to the loosing of the project of urbanism from its basis in traditional centers, and to the logics of camouflage and re-representation, the plannerly imagination was free for unprecedented acts of recombination and reinvention. The complex against which Eisenhower cautioned in his valedictory address was, after all, multinational, and—at the apex of the American Century—it was only logical that an acquisitive, commercial, quickly depreciated, image-saturated urbanism should flourish.

Disneyland (opened in 1955, now physically incarnate on three continents, ubiquitous on TV) is both the leading fact and the dominant metaphor for this transformation. Its creative geographical practices—which allow the free juxtaposition of the elements within the park as well as the free juxtaposition of the parks within host cultures—participate in the great war-bred spatial departicularization of the postmodern city. But Disney finds its resonance not simply in the familiar mendacities of its counterfeit architecture but in its project of pure consumption, its vision of the city as a factory for leisure. In this, it perfectly parallels Ike's own passage from the trenches to the links, afflicted equally by the narrow dimensions of its recast purpose.

Hollin Hills

I grew up in a fantasy of a suburb. Hollin Hills was begun in the late 1940s and constructed in two major phases through the early 1970s. The project of developer Robert Davenport and architect Charles M. Goodman with a landscape scheme by Barney Voight, it stood out among its Fairfax County, Virginia, kith for the candor of its modernity. Indeed, it was legendarily different from the colonialoid carpet of its surroundings. After tooling through red-brick Alexandria in both its authentic and ersatz incarnations (the Georgian Gulf station . . . the Federalesque dry cleaner) and passing a legion of more typical suburban constructions, the split-levels and mini-Taras of the standard-issue American dream, one arrived at an unexpected Arden of the new. Glass walled and crisply lined, the houses were of the same materials—wood and brick—as the neighboring burbs but were radically unlike them in expression.

Although the basic plan types were limited, each house was inflected cosmetically or in configuration to produce a satisfyingly individual character. Variations in cladding and finish, orientation, elevation, roof type (flat, pitched, or "butterfly"), layout, and detail made up a brilliant and satisfying system of customization and variety. This sense of expression and elaboration within a consistent modern idiom was extended over the years by an amazing proliferation of additions (each vetted by a community architectural board) that served to house the growing families and prosperity of residents who thought themselves virtual citizens of the place.

Hollin Hills's modernity strongly shaped the character of its inhabitants. First settled by a cadre of civil servants and others drawn to Washington by the New Deal and the war, its politics were strongly liberal from the outset, reinforced by an infusion of New Frontierspersons after the Kennedy election. In this it stood out strongly from its surroundings—still in the Jim Crow throes—as a tiny demographic blip. In the early days the subdivision's liberalism imparted a fine sense of reciprocal beleaguerment and hostility: the roads were notoriously unplowed after snowstorms, icy for days after the surrounding streets were running free. Residents felt dramatically unrepresented at all levels of government. Adlai Stevenson was surely the post-Rooseveltian politician who most succinctly embodied the (frustrated) political dreams of Hollin Hillers.

In many ways, Hollin Hills was the postwar variation and resting place of the territorial imagination of the New Deal and the war, the extension of Radburn or Greenbelt by other means, transformed by a new postwar attitude toward collectivity and prosperity. Hollin Hills was the new town as suburb. It retained the organic site planning, the reverence for landscape, and the collective green spaces of the Greenbelt towns but replaced their apartment and attached architectural typologies with the single-family house. The collective activities of the new town were (in a familiar paring) reduced to recreation—community open spaces, swimming pool, and tennis courts. An interesting side debate about the mutual definition of community character occurred in the early sixties when a proposal was floated to augment the sports facilities with a squash court. The initiative was defeated because squash was considered to be too "elitist" a game. Similarly, efforts to install curbs, sidewalks, and streetlights were consistently rejected as inimical to the arcadian character of the community.

Although the hyperdevelopment of Fairfax County has now flattened the demographic anomaly of Hollin Hills, it strongly retains the character of its architectural and planning intentions. One might argue that mass suburbanization is the result of the war, of the simple calculus of prosperity plus automobilization plus the G.I. loan, but Hollin Hills is clearly a special case. If the war redeemed functionalism as the national mode of design, Hollin Hills retained the purity of this intention and carried on the collective fantasy of both prewar new-town planning and wartime collective housing. Like the experience of the Greenbelt towns, it thrived on its sense of experimental anomaly.

Mushroom Cloud

Observing the first blast at Alamogordo, Oppenheimer spake, following Shiva, "I am become death, destroyer of worlds." For the first time, global annihilation had a form: the mushroom cloud was death's placenta. My own first memories of the nuclear age are somewhat more benign, via Walt Disney's production "Our Friend the Atom," which I consumed both on television and in the tie-in book. The atom was civilianized by being reduced to its most minute, benign, and stable form. Its principal signifier in the early postwar era was the nucleus with its happy surrounding of elliptical orbits, the Trinity Site of proton, neutron, and electron.

The atom's invisibility suggested exactly that it could not hurt you. Unlike microbes—which (in contrast to the abundantly foregrounded images of the atom) were never presented as having any discernible form—the atom was made to seem harmless by its very representability. The image of the atom thus proliferated as a symbol of science and progress, visible everywhere from home appliance logos to drive-in restaurant marquees. The decor of the fifties is all bursts and orbits, nuclei and energetic spheres. The atom was fully relegated to the class of things, isolated from life. The most familiar depictions of the bomb's effects were strictly taken from the cosmos of objects, images of the old warships sunk at Bikini, of the test houses blown apart at the desert site. Of the bomb's effects on humans the image was of troops watching the blast through sunglasses or simply turning away. We were spared the sight of the hapless livestock vaporized in New Mexico or of the Hiroshima maidens. The paranoia (and the cancers) came a little later.

That the atom so readily became a chipper symbol of American modernity in the immediate aftermath of its use as the greatest instrument of mass death in human history speaks volumes about the relationship of the accomplishments of war to the formal culture of peace. The bomb is simply the extreme case of the necessary modifications. Of course, part of the agenda behind all of this was not just retrospective redemption but foundation-laying for the prodigies of military expenditure to come and for the great, failed buildup of the atomic power industry. But beyond that, the representations of the atomic, its breakneck passage into commercial folklore, describe a crucial mechanism of American understanding of the war: nothing bad could come of something so good.

Manzanar

War made America a monoculture. It encouraged us to "put aside our differences" in order to unite in the common purpose of victory. This unity had many happy consequences, including widespread prosperity, increased racial integration, and an opening of the work force to women. It also accelerated a pervasive discourse of visuality, a corporate identity for the nation, a commingling of the notions of sacrifice, virtue, and purpose. The message was not simply that we were fighting in defense of our values but that the order and means by which we defended them were our values.

The war was—inter alia—a remarkable feat of urbanization, an era of instant cities. From military camps to huge projects for armaments workers, millions were newly housed in the most unprecedented construction surge in the nation's history. At one level, this effort was a titanic success. Quantitatively, the sheer orderly enclosure of space, the provision of infrastructure, the organization of production was peerless. At another level, though, this was qualitatively an urbanism of total failure, a setup for failures to come.

These new cities were company towns raised to the nth power. Consecrated to a single function—housing troops, aircraft or atomic workers—they were conceived and valued in terms of the efficiency of their hermetic arrangements. Even those towns most generally singled out for praise—Oak Ridge, Linda Vista, etc.—are striking not for any special contribution to the richness of urban social life but rather for their relative sensitivity to the landscape, for their confirmation of the principles of the Garden City/Greenbelt movement, or for their prototypical suburban-style shopping centers.

The most extreme examples of these wartime single-purpose towns were to be found in America's own gulag, the internment camps into which Americans of Japanese origins were forced beginning in 1942. Here, in effect, was the dark side of Radburn and Greenbelt, preemptive prisons for a part of our citizenship that while having committed no crime was nonetheless viewed—for racial reasons—as harboring such a propensity. Modeled on military camps, these towns included none of the Garden City or architectural niceties of the better-designed war worker communities that were built concurrently with them. Like military camps and company towns, the internment camps were essays in the limits of architecture, the edges of elaboration and comfort necessary to ensure the disciplined and self-conscious behavior of their inhabitants.

The Janus of the monofunctional, monocultural settlement pervades the dominant settlement types of the postwar

American landscape. The suburbs—company towns for the project of consumption—owe their failures exactly to their incompleteness, to the invisibility of the workplaces necessary to sustain them. The animating fantasy of the suburbs is a rising and universal prosperity to which they, however, make no contribution, save as reward. In their own way, the suburbs require a discipline as sacrificial and exacting as any factory town, hemmed by a set of possibilities that forces the production of variety entirely into the domestic sphere.

The other great postwar phenomenon of American urbanism is the housing project of "urban renewal." The standard understanding surely overemphasizes the role of architectural urbanistic modernism in propagating the ethos that led to the construction of the drear archipelago of American public housing. To be sure, modernism, with its Cartesian, Enlightenment roots, was predicated on the notion of a universal subject, a new Everyman, prepared to sacrifice his or her individuality to the melting pot of the new culture of rationality. The war with its ideas of common purpose, universal service, and uniform(ed) expression, was the high-water mark of an optimistic vision for possibilities of such obliteration of difference as a strategy for happiness.

Manzanar, a Japanese internment camp in California, represents the means for the oppressive imposition of a virtuously rationalized sameness. The imprisonment of the Japanese "aliens" was but a modest experiment in comparison with the vast undertaking that was to transform so much of the American "inner city" after the war. The new subject was not Japanese Americans, of course, but African Americans. The war had provided the rationale for the monofunctional order of the spaces of production and culture. Such organization was both necessary and beneficial because the aims of warring were so self-evidently good. So too, in general, were the results: America was restored both to prosperity and to world leadership. The result was a sanctification of the forms that had produced the victory. On the one hand this led to the proliferation of consumer machinery and on the other to a rampantly univalent view of the environment. Unfortunately, the means of waging war, the kinds of social organization inspired by emergency, proved to be an equally adept means of waging a kind of internal warfare, of subjugating an internal population that was the object of both fear and revulsion. The argument for Manzanar—so easily accepted at the time—was brought under the banner of therapy and optimism to every city in America.

John Wayne

Among the premier media spectacles of the 1993–94 season were the twin trials of Lorena and John Wayne Bobbitt in Manassas, Virginia. As you may recall, both Bobbitts were acquitted, she of assault (the charge was cutting off her husband's penis) and he of rape. Although the spectacle was global, the trials took place in a town that was itself the object of controversy as the proposed site for a new Disneyland. That project also faced great trials: instead of the usual deployment of Tomorrowland, Fantasyland, Frontierland, etc., the new theme park was to be based on the re-creation of scenes from American history, including the battles of Bull Run, themselves fought nearby. As with any act of mediation, both struggles were over what was to be believed, what versions were to be included and which excluded. As the media produced show trials for the Bobbitts, so Disney proposed to convert history into show.

The trials mesmerized the world for their mythic—almost Greek—character, dominating both local and global media for weeks. They especially resonated as the desperate rising of a woman against a historic routine of domination, against a familiar imperial ordering of the world. The names (Bobbitt equals Babbitt plus the Hobbit?) were crucial and inescapable and served to enlarge and mediate the event. The emasculation of a former Marine named John Wayne by his Latin American wife thus also marked a cutoff of an axis of penetration of the image of World War II into American life. As Disney's effort to make Civil War carnage into an afternoon's fun was an inevitable aura-sapper, so Bobbitt's bad behavior (like that of his nominal brother John Wayne Gacy) only rewrote his make-believe war hero eponym as a brute.

America exited World War II with a sense of exhilaration. As a child, I experienced this in the countless war films that were a staple of Hollywood production until the endless, rivening folly of Vietnam made the bloodless optimism of these films impossible to sustain. No figure better embodied the blithe one-dimensionality of this perspective than John Wayne. In role after role, he portrayed the laconic heroism of America, fighting and cosmetically dying for a purpose that was simply beyond disputing, continuous with the democratic project of America itself. Emblematically, Wayne's *The Green Berets,* a final attempt to make a boosterish World War II–style film on the subject of Vietnam, marked the last gasp of the genre.

Wayne's minimalist politics found their way into the actual corridors of power in the person of Ronald Reagan. Reagan was the end of the line for the conversion of the war into an empty aspect of the national fantasy, the complete adolescent's version of the war-made policy. As an actor, Reagan had sat the war out in Hollywood, making films, parading around town in an impressive uniform. Although he lived through it, Reagan had—in a sanctioned version—the same relationship to the war that I had as a boy, rat-a-tat-tatting with a pretend machine gun, consumed with hardware, with the sheer weight of gadgetry, with the astounding adventures of secret weapons and international intrigues.

Indeed, the centerpiece of the Reagan presidency was his promotion of that incredible fantasy of cinema bellicosity: Star Wars. This program to spend our way to ultimate security was aptly named: Steven Spielberg's films recuperate the Waynesque war movie via genre bending. Those aliens marked for annihilation by their storm-trooper-style headgear collaborate in a project to reduce warfare to a matter of style and decor, to further inscribe the experience of the war into the realm of boyish play-acting and the sphere of the cartoon. With Star Wars, Reagan refined the postwar *propter war* fallacy to the ultimate degree: he completely identified prosperity with warfare. This was the delusion of Reaganomics, the supply-siders' inability to distinguish between spending and prosperity with the result that we simply waged economic warfare on ourselves in a potlatch of mutually assured bankruptcy.

As real memories of the war fade, its artifacts become more and more important, unattached mnemonics awaiting the valence of culture. The P-38 becomes the '48 Caddy becomes the Millenium Falcon becomes. . . . John Wayne becomes John Wayne Gacy becomes John Wayne Bobbitt becomes. . . . With each successive iteration, meaning is both lost and replaced and we more and more pass into the Disneyland of distorted recall. Fifty years after its end, the war's effects are everywhere, just less and less visible as they dissolve with a hiss and a rush into the memory of the nation.

Selected Bibliography

Prepared by Heather Burnham

Abbott, Carl. *The New Urban America: Growth and Politics in Sunbelt Cities.* Chapel Hill: The University of North Carolina Press, 1981.

Abenheim, Donald. "Never a Shot Fired in Anger, the Coastal Defenses of San Francisco." *Military Collector and Historian,* no. 3. (1976).

Ackerman, Frederick L. "Shelter to Speed War Work." *Architectural Record* (June 1942).

"Aircraft Engine Assembly Plant: Albert Kahn Associated Architects and Engineers, Inc." *Pencil Points* (March 1944).

"Aircraft Plant Has 150-ft. Timber Trusses." *Engineering News-Record* (October 1943).

"Airports." *Architectural Record* (July 1943).

"Albert Kahn—Defense Builder." *Architect and Engineer* (February 1942).

"Albert Kahn, Architect—A Tribute." *Architectural Record* (January 1943).

Allison, David K., Ben G. Keppel, and C. Elizabeth Nowicke. *D. W. Taylor.* Washington, D.C.: Government Printing Office, n.d.

"Aluminum City Terrace Housing." *Architectural Forum* (July 1944).

"Aluminum Goes to War." *Popular Mechanics* (January 1943).

Amirikian, Arsham. "Navy Develops All-Timber Blimp Hangar, Part 1. Unprecendented Design Problems Encountered." *Civil Engineering* (October 1943).

Amirikian, Arsham. "Navy Develops All-Timber Blimp Hangar, Part 2. Construction Procedure." *Civil Engineering* (November 1943).

Anderson, Karen. *Wartime Women: Sex Roles, Family Relations and the Status of Women during World War II.* Westport, Conn.: Greenwood Press, 1981.

"Annual Review and Forecast Section: War's Impact on Techniques." *Textile World* (February 1943).

"Architects and Defense." *Pencil Points* 22 (October 1941).

"Architecture for War Production—A Military Aircraft Plant in the East." *Architectural Record* (June 1942).

"Architecture for War Production—An Aircraft Parts Plant in the Midwest." *Architectural Record* (June 1942).

Armstrong, Ellis L., ed. *History of Public Works in the United States—1776–1976*. Chicago: American Public Works Association, 1976.

"Army and Navy Try Out 'Demountable' Houses." *American Builder and Building Age* (January 1941).

"Army Engineers Practice for War." *Popular Mechanics* (May 1941).

Augur, Tracy B. "Planning Principles Apply in Wartime. Planning the Postwar Community." *Architectural Record* (January 1943).

Bailey, Kristin Szylvian. "The Federal Government and the Cooperative Housing Movement, 1917–1955." Ph.D. diss., Carnegie Mellon University, 1988.

Barnes, Andrea M. "An Archival and Photographic Study of World War II Temporary Wooden Buildings, For Carson Military Reservation, Colorado." HABS Report, Centennial Archeology, Inc., April 1991.

Barnes, Andrea M. "Documentation and National Register Assessment of the Old Hospital Complex and Red Creek Ranch, Fort Carson Military Reservation, El Paso County, Colorado." HABS Report, Centennial Archeology, Inc., April 1992.

Bauer, Catherine. "Cities in Flux." *American Scholar* (1943–44).

Bauer, Catherine. "Wartime Housing in Defense Areas." *Architect and Engineer* (October 1942).

Bauer, David F. "Prefabricated Barracks for the Army." *Civil Engineering* (September 1945).

Berge, Wendell. *Economic Freedom for the West.* Lincoln: University of Nebraska Press, 1946.

"Better Building for Industry." *Architectural Record* (April 1943).

"Better Homes—More Ships." *Ameican Builder and Building Age* (April 1943).

"Big Berthas of the Coast Artillery." *Popular Mechanics* (December 1941).

"Big Defense Program Stimulates All Types of Hawaiian Home Building." *American Builder and Building Age* (March 1941).

Blakely, Jeffrey A., and John D. Nortrip. "World War II Structures at Fort Chaffee, Arkansas." HABS Report, Archeological Assessments, Inc., March 1991.

Blandford, John B., Jr. "NHA's War Housing Policy." *American Builder and Building Age* (April 1943).

Blum, John Morton. *V Was for Victory: Politics and American Culture during World War II*. New York: Harcourt Brace Jovanovich, 1976.

Bober, W. C. "The Home Building Wave of the Future." *American Builder and Building Age* (January 1943).

Boeing Company. *Pedigree of Champions: Boeing since 1916,* 4th ed. Seattle: Boeing Co., 1977.

Bogner, W. F. "Postwar House: Direction for Progress in House Building Techniques." *Architectural Record* (December 1944).

Bouman, Mark J., David Broderherson, Robert Bruegmann, Dennis P. Doordan, Neil Harris, Victor Margolin, Ross Miller, Deborah Fulton Rau, Sidney K. Robinson, Pauline Sagila, Franz Schulze, R. Stephen Sennott, Stanley Tigerman, Carol Willis, Wim de Wit, and John Zukowsky. *Chicago Architecture and Design 1923–1993: Reconfiguration of an American Metropolis*. Chicago: The Art Institute of Chicago, 1993.

Breihan, John R. "Between Munich and Pearl Harbor: The Glenn L. Martin Aircraft Company Gears Up for War, 1938–1941." *Maryland Historical Magazine* 88 (Winter 1993).

Brinkley, David. *Washington Goes to War*. New York: Alfred A. Knopf, 1988.

Brubaker, Stanley. "The Impact of Federal Government Activities on California's Economic Growth, 1930–1956." Ph.D. diss., University of California, 1959.

Bruce, Alfred, and Harold Sandbank. "Prefabrication," parts 1–6. *Architectural Forum* (July–December 1943).

"Builders Demand War Housing Action." *American Builder and Building Age* (February 1943).

"Builders Rush Defense Housing to Meet Growing Shortage." *American Builder and Building Age* (August 1941).

"Builder's Standby; Wider Use of Concrete Block." *Business Week* (June 1, 1946).

"Building Blocks for a New World." *Popular Mechanics* (May 1944).

"Building for Defense . . . A Propeller Plant in 68 Days." *Architectural Forum* (May 1941).

"Building for Defense . . . Packard's Detroit Plant." *Architectural Forum* (December 1941).

"Building for Defense . . . Seven Industrial Plants." *Architectural Forum* (August 1941).

"Building Types Study No. 128." *Architectural Record* (August 1947).

"Building Types: Wartime Construction of Factory Buildings; Reference Studies in Design and Planning," *Architectural Record* (December 1942).

Burns, Fritz B. "We're the Suicide Troops of the War Building Industry." *American Builder and Building Age* (December 1942).

Bush, Vannevar. *Science, the Endless Frontier.* New York: Arno Press, reprint, 1980.

Business Executives' Research Committee. *Impact of World War II Subcontracting by the Boeing Airplane Company upon Pacific Northwest Manufacturing.* Seattle: Washington State University, Bureau of Business Research, 1955.

"Cabrillo Homes Community Building: Community Facilities for War Housing, Long Beach, California." *Pencil Points* (February 1944).

"Call for Designs; War Housing." *Architectural Forum* (May 1942).

"Camp Chemical, the City Built from Scratch." *Dow Diamond* (September 1942).

"Canal and Terrace to Be Demolished." *Richmond Independent,* August 11, 1952.

Carmel, Kate, Martin Eidelberg, Marilyn B. Fish, David A. Hanks, Frederica Todd Harlow, Christine W. Laidlaw, R. Craig Miller, Lenore Newman, Marc O. Rabun, Gregory Saliola, Penny Sparke, Jennifer Toher Teulie, Christa C. Mayer Thurman, Christopher Wilk, Toni Lesser Wolf, and Alice Zrebiec. *Design 1935–1965: What Modern Was.* New York: Harry N. Abrams, Inc., 1991.

Carr, Lowell, J., and James E. Stermer. *Willow Run: A Study of Industri- alization and Cultural Inadequacy.* New York: Harper and Brothers, 1952.

Carter, Craig. "An Interview with Margaret Hottle, 1911–   ." San Diego: San Diego Historical Society Oral History Program, May 18, 1988.

Castillo, Edmund L. *The Seabees of World War II.* New York: Random House, 1963.

Castleman, Riva, ed. *Art of the Forties.* New York: The Museum of Mod- ern Art, 1991.

Charles, J. R. "Basic Magnesium—the Desert Giant 1. The Development of the Vast Project." *Civil Engineering* (January 1945).

Chase, David. "Quonset Point National Register of Historic Places Nomi- nation Form." Manuscript, Providence, R. I., 1974.

Childs, John W. "Emergency Bridge Superstructures." *American High- ways* 21, no. 4 (January 1942).

"City Planning: Battle of the Approaches." *Fortune* (November 1943).

Clark, Robert. "Coast Defenses of Hawaii." *Periodical of the Council on Abandoned Military Posts,* no. 16 (Summer 1973).

Clark, Robert J., David DeLong, Martin Eidelberg, J. David Farmer, John Gerard, Neil Harris, Joan Marter, R. Craig Miller, Mary Riordan, Roy Slade, Davira S. Taragin, and Christa C. Mayer Thurman. *Design in America: The Cranbrook Vision, 1925–1950.* New York: Harry N. Abrams, Inc., 1983.

Clary, David A. *Fortress America: The Corps of Engineers, Hampton Roads, and U.S. Coastal Defense.* Charlottesville: University Press of Vir- ginia, 1990.

Clawson, Marion. *New Deal Planning: The National Resources Planning Board.* Baltimore: Johns Hopkins University Press, 1981.

Clive, Alan. *State of War: Michigan in World War II.* Ann Arbor: Univer- sity of Michigan Press, 1979.

Coll, Blanche D. *United States Army in World War II, the Corps of Engi- neers: Troops and Equipment.* Washington, D.C.: Office of the Chief of Mili- tary History, United States Army, 1958.

Collison, Thomas. *Flying Fortress: The Story of Boeing.* New York: C. Scribner's Sons, 1943.

"Concrete Has What It Takes for War Construction." *New Pencil Points* (June 1943).

"Congress and the FHA." *American Builder and Building Age* (April 1943).

"Construction Outlook." *Architectural Record* (January 1945).

"Construction Outlook for 1942." *Architectural Record* (December 1941).

"Construction Potentials: Postwar Prospects and Problems, a Basis for Action." *Architectural Record* insert (December 1943).

Consumers Union. *I'll Buy That!: 50 Small Wonders and Big Deals That Revolutionized the Lives of Consumers.* Mount Vernon, N.Y.: Consumers Union, 1986.

"Contract for Constructing 5,000 Demountable Houses Awarded, Harris Announces." *Norfolk Virginian Pilot,* January 28, 1942.

Cookingham, L. P. "The Effect of the War upon Cities." *Planning,* Chicago (1943).

Corbett, H. W. "New Building Technique May Be a Solution for Post-War Industry." *Architectural Record* (December 1941).

Cortwright, Frank W. "Masonry for War Housing." *American Builder and Building Age* (December 1942).

Craig, Lois A. *The Federal Presence—Architecture, Politics, and National Design.* Cambridge, Mass.: The MIT Press.

Crandall, Lou R. *The George A. Fuller Company: War and Peace, 1940–1947.* New York: The George A. Fuller Company, 1947.

Cummings, Betty H., and Milt Bona, eds. *Housing in War and Peace.* Vancouver, Wash.: Housing Authority of the City of Vancouver, 1972.

"Curtiss-Wright Aircraft Plant, Columbus, Ohio." *Architectural Record* (November 1944).

Daniels, Douglas Henry. *Pioneer Urbanites: A Social and Cultural History of Black San Francisco.* Philadelphia: Temple University Press, 1980.

"Fast Construction for Fast Production—Aircraft Engine Plant." *Architectural Record* (February 1945).

Faure, A. M. "Post-War Planning as a Joint City-County Project." *American City* (October 1944).

"Federal Housing and World War II." *The Journal of Land and Public Utility Economics* (March 1944).

Feiss, Carl. "How Cities Are Preparing for the Post-War Era." *Planning*, Chicago (1944).

Ferry, W. Hawkins. *The Legacy of Albert Kahn,* 1970. Reprint, Detroit: Wayne State University Press, 1987.

Findlay, A. C. "Postwar Capacity and Characteristics of the Construction Industry." *Monthly Labor Review* (May 1944).

Fine, Lenore, Jesse A. Remington, and Maurice Mattoff, eds. *The United States Army in World War II—The Corps of Engineers: Construction in the United States.* Washington, D.C.: Office of the Chief of Military History, United States Army, 1972.

Finnie, Richard. *Marinship: The History of a Wartime Shipyard.* San Francisco: Marinship, 1947.

"500 House Experiment Project at Camden, N.J." *American Builder and Building Age* (August 1941).

Flebus, C. G., "Air Raid Shelters." *The Military Engineer* (January 1941).

"For Action—Join the Seabees." *American Builder and Building Age* (November 1942).

Fortune 33, no. 4 (April 1946), housing issue.

Fowle, Barry W. *Builders and Fighters: U.S. Army Engineers in World War II.* Fort Belvoir, Va.: United States Army Corps of Engineers, 1992.

"FPHA Dormitories for a Midwestern Bomber Plant." *Architectural Record* (July 1942).

"FPHA Duration Dormitories for Industrial War Workers." *Architectural Record* (July 1942).

"FPHA to Use Plastic Tubing." *Architectural Record* (June 1943).

"Functions, Factors, and Futures; Reshaping the Building Industry for its War and Post-War Tasks." *Architectural Record* (November 1942).

"Funds for Postwar Highway Planning Provided in New Federal-Aid Law." *Engineering News Record* (July 1943).

Funigiello, Philip J. *The Challenge to Urban Liberalism: Federal-City Relations during World War II.* Knoxville: University of Tennessee Press, 1978.

Garner, John S. "World War II Temporary Buildings: A Brief History of the Architecture and Planning of Cantonments and Training Stations in the United States." USACERL Technical Report CRC-93/01. Washington, D.C.: United States Army Engineering and Housing Support Center, United States Army Corps of Engineers, March 1993.

Gaskins, Susanne Teepe. "The Dam That Would Not Stay Put: Henry J. Kaiser and Shipbuilding on the Homefront." Ph.D. diss., California State University, Fullerton, 1987.

Gelfand, Mark I. *A Nation of Cities: The Federal Government and Urban America, 1933–1965.* New York: Oxford University Press, 1975.

Goodman, Percival. "Defense-Time Planning for Peace-Time Use." *Architectural Record* (November 1940).

"Good Planning, Attractiveness, and Extensibility under Title VI." *American Builder and Building Age* (March 1942).

Goodrich, Carter. *Government Promotion of American Canals and Railroads,* 1800–1900. New York: Columbia University Press, 1960.

Gordon, Walter. "Cities While You Wait: Housing in Washington and Oregon." *Pencil Points* (April 1943).

Groueff, Stephane. *Manhattan Project: The Untold Story of the Making of the Atomic Bomb.* Boston: Little, Brown and Company, 1967.

A Guide to Archival Sources for the Study of World War II Temporary Buildings. Washington, D.C.: United States Army Corps of Engineers, February 10, 1988.

Hagood, Gen. Johnson. "Our Defenseless Coast." *Colliers* (June 22, 1940).

Hamlin, Talbot F. "The Architecture of the Future. Part 1—Postwar Design: Architecture of Democracy." *Pencil Points* (March 1943).

Huie, W. B. "Navy Seabees Build the Roads to Victory." *Life* (October 9, 1944).

"Igloos for Munitions Storage." *Engineering News Record* (September 1941).

"Industrial Buildings to Speed Invasion." *Architectural Record* (July 1943).

"Industrial Buildings . . ." *Architectural Record* (January 1942).

"Innovations Dot Navy's Ship Model Testing Basin." *Engineering News Record* (July 10, 1941).

"Innovations Mark Construction of Experimental-Model Basin." *Architectural Record* (September 1939).

"In Time of War Prepare for Peace." *Pencil Points* (April 1942).

"Installation Building Survey: Report of Findings: Fort Leonard Wood, Missouri." HABS Report, Harland Bartholomew and Associates, Inc., St. Louis, May 1989.

"Jake on the Job for U.S.A." *American Builder and Building Age* (February 1943).

Jessup, M. E. "Trends in Housing during the War and Post-War Periods." *Monthly Labor Review* (January 1947).

"Job for the Engineers: Army Construction." *Time* (September 15, 1941).

"Jobs for Trained Men." *Pencil Points* (February 1942).

Johnson, A. E. "Seabees Can Do It." *Popular Science* (January 1944).

Johnson, Bernard L. "National Defense—Spending Billions—Will Lead to Enlarged Industrial Construction and Home Building." *American Builder and Building Age* (June 1940).

Johnson, Charles. *The Negro War Worker in San Francisco.* San Francisco, 1944.

Johnson, Marilynn S. "Urban Arsenals: War Housing and Social Change in Richmond and Oakland, California, 1941–1945." *Pacific Historical Review* (1991).

Johnson, Marilynn S. "The Western Front: World War II and the Transformation of West Coast Urban Life." Ph.D. diss., History Department, New York University, 1990.

Kahn, Albert. "Architecture in the National Defense Building Program." *Michigan Society of Architects Weekly Bulletin,* no. 52 (December 30, 1941).

"Kaiserville: Pop. 40,000." *Architectural Forum* (February 1943).

Keller, David Neal. *Stone and Webster 1889–1989, a Century of Integrity and Service.* New York: Stone and Webster, Inc., 1989.

Kelly, Barbara M. "The Politics of House and Home: Implications in the Built Environment of Levittown Long Island (New York)." Ph.D. diss., S.U.N.Y. Stony Brook, 1988.

Kelly, Burnham. *The Prefabrication of Houses: A Study by the Albert Farwell Bemis Foundation of the Prefabrication Industry in the United States.* Cambridge, Mass.: The MIT Press, 1951.

Kempner, M. J. "Builders at War: Seabees Beat Time and Terrain." *House and Garden* (September 1945).

King, Gregory. "Historic Property Survey Report, Volume 4, Part VII, E, Subarea E: Naval Supply Center, Oakland," August 1990.

Kirchner, David P., and Emanuel Raymond Lewis. "American Harbor Defenses: The Final Era." *U.S. Naval Institute Proceedings* (January 1984).

Krakauer, John. "Ice, Mosquitos and Muskeg—Building the Road to Alaska." *Smithsonian* 23, no. 4 (July 1992).

Kriv, Arlene R., ed. "World War II and the United States Army Mobilization Program: A History of 700 and 800 Series Cantonment Construction," Legacy Resource Management Program, United States Department of Defense, HABS Report, 1994.

"Laminated Lumber Speeds Huge Expansion at Great Lakes Naval Training Station." *American Builder and Building Age* (May 1942).

"Landscape Architects at War. The ASLA in the Armed and Civilian Services, as Revealed by Questionnaire." *Landscape Architecture* 33 (October 1942).

Lane, Frederick C. *Ships for Victory: A History of Shipbuilding Under the U.S. Maritime Commission in World War II.* Baltimore: The Johns Hopkins University Press, 1951.

Larkin, W. B. "Steel-Frame Portable Airplane Hangars." *Engineering News-Record* (May 6, 1943).

Larrabee, Eric. "The Six Thousand Houses That Levitt Built." *Harper's Magazine* 197 (September 1948).

Lemmon, Sue. "Homoja Huts." *Grapevine* (publication of Mare Island Navy Yard) (September 4, 1992).

"Levitt & Sons of Virginia Set New Standards in Title VI War Homes." *American Builder and Building Age* (June 1942).

"Levitt's Progress." *Fortune* (October 1952).

Lewis, Emanuel Raymond. *Seacoast Fortifications of the United States: An Introductory History.* Annapolis: Leeward Publications, Inc., 1979.

Lewis, Emanuel Raymond, and David P. Kirchner. "The Oahu Turrets." *Warship International* 1 (1992).

Lifshey, Earl. *The Housewares Story: A History of the American Housewares Industry.* Chicago: National Housewares Manufacturers Association, 1973.

"Lighting of Industrial Plants." *Architectural Record* (September 1942).

Littlefield, Joan. "Prefabricated Houses of Aluminum." *Metal Progress* (September 1945).

Longstreth, Richard. "The Lost Shopping Center." *The Forum, Bulletin of the Committee on Preservation,* no. 20. Society of Architectural Historians (October 1992).

"Looking Ahead to the Postwar Home." *American Builder and Building Age* (September 1942).

"Looking Ahead to the Postwar Home." *American Builder and Building Age* (October 1942).

"Looking Ahead to the Postwar Home." *American Builder and Building Age* (November 1942).

Lorimer, Gordon. "The Industry Engineered House." *Architectural Record* (September 1947).

Lotchin, Roger W. *Fortress California 1910–1961: From Warfare to Welfare.* New York: Oxford University Press, 1992.

Maben, Manly. *Vanport*. Portland: Oregon Historical Society Press, 1987.

MacDonald, J. "Men Who Work the War." *New York Times Magazine,* November 28, 1943.

"Machine Shop and Assembly Building for a War Plant in Maine, Alonzo J. Harriman, Architect-Engineer." *Pencil Points* (March 1944).

Mackesey, Thomas W. "The Conception of a Community to House Workers near Willow Run and How it Developed Technically Until Its Program Was Changed." *Architectural Record* (January 1943).

"Marin City, California." *Architectural Forum* (December 1943).

Mason, Joseph B. "Not Boxes, Not Barracks, but Homes." *American Builder and Building Age* (August 1942).

"Mass Production Airplane Plant." *Architectural Forum* (June 1942).

McCloskey, Joseph F. "Military Roads in Combat Areas: The Development of Equipment and Techniques by the Corps of Engineers, United States Army, during World War II." Ph.D. diss., University of Pittsburgh, 1949.

McNamara, John E. "A Plan for Providing National Defense Housing without Government Subsidy." *American Builder and Building Age* (January 1941).

McVoy, Arthur. "How Cities Are Planning for the Post-War Period: Portland." *Planning,* Chicago (1944).

Menefee, Selden. *Assignment: U.S.A.* New York: Reynal and Hitchcock, 1944.

Meyer, Agnes. *Journal through Chaos*. New York: Harcourt, Brace and Co., 1944.

"Michigan Builds War Roads." *Engineering News Record* (January 14, 1943).

"Military Hospitals Are Planned in Pavilion Units Here and Abroad." *Architectural Record* (August 1941).

Moffet, Marian, and Lawrence Wodehouse. *Built for the People of the United States—Fifty Years of TVA Architecture*. Knoxville: The University of Tennessee, 1983.

"Monticello Village—Fast Moving Title VI Victory Home Job." *American Builder and Building Age* (April 1942).

Moore, Shirley Ann. *The Black Community in Richmond, California.* Richmond, Calif.: Richmond Public Library, 1987.

"More Cars, Superhighways Will Set Post-War Pattern for Commercial Building." *American Builder and Building Age* (June 1943).

"More War Homes Under FHA, Title VI." *American Builder and Building Age* (February 1942).

Mott, James W. "Highways in Relation to National Defense." *American Highways* 19, no. 4 (January 10, 1940).

"Multiple-Arch Concrete Roof Saves Steel." *Engineering News Record* (January 14, 1943).

Murphy, Kathryn R. "Housing for War Workers." *Monthly Labor Review,* serial no. R. 1464. (June 1942).

Nash, Gerald D. *The American West Transformed: The Impact of the Second World War.* Bloomington: Indiana University Press, 1985. Reprint, Lincoln: The University of Nebraska Press, 1990.

National Archives. Records of the United States Army Operations Division. Record Group 165, OPD 662. United States Army Corps of Engineers. "Progress of Construction of Seacoast Batteries." (August 31, 1942).

National Archives. Records of the United States Army War Plans Division. Record Group 165, WPD 4279-21. "16-Inch Seacoast Battery Program" (July 25, 1941).

National Archives. Records of the United States Army War Plans Division. Record Group 165, WPD 4279-15. "Modernization of Existing Seacoast Batteries in the Continental United States" (August 25, 1941).

National Archives. Records of the United States Army War Plans Division. Record Group 165, WPD 4279-12. "Notes on Type Harbor Defense Installations" (February 1941).

"Naval Air Stations." *Architectural Concrete* 8, no. 2. (1942).

"Navy Prefabricates; Standard Housing Plan Gets Tryout in 50 One-Family Units at Norfolk Base." *Business Week* (September 21, 1940).

"Navy's Fighting Seabees." *Popular Mechanics* (April 1943).

"Need for Wartime Materials Met with New Products." *American Builder and Building Age* (July 1943).

"New House, 194X." *Architectural Forum* (September 1942).

"New Markets for Plastics." *Canadian Chemistry and Process Industries* (September 1945).

"New Plastic Fibers and Materials Bear Watching." *Rayon Textile Monthly* (November 1944).

"New Power Equipment and Materials for War Jobs." *American Builder and Building Age* (September 1943).

"New Procedures, Standards, Speed Up War Housing; Ask for 250,000 Units This year." *American Builder and Building Age* (May 1943).

"New Products and New Ideas Speed War Building." *American Builder and Building Age* (May 1943).

"New War Plants Will Be Rushed to Make What Army Needs Most." *Newsweek* (December 25, 1944).

"New Wartime Products Help Builders Do the Job." *American Builder and Building Age* (June 1943).

"New Ways to Save Steel in Concrete." *Architectural Record* (February 1942).

"1942 Construction Estimates Again Boosted." *American Builder and Building Age* (May 1942).

Ockman, Joan, ed. *Architecture Culture 1943–1968: A Documentary Anthology.* New York: Rizzoli International Publications, Inc., 1993.

O'Connell, Charles F., Jr. "Quonset Point Naval Air Station." *Historic American Engineering Record* (January 1979).

"Ohio Builder Does His Best on War Housing." *American Builder* (December 1, 1942).

Olzendam, Roderic. "After the War. . . . Wood." *Pencil Points* (January 1943).

"Our Coastline Wall of Steel." *Popular Mechanics* (October 1941).

"Our Hospitals are Preparing." *Pencil Points* 21 (November 1940).

"Packed Full of Postwar Ideas." *American Builder and Building Age* (July 1945).

Palmer, Charles F. "Defense Housing Progress and Outlook." *American Builder and Building Age* (July 1941).

"Panel-Built Homes for Quantico Marines." *American Builder and Building Age* (April 1941).

Panhorst, F. W. "Lack of Material Forcing Engineering to Adopt Unusual Bridge Designs." *California Highways and Public Works* 20, no. 2 (February 1942).

Payne, Judd H. "Building's Part Is Big." *Architectural Record* (November 1941).

"Peacetime Fate of War Plants Presses for Prompt Solution." *Newsweek* (October 4, 1943).

Peltier, Eugene J. *The Bureau of Yards and Docks of the Navy and the Civil Engineering Corps.* New York: The Newcomen Society in North America, 1961.

"Permanent Plant for Torpedoes." *Architectural Record* (April 1944).

"Plane Engine Plant Sets New Precedent." *Engineering News Record* (July 1941).

"Planning for the Peace." *Pencil Points* (June 1942).

"Plastic Electric Drill." *Engineering News Record* (March 11, 1943).

"Plywood Soars: Gears for an Expanded Post-War Market." *Business Week* (January 2, 1943).

"Plywood, an $80,000 Industry That Wants to Revolutionize the Construction of Everything." *Fortune* (January 1940).

Polenberg, Richard. *War and Society: The United States, 1941–1945.* New York: J. P. Lippincott Co., 1972.

"Power Equipment Helps in Defense Rush." *American Builder and Building Age* (October 1941).

"Power Equipment Speeds Big War Housing Job in Face of Serious Delays." *American Builder and Building Age* (December 1942).

"Power Plants for Wartime Production." *Architectural Record* (May 1944).

"Power Saws Speed Norfolk Victory Homes." *American Builder and Building Age* (April 1942).

"Precast Concrete in Wartime Building." *Architectural Record* (March 1942).

"Prefab Methods Speed Seattle Housing." *American Builder and Building Age* (December 1942).

"PreFab PreView." *American Builder and Building Age* (January 1942).

"Prefabrication." *Architectural Record* (June 1943).

"Prefabrication: All-Masonry House Is Quickly Assembled with Wall and Roof Units of Light Reinforced Concrete." *Architectural Forum* (May 1945).

"Prefabrication Rushed with Power Tools." *American Builder and Building Age* (April 1942).

"Prefabrication Up-to-Date." *American Builder and Building Age* (January 1943).

"Prefab Sections Create Quick Housing." *American Builder and Building Age* (November 1942).

Price, Burr. "Paints: Present and Postwar." *Architectural Record* (June 1943).

"Producer of Production Lines." *Architectural Record* (June 1942).

"Products for Postwar Plans, 255 Manufacturers Summarize Their Definite Plans." *Architectural Record* (December 1944).

"Programming Highway Construction to Meet Post-Defense Needs." *Engineering News Record* (November 1941).

"Properties of Fiberglas Fibers and Fabrics." *Textile Research* (September 1944).

"Prospects for 1941: Everybody BUSY." *American Builder and Building Age* (January 1941).

Pubic Roads Administration, "Highways for the National Defense." *Senate Committee Print,* 77th Congress, 1st Session. Washington: U.S. Government Printing Office, 1941.

Pulos, Arthur J. *The American Design Adventure.* Cambridge, Mass.: The MIT Press, 1988.

"QuarterMaster and M-Drawing Mobilization Construction Comparison." HABS Report, Harland Bartholomew and Associates, Inc., St. Louis, May 1989.

"Quickly Converted for Casualties." *Architectural Record* (January 1944).

"Quonset Huts Are Back from the War." *Architectural Record* (January 1947).

Ragon, Michel. *Goldberg: Dans la ville. On the City.* Paris: Paris Art Center, 1985.

Rainey, F. "Alaskan Highway an Engineering Epic." *National Geographic Magazine* (February 1943).

Rathbone, A. D. 4th. "Pier in Time: 700 ft. Utility Pier for the U.S. Navy Built in 43 Days." *Scientific American* (July 1942).

Rathbone, A. D. 4th. "We Defend What We Build; Seabees, the Fighting Technicians of the Navy." *Scientific American* (February 1943).

"Rebuilding America after the War." *Michigan Society of Architects Weekly Bulletin* (April 15, 1944).

Reed, Harold E. "Fabric Laminates—Growing Outlet for Textiles." *Textile World* (October 1945).

Reeves, John. "Structural Materials Made from Fiberglas Fabrics." *Textile World* (October 1945).

Reid, Kenneth. "Year of War and Work." *Pencil Points* (January 1942).

"Relocation Will be Probed by Committee Here." *Richmond Independent,* April 4, 1952.

"Rental Decision to Await Survey." *Richmond Independent,* August 5, 1952.

"Rental Duplex Units Pre-Built on Site." *American Builder and Building Age* (June 1942).

"Replanned for Wartime Construction, Arlington Hospital, Virginia." *Architectural Record* (August 1944).

"Residential Building Potentials, by the Committee on Postwar Construction Markets, F. W. Dodge Corporation." *Architectural Record* (June 1944).

Reybold, E. "This Is Definitely an Engineer's War." *Popular Science* (May 1945).

Rodney, Marguerite C. "Oakdale Farms: Levitt's Prototype for Postwar Suburban Housing." Department of American Studies, George Washington University, Washington, D.C., April 1993. Photocopy.

Rogers, T. S. "Statement on Postwar Building Materials and Design, by the Technical Committee of the Producers' Council." *Architectural Record* (November 1944).

"Roosevelt Naval Base, Terminal Island." *Architectural Record* (May 1944).

Rose, Mark H. *Interstate: Express Highway Politics, 1941–1956.* Lawrence: Regents Press of Kansas, 1979.

Rosenman, Dorothy. "Defense Housing—Are We Building Future Slums, or Planned Communities?" *Architectural Record* (November 1941).

Rosenman, Dorothy. "Housing to Speed Production." *Architectural Record* (April 1942).

Ruble, Kenneth D. *The Magic Circle: A Story of the Men and Women Who Made the Most Respected Name in Windows.* Bayport, Minn.: North Central Publishing Co., 1978.

Ruml, B. "Construction Industry's Place in Post-War Employment." *American City* 59 (March 1944).

"San Francisco: Gibraltar of the West Coast." *National Geographic* 83, no. 3 (March 1943).

"Seabees." *Newsweek* (October 19, 1942).

"Seabees: The Navy: Fighting Builders." *Architectural Forum* (February 1944).

"Seattle War Workers Get Homes—Not Mere Housing." *American Builder and Building Age* (June 1942).

Sherman, Don. "Willow Run." *Air & Space* (August 1992).

"Shopping Facilities in Wartime." *Architectural Record* (October 1942).

Sill, Van Rensselaer. *American Miracle; The Story of War Construction around the World.* New York: Odyssey Press, 1947.

"63-Man Barracks Built in a Day." *American Builder and Building Age* (November 1942).

Sleeper, H. R. "Drywall Construction." *Architectural Record* (October 1943).

"Sliding Form Used to Construct Walls of 77-ft. Pit." *Engineering News Record* (August 1941).

Smith, Beth Laney, and Karen Trogdon Kluever. *Jones Construction: Looking Back, Moving Forward.* Charlotte, N.C.: Laney-Smith, Inc., 1989.

"Special Defense Issue Devoted to the Work of Albert Kahn." *Michigan Society of Architects Weekly Bulletin* 15, no. 52 (December 30, 1941).

"Statement of Postwar Building Materials and Design." *Architectural Record* (November 1942).

Stein, Charles M. A. "Today We Produce to Destroy, but Tomorrow We Will Produce to Build." *Pencil Points* (January 1943).

Sternberg, B. M. "New Opportunities in Postwar Markets." *Modern Plastics* (April 1945).

Stokes, K. C. *Regional Shifts in Population, Production, and Markets, 1939–1943* Washington, D.C.: Bureau of Foreign and Domestic Commerce, 1943.

Stowell, K. K. "Design for Democracy Now!" *Architectural Record* (August 1942).

Stowell, K. K. "Evolution in Building." *Architectural Record* (September 1943).

Stowell, K. K. "More and Faster—Now." *Architectural Record* (March 1942).

Stowell, K. K. "There's No Place Like Home! Just What It Will Be Like in the Postwar Period." *Architectural Record* (December 1943).

Straub, Eleanor, "U.S. Government Policy toward Civilian Women during World War II." *Prologue* 5 (Winter 1973).

"Suburban Hospital, Bethesda, Maryland; Faulkner & Kingsbury, Architects." *Pencil Points* (March 1944).

"Suitcase House." *Architectural Record* (June 1944).

"Survey of War Building to Be Done in the Months Ahead." *American Builder and Building Age* (April 1942).

Taschner, Mary. "Boomerang Boom: San Diego 1941–1942." *Journal of San Diego History,* no. 28 (1982).

"Technical Teams with War Work." *Architectural Record* (June 1942).

"Tenite Tubing Available." *American Builder and Building Age* (May 1942).

"These Are the Houses That Sam Built, Vallejo, July 1942–January 1944: First Report of the Housing Authority of the City of Vallejo, California, Supplement." Vallejo: Housing Authority of the City of Vallejo, California, July 1942.

"These Are the Kinds of Defense Homes That Will Still Be Good after the Emergency." *American Builder and Building Age* (September 1941).

"Three Billion Dollars Asked for Postwar Highway Projects." *Engineering News Record* (July 29, 1943).

"Title VI Defense Home Boom Hits Norfolk, Virginia." *American Builder and Building Age* (April 1942).

"Title VI Rows Recommended by FHA." *American Builder and Building Age* (March 1942).

Tompkins, Maurice Albert. "Military and Civilian Aspects of San Diego during the Second World War." Master's thesis, San Diego University, 1982.

Torgerson, Ralph S. "War Housing Projects to Use Concrete Products." *Rock Products* (August 1943).

"Total War Means All-Out Conservation." *Architectural Record* (January 1942).

"Transparency in the Home." *Modern Plastics* (October 1945).

"Treated Lumber in Los Angeles War Homes." *American Builder and Building Age* (June 1942).

"Two Traveling Tower Derricks Erect Huge Timber Blimp Hangars." *Engineering News-Record* (April 1943).

United States Army. *Engineers of the Southwest Pacific, 1941–1945.* Washington, D.C.: United States Government Printing Office, 1947.

United States Army. *Unit History/31st Signal Heavy Construction Battalion.* Manuscript, January 1945.

United States Army Corps of Engineers. *The United States Army in World War II—The Corps of Engineers: The War Against Japan.* Washington, D.C.: Office of the Chief of Military History, United States Army, 1987.

United States Army Corps of Engineers. *Unit History, 1139th Engineer Combat Group, 1 July 1944 to 8 May 1945.* Munich, 1945.

United States Army Service Forces. "Strategic and Critical Raw Materials." *Army Service Forces Manual, M 104.* Washington, D.C.: U.S. Government Printing Office, 1944.

United States Navy, Bureau of Yards and Docks. *Building the Navy's Bases in World War II: History of the Bureau of Yards and Docks and the Civil Engineering Corps, 1940–1946.* 2 vols. Washington, D.C.: United States Government Printing Office, 1947.

United States Congress. House. 77th Congress, 1st session. Committee on Banking and Currency. *Hearings on Conversion of Small Business Enterprises to War Production.* Washington, D.C.: United States Government Printing Office, 1948.

United States Congress. Senate. 78th Congress, 1st session. Subcommittee on Military Affairs. *Hearings on Scientific and Technological Mobilization.* Washington, D.C.: United States Government Printing Office, 1943.

United States Congress, Senate. 77th Congress, 1st session. Special Committee to Study and Survey Problems. *Hearings on Small Business and the War Program,* 94 parts. Washington, D.C.: United States Government Printing Office, 1948.

"USHA Offers Plans for Defense Housing." *American Builder and Building Age* (January 1941).

"Valencia Gardens: USHA War Housing in San Francisco." *Pencil Points* (January 1944).

Vancouver Housing Authority. *Vancouver's Plan.* Vancouver, Wash: Vancouver Housing Authority, 1945.

"Vanport City." *Architectural Forum* (August 1943).

Vawter, Roderick, *Industrial Mobilization: The Relevant History*. Washington, D.C.: National Defense University Press, United States Government Printing Office, 1983.

Verge, Arthur C. "The Impact of the Second World War on Los Angeles, 1939–1945." Ph.D. diss., Univeristy of Southern California, 1988.

Vermilya, H. P. "Technical Advances: Present and Postwar." *Architectural Record* (June 1943).

"Victory Wiring Layout Saves Copper." *American Builder and Building Age* (September 1943).

Walker, Gregg, David Bella, and Steven Sprecher, eds. *The Military-Industrial Complex: Eisenhower's Warning Three Decades Later.* New York: P. Lang, 1992.

"Wall Sections for War Homes Built in Local Lumber Yards." *American Builder and Building Age* (March 1942).

Wallis, Allan D. *Wheel Estate: The Rise and Decline of Mobile Homes.* New York: Oxford University Press, 1991.

Walsh, Vandervoort. "House Building Materials Reappraised." *Architectural Record* (November 1947).

"War and the Building Outlook for 1942." *American Builder and Building Age* (January 1942).

"War Board's Building Conservation Order." *American Builder and Building Age* (May 1942).

"War Construction Hits Its Stride." *American Builder and Building Age* (August 1942).

"War Housing Construction Is Still One of the Country's Leading Industries." *Engineering News-Record* (September 1943).

"War Housing. . . ." *The Architectural Forum* (May 1942).

"War Needs . . . Community Buildings." *Architectural Record* (May 1942).

"War Needs . . . Housing." *Architectural Record* (April 1942).

"War Opens a New Day in Interior Wall Structure." *The Empire State Architect* (November 1942).

"War Plants after the War." *American Institute of Architects Journal* 2 (August 1944).

"Wartime Advance in Welding." *Architectural Record* (July 1946).

"Wartime Construction of Factory Buildings." *Architectural Record* (December 1942).

"Wartime Wiring Will Cut Costs and Promote Safety." *American Builder and Building Age* (April 1942).

Wasch, Diane Shaw, and Perry Bush. "The Historical Context of World War II Mobilization Construction, Part 1." Manuscript.

"Washington Building to Provide 4,000,000 sq. ft. of Space." *Engineering News Record* (August 21, 1941).

"Washington Report." *American Builder and Building Age* (August 1941).

Weaver, Robert C. *Negro Ghetto*. New York: Harcourt, Brace and Co., 1948.

Weinart, Richard, and Arthur, Robert. *Defender of the Chesapeake: the Story of Ft. Monroe*. Annapolis, Md.: Leeward Publications, 1978.

Welles, George D., Jr. "It's True What They Say about Lake Jackson." *Dow Diamond* (May 1944).

Wharton, D. "Builders for the Army." *Scientific American* (December 1941).

"What Builders Are Doing in Wartime." *American Builder and Building Age* (February 1943).

"What Does Military Design Offer the Architecture of Peace? (#2)." *Architectural Record* (March 1939).

"What Housing for Willow Run?" *Architectural Record* 92, no. 3. (September 1942).

"What Types of New Construction are Essential . . . Today." *Architectural Record* (December 1941).

White, Gerald T. *Billions for Defense: Government Financing by the Defense Plant Corporation during World War II*. University, Ala.: University of Alabama Press, 1982.

"Willow Run Bomber Plant." *Architectural Record* (September 1942).

Wilson, C. M. "Defense Brings a New Age of Rubber." *Popular Science* (September 1941).

Wilson, Francis Vaux. *Tomorrow's Homes.* Trenton, N.J.: Homasote, Inc., 1939.

Wollenberg, Charles. *Marinship at War: Shipbuilding and Social Change in Wartime Sausalito.* Berkeley: Western Heritage Press, 1990.

Woodbridge, Sally B. "Historic Architectural Resources Inventory for Naval Air Station, Alameda." Historic Structures Report Commissioned by the Department of Defense, 1992.

Woodbury, David Oakes. *Battlefronts of Industry.* New York: J. Wiley, 1948.

Woodbury, David Oakes. *Builders for Battle: How the Pacific Air Naval Bases Were Constructed.* New York: E. P. Dutton and Co., 1946.

"World War II Temporary Structures: The United States Army." HABS Survey, March 1989.

"World's Biggest Prefab Job." *American Builder and Building Age* (June 1942).

"Worthy Ideas from Wartime Housing." *Architectural Record* (November 1943).

Wright, Gwendolyn. *Building the Dream: A Social History of Housing in America.* Cambridge, Mass.: The MIT Press, 1981.

"Wright Plant Sets New Size Record." *Engineering News Record* (3 July 1941).

Wurster and Bernardi, Ernest J. Kump, Architects Association. "Prefabrication for Flexible Planning." *Architectural Record* (August 1945).

Wurster, William Wilson. "Carquinez Heights." *California Arts and Architecture* (November 1941).

"Your Postwar Home." *Ladies Home Companion* (June 1943).

Contributors

Donald Albrecht, Exhibition Curator and Catalog Editor, is an independent curator and writer who lives in New York. He is a contributing editor of *Architecture,* the author of *Designing Dreams: Modern Architecture in the Movies,* and has written for the *New York Times, HG,* and *Metropolitan Home.*

Margaret Crawford is Chair of the History and Theory of Architecture Program at the Southern California Institute of Architecture. She is the author of the forthcoming book *Constructing a Workman's Paradise: The Architecture of the American Company Town* and a contributor to *Variations on a Theme Park: The New American City and the End of Public Space.*

Joel Davidson was Guest Historian at the National Building Museum for *World War II and the American Dream.* His doctoral dissertation at Duke University analyzed the political struggles over military resource allocations during World War II. He also holds a J.D. from the Yale Law School.

Robert Friedel is Professor of History at the University of Maryland. His books include *Pioneer Plastic: The Making and Selling of Celluloid, Zipper: An Exploration in Novelty,* and *A Material World.*

Greg Hise is Assistant Professor in the School of Urban and Regional Planning, University of Southern California. He has published in the *Journal of Urban History, Perspectives in Vernacular Architecture,* and *Center: A Journal of Architecture in America.* A book expanding upon the themes of his essay is forthcoming from Johns Hopkins University Press.

Peter S. Reed is Associate Curator in the Department of Architecture and Design at the Museum of Modern Art in New York. He was co-organizer of the Museum's 1994 exhibition on Frank Lloyd Wright. He contributed essays to the exhibition catalog *Louis I. Kahn: In the Realm of Architecture.*

Michael Sorkin is Principal of Michael Sorkin Studio in New York City and Professor and Director of the Institute of Urbanism at the Academy of Fine Arts in Vienna. He is the author of *Exquisite Corpse* and editor of *Variations on a Theme Park: The New American City and the End of Public Space.* He designed the exhibition "World War II and the American Dream" with J. Abbott Miller of Design Writing Research.

Index

Page numbers in italics indicate illustrations.